Object-Oriented Software Development

Engineering Software for Reuse

John D. McGregor
David A. Sykes

Department of Computer Science
Clemson University

VAN NOSTRAND REINHOLD
An International Thomson Publishing Company

York • London • Bonn • Boston • Detroit • Madrid • Melbourne • Mexico City
Paris • Singapore • Tokyo • Toronto • Albany NY • Belmont CA • Cincinnati OH

Copyright © 1992 by Van Nostrand Reinhold

Library of Congress Catalog Card Number 92-1382
ISBN 0-442-00157-6

Eiffel is a trademark of Interactive Software Engineering, Inc.. Excelerator is a trademark
of Index Technology. IBM is a trademark of International Business Machines Corporation.
Monopoly, Sorry, Risk, and Clue are trademarks of Parker Brothers. NeXT is a trademark
of NeXT Computer. ONTOS is a trademark of Ontologic, Inc. ParcPlace and Objectworks
are registered trademarks of ParcPlace Systems, Inc. Scrabble is a trademark of Milton
Bradley. Smalltalk-80 is a trademark of ParcPlace Systems, Inc. Smalltalk/V is a trademark
of Digitalk, Inc. Software Through Pictures is a trademark of IDE. Trivial
Pursuit is a registered trademark of Horn Abbot Ltd. UNIX is a trademark of AT&T in the
USA and in other countries. SaberC++ is a trademark of Saber Software, Inc.

I(T)P Van Nostrand Reinhold is an International Thomson Publishing company.
       ITP logo is a trademark under license.

Printed in the United States of America

Van Nostrand Reinhold
115 Fifth Avenue
New York, NY 10003

International Thomson Publishing GmbH
Königswinterer Str. 418
53227 Bonn
Germany

International Thomson Publishing
Berkshire House,168-173
High Holborn, London WC1V 7AA
England

International Thomson Publishing Asia
221 Henderson Bldg. #05-10
Singapore 0315

Thomas Nelson Australia
102 Dodds Street
South Melbourne 3205
Victoria, Australia

International Thomson Publishing Japan
Kyowa Building, 3F
2-2-1 Hirakawacho
Chiyoda-Ku, Tokyo 102
Japan

Nelson Canada
1120 Birchmount Road
Scarborough, Ontario
M1K 5G4, Canada

ARCFF 16 15 14 13 12 11 10 9 8 7 6 5 4 3

Library of Congress Cataloging-in-Publication Data
McGregor, John D.
      Object-oriented software development : engineering software for
   reuse : manuscript / John D. McGregor, David A. Sykes.
          p.   cm.
      Includes bibliographical references and index.
      ISBN 0-442-00157-6
      1. Object-oriented programming (Computerscience) 2. Computer
   software—Development. I. Sykes, David A. II. Title.
   QA76.6.M416   1992
   005.1—dc20   92-1382
                                                  CIP

Contents

List of Figures

List of Tables

Preface

Object-oriented technology has evolved into a mature discipline for the design and implementation of software applications. Many systems have been developed using the techniques of the object-oriented paradigm. Statistics substantiate many of the claims that have been made about this style of software development. A growing number of companies are investigating the technology and considering the implications for their products and development techniques.

This text is intended to provide an entree into the world of objects for computing professionals who either develop systems or manage those who do. Many books are currently on the market that provide techniques for the design of object-oriented systems or that present the syntax of a language that supports object-oriented implementation. We believe that the contribution of this text is the breadth of its coverage. We present a system-development methodology that spans the process from analysis to maintenance. By considering all of these phases in one text, the interfaces between them can be explored as well. The progression from analysis to design, for example, can be rough. Object technology provides support that smoothes this transition considerably.

The development methodology presented here is not a radically new approach. It simply collects and coordinates the efforts of many. Each chapter will be loaded with pointers into the object-oriented literature where the reader can find additional details. In several cases more than one approach to a particular phase of the development process will be presented. We give pros and cons of each approach to aid readers in analyzing and adapting the technology to their environment.

The material is divided into three parts. Chapters One through Three provide an introduction to and overview of the material. Chapter One considers goals for the software development process and why changing to an object-oriented style may help achieve those goals. Chapter Two provides a preliminary set of definitions for the concepts behind object technology. Chapter Three provides an overview of the C++ language. This is not a book on C++, nor does most of the methodology depend on a specific language. However, C++ is the language in which implementation details are presented.

Part Two of the text presents the methodology. Chapter Four provides an overview by considering the various phases of the life cycle. Following chapters consider the phases in more detail. Techniques for object-oriented analysis (OOA), object-oriented design (OOD), and object-oriented programming (OOP) are explored. Chapter Eight covers different types of object-oriented languages and the difference in the object models supported by each.

Part Three of the text presents several special issues. The relationships between types and classes are considered from the perspectives of language and design. The special problem of persistence of objects – where the object model differs from the data model of the file system – is considered. The support for the paradigm from CASE tools and other types of development environments is considered by looking at currently available technology and by suggesting tools that are needed.

The text is based on a three-day course developed by John D. McGregor for AT&T Bell Labs. We would like to thank the many students who took the course and made many helpful suggestions about content and presentation. John D. McGregor would like to thank Barry Peiffer and Stan Habib of the Kelly Education Center for AT&T Bell Labs for their support and patience and Tim Korson of Clemson University and Jim Coplien of AT&T Bell Labs for teaching numerous sections of the course and providing important feedback.

John D. McGregor would like to thank Gayle and Mary Frances McGregor for their patience and love during the long hours of work and absence necessary to make this book a reality. He would also like to thank his parents for their guidance and support over many years.

David A. Sykes would like to gratefully acknowledge the support of his family and friends throughout the process of writing this book and throughout the many other adventures he has undertaken.

1

Software Development Paradigms

Our primary goal in this book is to present a particular software development methodology. The central focus of this style is the use of object technology. Object technology comes in many flavors and does not, by itself, provide a comprehensive approach to software development. For that reason, we will also incorporate several other ideas into our methodology. These include:

- Problem-driven techniques
- Reuse techniques
- Software engineering principles

The methodology we discuss in this text owes many features to the work of others. The uniqueness of the methodology comes from the comprehensive approach of considering all phases of the system development process. An important element of object technology is the high degree of continuity from one stage of the life cycle to the next. This is made possible because the pieces used in one stage are the same as the pieces used at the next stage. This makes a comprehensive approach feasible, so that techniques do not change after each phase of the life cycle. Our methodology integrates the techniques of object-oriented analysis (OOA) , object-oriented design (OOD), and object-oriented programming (OOP) into the appropriate phases of our life cycle.

Our methodology is driven by the problem to be solved rather than by the solution to that problem. By that we mean that the methodology provides support beginning with the development of a clear statement of the problem and carries that statement through the entire development effort. The software product incorporates objects and connections between them that provide a model of the problem as an integral part of the solution to the problem. When requirements change—and they will—these changes will begin with the model of the *problem*. Changes to this model will, in turn, point to the changes that are necessary in the remainder of the system. This model will also make the tracing of requirements much easier and more accurate.

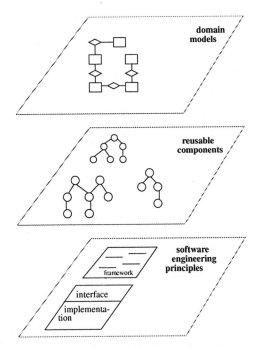

Figure 1.1: A philosophy for system design.

Our methodology emphasizes and facilitates reuse at all levels. Techniques in the analysis, design, implementation, and testing phases will be presented that will take advantage of the economies of reuse. In the text we will also discuss the role of management in supporting these types of reuse. To be maximally successful, our methodology must be accompanied by changes in management perspectives and expectations. For example, it has been verified in studies that the approach we will present requires more time in the analysis and design phases than does the structured development process. The layered nature of the design requires less time in integration testing. These changes need to be reflected in changed metrics and schedules for project management.

Finally, the discipline of software engineering supplies principles, formalisms, and metrics to our methodology. The advances made in recent years in the systematic development of applications should not be discarded by a change in paradigm. Development tools that support the object model will assist the developer in making optimal design decisions. The language model supports strong type checking to ensure the appropriateness of messages and arguments. The discipline provides techniques for organizing the production and management of software components.

Much of what we present will not be new. The inclusion of one or more of the pieces described here has led to a number of different object-oriented methodologies. Our effort in this text is to blend all of these ideas together into a comprehensive methodology so that the benefits of all these techniques are compounded.

APPLICATION DEVELOPMENT

As computer applications have become more complex, the emphasis has shifted from programming to application development. What's the difference? One difference is that of magnitude:

- *The size and composition of the development team has multiplied.* The solitary programmer has been replaced by a team of system developers. The software development process has become more structured and the tasks of team members has become more specialized. This has led to a greater need to communicate with other team members and to share and reuse the output of others in the team.
- *The complexity of the application has exploded.* Early applications were batch systems that had a relatively fixed flow of control. Menu-based, user-oriented systems have greatly increased the complexity of the flow through a system. Early applications on personal computers fit easily in 64K of RAM. Now special techniques are used to bypass the 640K limitation found on many microcomputers. Software systems with 500,000 lines of code are now commonplace. Multiple processor machines are being employed to perform the growing number of instructions.
- *Software factories produce multiple software applications for multiple hardware platforms.* New releases of the system must be made available on all platforms as quickly as possible. New features are propagated across all versions. New applications should be added to the family as quickly as possible.
- *System development crosses hardware generations.* The length of time between new generations of hardware has shortened as the time required for application development has lengthened. Applications must be as device independent as possible. Hardware dependencies that cannot be eliminated should be as isolated as possible. This requires an increased level of abstraction in the software components.
- *Software companies are taking a long-term view of the application development process.* Code developed for one application is the basis for the next application to be produced. The economics of software development requires that software companies develop a base of reusable components. These components constitute a portion of the company's inventory. The software components must be designed in a way that supports this reuse.

SOFTWARE QUALITIES

In this section, we want to take a brief look at those qualities of software that are desirable no matter which techniques are used for its production. Everyone has a list of software characteristics that they consider important. This list is not intended to be a complete taxonomy, but only a few items that we believe are illustrative.

Application Systems

Ultimately the true value of our application systems are judged by their purchasers and users. The design technique used to formulate the software and the language used to implement it are only of interest to the user of a system insofar as these characteristics support the development of a superior product. The following preliminary discussion was provoked by a question from a marketing person who asked a system developer, "What does this object-oriented technique mean to my customers?" We will come back to these qualities later and investigate the support provided for each by the object-oriented paradigm.

- *Usable*—Studies, which are admittedly somewhat dated now, once showed that over half of all software delivered was never used. A variety of reasons have been hypothesized for this phenomenon. One predominant cause seems to be that the users claim the software does not perform the desired functions. System designers complain that users change their mind during the long process of system development. Users are not sure what they want, but they know what they don't want when they see it! Techniques such as prototyping systems before full implementation have been proposed to provide closer and better communications between system user and developer. The role of object-orientation in prototyping will be considered later. Analysis and design techniques that anticipate changing requirements will also be discussed.

  Software applications—such as spreadsheets—for personal computers were touted as user-oriented products. The market for self-help books and hands-on seminars addressing the uses of these applications make that claim doubtful. Recent object-oriented interfaces and toolkits have greatly improved the user orientation of these systems.

- *Extensible*—Users' needs change. The presence of a new software system may answer some needs, but it may also point out additional features that are highly desirable. New systems can cause a revision of the user's operation, which in turn leads to a need for additional tools. Software systems should be designed not just to tolerate change, but to facilitate change. Adding new features to an existing, successful application can retain a recognizable interface while answering the requests of system users. We will consider how object-oriented techniques support extending existing systems, including how to provide procedurally designed systems with object-oriented extensions.

- *Maintainable*—The most carefully designed and implemented systems contain errors. Systems should be designed to make the isolation and correction of errors as easy as possible. One technique that aids in maintenance is information hiding. The more isolated data items are, the less likely it is that changes to an item will cause other problems to arise. We will give much attention to information hiding in our discussions on design.

- *Economical*—We have seen a number of systems advertised or demonstrated at trade shows that never sold many copies due to their cost. We have also heard many good ideas that never made it into code due to the complexity of the idea. Part of this cost is our approach of starting each new application as if it were the first ever written by the company. The ability to reuse specifications, designs, or code from one application to another is essential if the production of software is to be economical. Reuse is certainly possible with a number of software design techniques. However, object-oriented design procedures and languages have specific features that support reuse. Reuse at the analysis, design, and implementation levels can each contribute to the long-range economical development of software systems. Later discussions will consider how to exploit reuse to contribute to the economical development of software.

Software Components

In the previous discussion, the focus was on a complete application. This text will argue that reuse is—or should be—a priority concern of software companies. It will also make the case that if reuse is a priority, more attention should be paid to the individual modules—the units most likely to be reused—that comprise an application. Therefore, we now want to consider desirable characteristics of *individual* software components. As before, we will come back to this discussion to investigate how object-oriented techniques contribute to the production of quality software components.

- *Abstract*—Each software component should be the realization of an abstraction. That is, the component should represent a set of real world entities, rather than a single, very specific entity, by providing a general description of their common characteristics. This underlying concept provides a basis for validating the component. The component is complete, for example, if it is a complete model of the concept. The importance of abstraction will be seen in much of the discussion that follows. The differences in the types of abstraction that the procedural and object-oriented paradigms produce will also be considered.
- *Focused*—Each software component should be narrowly focused. In fact it should represent only one concept. It is often expedient to consider expanding a module to handle new, similar situations. The end result, though, is a component that is too large and too fragmented to be easily understood. By concentrating on one concept per module, the resulting component is an easily understood unit that is more likely to be reused by another designer. More efficient applications can be built if the components used represent single concepts. Only code that supports the needed functionality is included in the component.
- *Complete*—The software component should be a comprehensive model of the concept represented by the module even if some of the facets are not relevant to a particular application. There are at least two reasons for completeness. First, a complete component is more likely to be reused. If services are missing from a component, a paraphrase of Murphy's Law would imply that these are precisely the services that

will be needed by the next user. Second, a complete component is more economical to develop. It is widely accepted that maintenance programming costs more per line than does original system development. The cost of adding additional services to a module later is more than developing a complete implementation originally, particularly since changes to a module frequently affect components that already use it in its incomplete implementation.

- *Correct*—The software component should be a correct model of the target concept. This seems to be a very obvious criterion, but it is one that is seldom achieved in practice. This text examines the possibility that correctness is more easily attainable with object-oriented modules. The size and encapsulation of object-oriented modules make testing and validation a more manageable task.

PROBLEM SOLVING AND PARADIGMS

Our job is to solve problems. The problem solutions are represented in specifications, designs, and code. There are many approaches to problem solving and many ways to think about the solution to a given problem. This section considers how to formalize these differences and take advantage of them. It also suggests ways to be more efficient by choosing the most appropriate problem-solving techniques for pieces of the overall problem.

Paradigm

Webster's says a **paradigm** is a pattern. From our perspective in software development, a paradigm is a pattern for a problem-solving technique. In particular, a software development paradigm specifies the steps to be followed in developing a problem into a software application. The paradigm selected determines the types of pieces that are used to represent the problem and its solution. These pieces may represent abstractions related to the solution of a problem, as with procedural abstractions. Alternatively, the pieces may directly reflect the structure of the problem as we will see in the object-oriented paradigm.

The selection of a paradigm impacts the complete software development life cycle. That is, it directs the selection of design methodologies, coding languages, and testing and verification techniques.

Current Paradigms

A number of paradigms are in active use. They provide the system developer with a large number of approaches to system decomposition. Although all are represented by some form of language support, not all have advanced enough to have formal support at each stage in the application-development life cycle. Some of the paradigms in use are:

Procedural
Logic
Access-oriented
Process-oriented
Object-oriented
Functional
Declarative

Each of these paradigms has its supporters and users. Each is particularly suited to a certain type of problem or subproblem. The logic programming paradigm is the basis for the so-called *rule-based* systems. The access-oriented paradigm has proved a useful technique for structuring user interfaces. Each is a different way of thinking about problems, each uses a different approach to decompose a problem, and each results in different kinds of pieces, procedures, production rules, and so on. The logic paradigm, for example, decomposes knowledge about the problem into a set of discrete rules often represented in a language as "if-then" structures.

In the following sections we will examine three of the paradigms briefly. The purpose of this examination is to help you see that the starting point for solving problems is to slowly move away from, "Let's see how I can solve this problem in FORTRAN" to "What design technique will best support solution of this problem?" We will begin with the well known procedural paradigm and use this as a baseline for comparison with two other paradigms: object-oriented and process-oriented. Each will be considered from the perspective of the types of pieces it produces, their characteristics, and the paradigm's support and use.

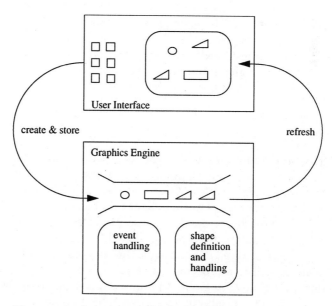

Figure 1.2: A conceptual model of the draw program.

Procedural System

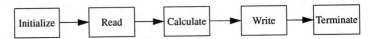

(a) System architecture is based on tasks to be performed. Changing
     one may require changes to all others.

Object-Oriented System

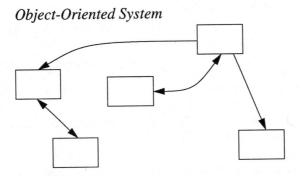

(b) System architecture is based on interactions between objects.
     Changing one usually has only local impact.

Figure 1.3: The basic architectures of procedural and object-oriented systems.

To provide a basis for comparison, we will consider a simple "draw" program that
allows the user to draw simple shapes on the screen. Figure 1.2 shows a conceptual
design for such a system. Its implementation uses an event-driven approach. The
program is considered at a very high level here and will be used as a continuing
example throughout the book. For each paradigm, we will discuss what the basic
architecture is and how it is developed.

Procedural Paradigm

The procedural paradigm is the most widely used and longest lived of the software
development paradigms. Many of us worked for many years believing that this was
"software development." Only relatively recently have we come to realize that there
are many other ways to think about problem decomposition.

The procedural design process produces procedural abstractions as its main result. These abstractions are developed by considering software as a stream of actions.
Perhaps it is a well defined algorithm that consists of a sequence of steps. Each step
is abstracted to a procedure with predefined inputs and specific outputs. The procedures are chained together to produce a reasonably stable flow of control through the
program. This results in an architecture that has a very simple but static structure,
as illustrated in Figure 1.3(a). The demands for more flexible systems have led to

Pseudocode Algorithm

1. Initialize system;

2. Create and draw interface;

3. **while** QUIT not selected **do**

       case

         Mouse event:
           create shape structure;
           read mouse movements for data;
           store newly created shape on list of shape records;

         KeyPress event:
           if key = 'q' **then exit loop;**
           else ignore;

         Expose event:
           refresh display by drawing each shape structure;

4. Shut down system;

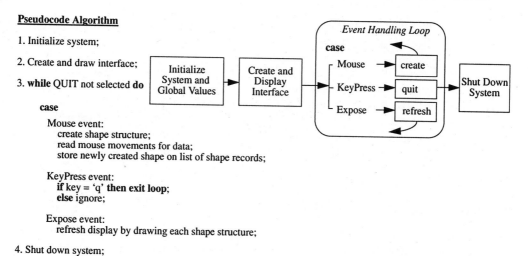

Figure 1.4: A procedural architecture for the draw program.

architectures that are more complex. The complexity is intensified by the fact that most of the details of this architecture are public and all must be understood if any is to be understood.

In the procedural paradigm the priority is on this stream of actions that constitutes the solution to the target problem. Data abstractions are not absent, however. Data structures are developed as the need arises to support the steps of the algorithm. The data structures are passed among the procedures to provide the information that the procedure needs to carry out its operation. The state of the system is the set of global variables that maintain their value as control moves from one procedure to another.

The amount of support for the procedural paradigm is impressive. A large number of are professionals trained in its use. These professionals have considerable experience developing systems from "Hello world" to million-line systems. Heuristics and optimizations have been developed and perfected to produce efficient systems.

There is a large number of supporting tools for the paradigm. The most obvious of these are the languages. From COBOL and FORTRAN to Ada and C, a number of languages have been widely used and refined for years. These languages have symbolic debuggers, optimizers, and libraries to support their use. There is also a complete array of design techniques such as top-down design and structured design, as well as techniques such as flowcharts and pseudocode compilers for recording the algorithms.

Figure 1.4 presents a possible procedural architecture for the draw program. It also presents the basic algorithm for the system. Many variations on this are possible and many details are omitted, but the basic principle can be seen. Tasks are the main pieces of the architecture. In this example, they are placed sequentially although there are possible places for some concurrency. The system is designed by first determining the overall sequencing, followed by defining data to support the basic operations of the procedures.

In summary, the procedural paradigm is a mature application development process. There is much support for this approach to system development. However, there have been problems in the development of very large systems as well as in the construction of user-oriented systems. Techniques to improve the development of large systems have centered around developing data abstractions. The increased attention on the use of Abstract Data Types (ADTs) has evolved the procedural system development process into a more data-driven approach. Continuing problems with large-system development have led to the need to combine the approaches of procedural abstractions and data abstractions. This need has led to the development of the following paradigm.

Object-Oriented Paradigm

The object-oriented paradigm is the result of an evolution in the way we decompose problems. Where procedural abstraction is the priority in the procedural paradigm, entities—problem domain objects—are the priority of the object-oriented paradigm. In the object-oriented paradigm, the major entities in the problem domain are identified and modeled as the starting point in system development. The behavior of objects is the focus instead of the sequence of actions that must be performed.

The objects in an object-oriented system are a unique blend of procedural and data abstractions. The data abstractions representing these entities are a major product of the object-oriented design process. The state of the system is maintained through the data stores defined at the core of each data abstraction. These values are maintained for the life of the abstraction. Flow of control is divided into pieces and is included inside each of the operators defined on the data abstractions. Instead of data being passed from one procedure to another, as in the procedural paradigm, flow of control is passed from one data abstraction to another. The resulting system architecture, illustrated in Figure 1.3(b), is more complex yet more flexible. Isolating flow of control in pieces allows complex actions to be viewed as local interactions which are more easily understood. Details of this architecture are discussed in the chapters that follow.

Support for the object-oriented paradigm is limited but growing. The number of professionals trained in its use is relatively small but increasing rapidly. The languages that are available are useful but do not have the long history of refinement that procedural languages have. Smalltalk has one of the longest histories of development, but other languages such as C++ are also seeing tremendous gains in popularity. These and other languages will be discussed later in greater depth. Building on the technology developed for the procedural paradigm, tools for the object-oriented paradigm have been more rapidly developed. There is still a need for environments specifically for this paradigm.

Figure 1.5 presents an object-oriented architecture for the draw application. The arrows in the diagrams indicate messages from one object to another. All of the required messages are not shown to simplify the diagram. A basic difference between this architecture and that shown in Figure 1.4 is the emphasis on "things," physical entities such as the mouse and the display and conceptual entities such as events and shapes. No algorithm is given here because it is really distributed into the various objects. We will see much more detail on the object-oriented design of this system in

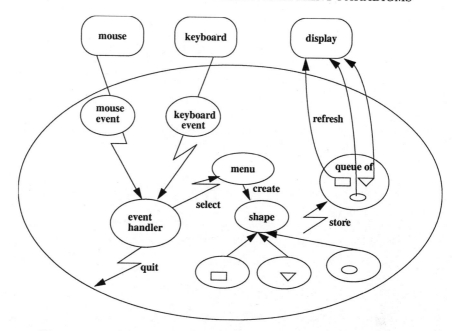

Figure 1.5: An object-oriented architecture for the draw program.

subsequent chapters.

　　To summarize, the object-oriented paradigm gives priority to data abstraction and looks secondarily at procedural abstraction. It is a new technique that has evolved from the increasing interest in ADTs. The entities of the target problem domain are the starting point for system design; implementing them drives the details of system development.

Process-Oriented Paradigm

The process-oriented paradigm is receiving increased attention as multiprocessor computers become more widely available. The focus of this paradigm is on the decomposition of a problem into independently executing modules—using more than one program running simultaneously in some sense. These programs—or more correctly *processes*—cooperate to solve the problem. We can think of a process as a module (or component) in the process-oriented paradigm. An interesting aspect of this paradigm is that a process will contain portions of an applications that may have been developed using any of the other paradigms as long as they support the protocols for the exchange of information between processes.

　　The major pieces produced by the process-oriented paradigm are processes. These pieces represent the most independent entities of any we have considered. The activity in one process is totally independent of that of any other process except for the need to obtain information from or provide information to other processes. Even this may be handled asynchronously, requiring only that the process pause to send or receive

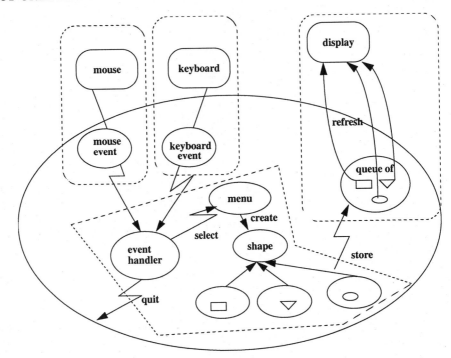

Figure 1.6: A process architecture for the draw program.

information. In the object-oriented paradigm, the separate objects are relatively in-dependent but there is still a single thread of control. The process-oriented paradigm can support the encapsulation of identity found in the object-oriented paradigm, but goes on to also provide multiple threads of execution. This provides the designer with an additional level of independence and complexity.

The support for the process-oriented paradigm is narrow but deep. By *narrow* we mean that the paradigm is limited to a relatively small community of users. By *deep* we mean that those who do use the paradigm have very mature techniques. An increasing number of mainstream languages such as Ada support the paradigm through a "tasking" facility. A language such as Ada provides an abstract interface to the production of processes while the C/Unix environment allows the designer direct access to operating-system-level services.

Figure 1.6 presents one possible process architecture for the draw application in which each process is developed using the object-oriented paradigm. In this case the internals of each process are objects. Each process should contain a set of objects that communicate with each other often while there should be much less need to move information from one process to another. A process architecture is often used to simplify the name space of an application and to provide the operating system with manageable pieces. This application is too simple to illustrate that purpose; however, another use is to support concurrency. The mouse and keyboard are separate devices, either of which might be used next. This design provides autonomy for the individual

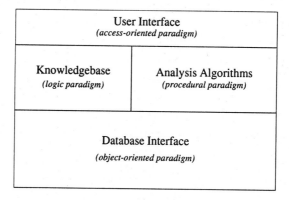

Figure 1.7: An intelligent data analysis system.

devices.

In summary, the process-oriented paradigm provides the designer with the ability to decompose a problem into a set of entities independent under the operating system. These entities can operate in parallel and may communicate with each other in a variety of ways. The process paradigm closely resembles the object-oriented paradigm in its information hiding and abstraction.

BLENDING PARADIGMS

In large system development, it is seldom the case that one paradigm is best for the entire problem. System development now has an extra step in which the large problem is decomposed into a set of subproblems. For each subproblem the appropriate software development paradigm can then be chosen. This design must be supported by some implementation language or a set of cooperating languages. A growing number of languages are in use that support more than one design paradigm.

There are a number of techniques for blending paradigms. Languages like C++ and Concurrent C are multiparadigm languages, supporting both the procedural and the object-oriented paradigms. Concurrent C also supports the process paradigm. Systems can be written in a single language to use elements of two or more paradigms. Often a number of languages are developed that share data representation and linkage conventions. Pieces written in these languages can then be linked into a single application. In this scenario, each piece is written in a language that supports the paradigm chosen for it. Each piece is then compiled by the appropriate compiler and then all are linked. Zave[106] describes another approach to multiparadigm system design. Later we will consider this idea as it pertains to merging new object-oriented code with existing procedural code.

Consider the design of an intelligent data analysis system which can be viewed as four subsystems, as illustrated in Figure 1.7. The system has an interface to a database that might be designed using the object-oriented approach, an intelligent analysis system designed in the logic paradigm, and a set of analysis algorithms that are procedural. The system is utilized via a user interface which was designed using the access-oriented paradigm.

SUMMARY

This first chapter has covered a number of subjects. Much of the discussions on criteria for software components and systems will be repeated later to evaluate pieces produced by the object-oriented techniques. The most important idea of this chapter is that of *paradigm*. This concept raises the decisions made in software development to a new level of abstraction. System developers begin to make selections from an array of problem decomposition tools much as we have selected language tools for some time. The introduction of this concept should put you in the proper frame of mind to consider the total impact of the use of object-oriented techniques.

It is not just a matter of new syntax for a different language. The change from one paradigm to another actually impacts the entire application development life cycle. In the following chapters we will consider a number of changes to the way system designers think and act while using object-oriented system development techniques.

FURTHER READING

While much has been written about "how-to" for each of the paradigms, little has been written that compares the various paradigms. Bertrand Meyer[72] contrasts the procedural and object-oriented paradigms. Stefik, Bobrow, and Kahn[86] discuss the access-oriented paradigm and how it can coexist with other paradigms in an application. A special issue of *IEEE Software*[40] considers several languages that support more than one paradigm. We will have more to say about this in Chapter 7. Strom[87] compares the object-oriented and process paradigms. Finally, as already cited, Zave[106] considers how to compose programs from pieces written in different paradigms.

2

An Overview

In this chapter we will provide the context for the study of object-oriented system design and implementation by presenting an overview of the topics and terminology of object-oriented software development. The meanings of terms presented here are intended as intuitive characterizations and not as complete, rigorous definitions. Each of the topics presented will be discussed again in greater detail later in the text. In this chapter we provide a beginning understanding of all the terms and how they fit together.

Object-oriented—as with any paradigm—cannot be characterized by considering only one phase of the development life cycle such as implementation. Nor can a paradigm be described with a set of concepts that are totally disjointed from those of any other paradigm.

WHAT IS *OBJECT-ORIENTED*?

Object-oriented is the buzzword of the late 1980s and early 1990s. The marketing campaigns for many programming languages, software tools, and end-user applications proclaim products that are object-oriented. An advertisement usually does not explain what makes a product object-oriented, nor does it explain why being object-oriented is a desirable characteristic for a particular product.

Indeed software professionals do not agree as to exactly what constitutes object-oriented software. In this text, we adopt Wegner's[95] definition, which requires that a language support these three concepts to be considered object-oriented:

- Objects
- Classes
- Inheritance

We will consider a software system to be *object-oriented* if it is designed and implemented using these three concepts. An object-oriented program is a software system whose components are objects. Computation is performed via the creation of new objects and the communications between them.

Our reliance on Wegner's definition is not intended to imply that techniques that do not utilize all three methods are not useful, but simply that they are not what we would term object-oriented. We will claim that design techniques that do not utilize all three do not provide the designer with the full power of object-orientation. Further, we will examine how the concepts of objects, classes, and inheritance affect the entire life cycle.

Objects

An *object* is the basic component of the object-oriented paradigm. Each object is characterized by its own set of attributes and by a set of operations that it can perform. The attributes may change as a result of the application of the operations and, in general, only through the operations. Operations are referred to as *methods* (or *member functions* in C++) and are applied via the process of *message passing* (or *messaging*). A message sent to an object specifies a method name and a (possibly empty) list of arguments, each of which designates some object. A message received by an object causes code associated with the method named in the message to be executed with its formal parameters bound to corresponding values in the argument list. The processing of a message by the receiving object might result in a state change—that is, a change to one or more of the receiving object's attributes—and/or the sending of a message to itself or some other object. It is useful to think of message passing as being roughly equivalent to function calls in the procedural paradigm. However, the purpose of the method invoked as the result of a message is intended to modify the internal state of the object to which it is attached rather than to modify its arguments and return them. An object may even send itself a message. Some languages provide special terminology to allow the object to refer to itself—for example, *self* in Smalltalk—or let the object be the default if another object is not explicitly referenced.

As an illustration, consider polygons drawn on a computer screen. Each polygon is an object defined by an ordered collection of vertices. The order specifies how the points are connected. The vertices define the state of a polygon object, both its shape and its location on the screen. Operations on a polygon include "draw" (display it on the screen), "move" (erase it from its current location and redraw it at some specified distance in the x and y directions), and "contains?" (a check whether some specified point is inside the polygon). Figure 2.1(a) shows three polygon objects on a computer screen and the points that define them. Figure 2.1(b) shows how these polygons are represented as objects.

Note that in describing polygon objects we have used other objects—namely, a screen and points. A screen is a physical object that for our needs here comprises an arrangement of picture elements (or *pixels*) that we can manipulate to draw shapes. A screen object provides methods to turn pixels on and off, to access the current state of a specified pixel (on or off), and to draw lines between any two points, where the screen maps points to pixels. A point represents a specific pixel according to some

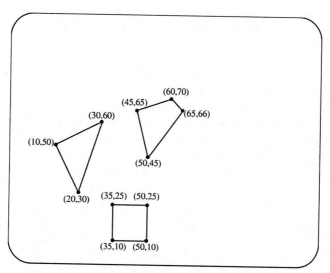

(a) Three polygons on a computer screen.

triangle	**quadrilateral₁**	**quadrilateral₂**
(10,50)	(35,10) (50,10)	(45,65) (50,45)
(30,60)	(35,25) (50,25)	(65,66) (60,70)
(20,30)		
draw	draw	draw
move $(\Delta x, \Delta y)$	move $(\Delta x, \Delta y)$	move $(\Delta x, \Delta y)$
contains?(aPoint)	contains?(aPoint)	contains?(aPoint)

(b) Three objects representing polygons.

Figure 2.1: Polygon objects.

x and y coordinate system. A point object provides methods to access its x and y components and perhaps to compute its distance from another point.

There is no reason why objects must only represent physical objects. They may be instances of any sort of conceptual entity. Processes in an operating system, the level of illumination in a room, and the role of being a lawyer in a particular trial are all examples of objects.

Two views of "object" represent the design and implementation perspectives, respectively. From a design perspective, objects can be thought of as instances of concepts that model entities of interest. These objects often directly correspond to physical entities in the problem domain. This view of objects as entities leads to a somewhat declarative design process: Rather than functionally describing a sequence of actions, the designer describes the entities that should be present, including attributes and operations they can perform. For example, in a simulation application there would be an object for each of the entities to be simulated. These entities are thought of as being independent, functioning units that have relationships with other objects in the domain of interest. The result of declaring all the entities needed to model the problem domain is sufficient functionality to solve the target problem.

From an implementation perspective, an object is the actual data structure used to represent an entity in the executable code of an object-oriented application program. For entities "in memory," the underlying object is a protected region of memory. Inside this region of memory is the data—instance variables—for that particular entity and some means of accessing the operators—methods—associated with that data. These objects are unique blends of data and operations that are instantiations of data abstractions, but they also maintain state throughout their lifetime. For entities "on disk" or that are being stored on some other form of secondary storage, some protocol for the storage of bit patterns is followed that treats the object as a unit. Issues about this persistent storage of objects will be discussed later in Chapter 14.

Classes

A *class* is a set of objects that share a common conceptual basis. The definition of a class includes a set of data attributes plus the set of allowable operations on that data. A class definition can be viewed as a template that is used for the production of objects. All objects in a given class have matching attributes and operations. Each object is an *instance* of some class, and the state of an object is contained in its *instance variables*.

For example, the two quadrilaterals in Figure 2.1—and every quadrilateral object— have the same properties, so we can define a class Quadrilateral shown in Figure 2.2 to specify these properties. Every object of class Quadrilateral has the same set of instance variables and methods defined by the class. In this sense, the class Quadrilateral provides a template for our representation of all four-sided polygon objects, specifying both the variables in each *instance* of a Quadrilateral and the set of methods that can be sent to any instance.

An instance creation operator must be provided in order to produce objects from a class definition. A number of approaches have been taken by object-oriented programming languages. Both Smalltalk and C^{++}, for example, define an explicit *new*

Quadrilateral	
point$_1$	point$_3$
point$_2$	point$_4$
draw	
move ($\Delta x, \Delta y$)	
contains?(aPoint)	

Figure 2.2: A class definition for quadrilaterals.

operation that creates a new instance of a specified class. C++ also incorporates a constructor concept in which instances are created implicitly when an object is declared.

Programming languages take different approaches to instance destruction—that is, the deletion of objects when they are no longer useful so memory can be made available for other objects. C++ provides a *delete* operator that can explicitly free up the space used by an object, thereby relying on the programmer to manage objects in memory. C++ also allows each class to define a destructor method that is called implicitly when an object is destroyed. Smalltalk, on the other hand, does not provide a mechanism to destroy objects, but relies instead on garbage collection.

A class is often considered to be a realization of an abstract data type (ADT). This definition is not quite sufficient. It is more appropriate to consider a class as a model of some concept. This model is provided to a software system in a form that is different from that of any other approach. The fact that the class is a single syntactic unit makes the manipulation of objects in a system more natural than requiring the system developer to match data definitions and the operations on them. The class is the primary tool of object-oriented design, so maybe it should have been called class-oriented design!

Most languages that support the object-oriented paradigm provide data abstraction mechanisms. The mechanism for class definition provides a means for designating the operations that users of the class will be able to access. This set of operations is termed the *class interface*. The remainder of the class definition provides data definitions and auxiliary function definitions that comprise the *class implementation*. This separation isolates the users of the class from the effects of changes to the internals of a class.

The class interface is the set of operations that instances of the class can be requested to perform. The simplified public interface for the Quadrilateral class, Figure 2.2, shows the messages to which instances of the Quadrilateral class can respond. Sending the message *draw* to an instance of class Quadrilateral results in that instance executing its draw operator. The draw operator would be designed to draw a quadrilateral having shape and location determined by the point data inside the instance.

The class implementation often includes instances of other classes that provide services the new class requires. These instances should be defined in such a way that they are inaccessible from other objects—that is, protected from access by other objects, including other instances of the same class. In the quadrilateral example, the four points that specify a quadrilateral are point objects defined within the quadrilateral object. These point objects are intended to be inaccessible from other objects. If we decide that it is important for other objects to be able to access these points, then we can add methods to the class interface to provide this access. For example, we might want to designate one point—perhaps the point closest to point $(0,0)$ on the screen—as a reference point. We would define a method, say referencePoint, to provide that value rather than allowing other objects to compute it from the values of $point_1$, $point_2$, $point_3$, and $point_4$. A class implementation might also include some private methods—for use in implementing the class, but not intended for use by any other object. For example, we might want a private method that, when given a list of points, determines the point that is closest to $(0,0)$.

A class is similar to—but also very different from—a record in Pascal or a structure in C in the sense that it is an aggregation of data values. Classes normally extend the usual semantics of records to provide varying levels of visibility—that is, some components of the record may not be accessible by every component that has visibility to the record type. Classes differ from records in that they include definitions of operators with the same status as the data values declared within the class. These are not equivalent to function pointers that are defined independently of the class and stored in the class instances.

A class is a unique combination of data and operators that supports building complete models of real-world entities in a more natural way than the Ada package or a Modula-2 module. The class can serve as a type, a compilation unit, and a modeling unit all in one. The type checking of a compiler uses the class name and definition as it would a type name to check for compatibility of expressions. Classes can be compiled separately in many object-oriented languages, and a class can represent a real-world concept by defining the appropriate attributes and operators.

The Ada package closely resembles the class, yet there are differences here as well. The package is an efficient compilation unit, but not an adequate conceptual modeling unit. Within its specification, a package may define a data type and the operations that are to be allowed on instances of the type. However, the instances of the type and the operators are separate. A user of the type must create objects of that type and then pass these objects to the subprograms that operate on objects of that type. The use of Ada *generic* packages circumvents the need to pass objects as parameters because the package instance can maintain its own private state variables, but the generic package feature provides no support for inheritance.

Virtually all object-oriented languages use objects as the representation of the instances that make up an application. Some languages, such as Smalltalk, also implement the classes themselves as objects. Since objects are the manipulatable entities in an object-oriented application, the implication is that languages that implement classes as objects allow the manipulation of classes by an application. This capability supports the flexibility needed in many application areas such as artificial intelligence.

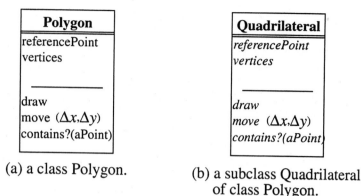

(a) a class Polygon.

(b) a subclass Quadrilateral
of class Polygon.

Figure 2.3: An example of the use of inheritance.

Inheritance

Up to this point, if you use a language with good support for data abstraction, you may wonder why all the excitement about object-orientation. The title of Brad Cox's book[23], *Object-Oriented Programming: An Evolutionary Approach*, implies that object-oriented techniques simply extend existing technology as opposed to being totally new. *Inheritance* is the major, unique extension to ADT technology by object-oriented technology.

Inheritance is a technique for using existing definitions as the basis for new definitions. The definition of the new class is a combination of the data and operation declarations from the existing class(es) and any declarations added by the new class. The new class reuses the existing definitions without any need to modify the existing classes. It is less expensive to develop this way because a portion of the class has already been implemented and tested. The existing class is referred to as the *parent class*, the *base class*, or the *superclass*. The new class is correspondingly referred to as the *child class*, the *derived class*, or the *subclass*.

Consider the Quadrilateral class. If the class Polygon shown in Figure 2.3(a) existed when class Quadrilateral was defined, then the definition of Quadrilateral could have looked like Figure 2.3(b). The italicized items in Figure 2.3(b) have been defined in class Polygon and added to the definition of class Quadrilateral through the inheritance mechanism. Presumably these elements have already been tested as part of class Polygon and may not need to be retested as rigorously as newly written code.

Inheritance is a very general technique. There is a variety of ways that existing classes can be combined with the new definitions to define a new class. We will investigate this concept in detail in Chapter 4. For now we will present a design discipline for using inheritance and justify it later.

Defining a new class using inheritance can be viewed as describing a new set of objects that is a subset of the objects described by the existing class. This new subset can be thought of as a *specialization* of the existing class. For example, the Quadrilateral class in Figure 2.3 is a specialization of the Polygon. A quadrilateral is a polygon restricted to four sides. We could further specialize a quadrilateral into a rectangle which is a quadrilateral having special properties. The interface for the Quadrilateral class might be identical to that of the Polygon class, and the interface for a Rectangle might be the same as that of the Quadrilateral.

The new class can also be viewed as having an interface that is an *expansion* of the interface of the existing class. For example, deriving a four-wheel drive vehicle class from an existing vehicle class would not only specialize the definition to a subset of vehicles, but probably also introduce new capabilities in the new class interface. Continuing with our example, we might wish to add more operations for a rectangle— for example, a method that would answer the largest ellipse that can be enscribed in that instance.

How much of the existing definition is available to be added to the new definition varies from one language to another. Many languages give the implementor control over which attributes are actually inherited and how they are inherited. Typically, the system developer may choose to either inherit only the interface and not the representation or to inherit both the interface and the representation. We will see later how this control provides better support for data abstraction.

In summary, our discipline for the use of inheritance is to include all the attributes of the existing class in the new class definition. This leads to the development of inheritance structures that are conceptually rational and understandable.

Additional techniques

Objects, classes, and inheritance characterize the object-oriented paradigm, but other techniques are used in conjunction with them to provide additional power. Two of these are *polymorphism* and *dynamic binding.*

Polymorphic techniques provide the designer with the flexibility to build structures that accommodate objects that are of separate but related types in a type-safe environment. *Inclusion polymorphism* is an attribute of a type system that introduces flexibility in the type checking of subprogram parameters. In a polymorphic language, actual parameters are checked against the formal parameters as usual. However, instead of requiring an exact match between the type of the formal parameter and that of the actual parameter, the actual parameter may be an instance of any of several types belonging to a specified set. In an object-oriented polymorphic language, the set of types that may be substituted for a specified type is the set of its subclasses.

Figure 2.4 shows an inheritance hierarchy for four classes. With this inheritance structure, an actual parameter of class Quadrilateral could be substituted for a formal parameter of class Polygon. This is reasonable if the discipline of inheritance presented above is followed because the interface for class Quadrilateral is compatible with the interface for class Polygon—that is, instances of class Quadrilateral respond to all of the messages in the interface for class Polygon. Similarly, an actual parameter of class Rectangle can be bound to a formal parameter of class Polygon or Quadrilateral.

An example that illustrates the benefits of inclusion polymorphism is a collection class such as a list of polygons to be drawn on a screen. The kind of strong typing supported by procedural languages such as Pascal and Ada requires the use of a single variant record type to represent a list element or requires the use of some

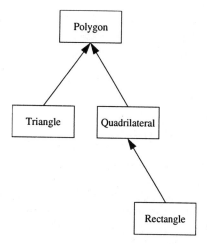

Figure 2.4: An inheritance hierarchy for some polygon classes.

"untyped" pointer to bypass type checking when accessing list elements. The kind of polymorphism supported by object-oriented techniques allows an object to be treated as belonging to several types at one time. This allows a structure such as a list to hold elements from a designated set of types rather than just one type. The designated set is considered to be a family of classes that are related through inheritance to the formal type specification for the elements of the list. We can "draw" all of the entries in the list of polygons by traversing the list, sending each element the *draw* message, which is understood by any polygon. When you consider that one of the subclasses may have been developed days, weeks, or even months later but can still be held by the list without modification, the usefulness of this technique becomes obvious.

Polymorphism combined with the language implementation technique of dynamic binding supports the system developer in building systems that are flexible and easily extended. Dynamic binding delays the association of a function call to a destination code block until execution time. A number of languages, such as Smalltalk and CLOS, utilize dynamic binding exclusively because they are interpreted languages. Compiled languages such as C++ and Eiffel selectively alternate between static and dynamic binding to support polymorphism where it is useful and to retain the efficiency of static binding where possible. Some compiled languages, such as C++, do compile-time checking that ensures every message sent can be understood by the object receiving the message, even when dynamic binding is used. Some interpreted languages, such as Smalltalk, cannot guarantee that an object can answer a message.

As an example of dynamic binding, consider the contains?(aPoint) method in our polygon class. This method could be reimplemented at each level in the class hierarchy in order to make use of special characteristics of each subclass. For example, it is more efficient to check if a rectangle contains a point than if a general quadrilateral contains a point while assuming that a rectangle must have sides that parallel the sides of the screen. If we have a polymorphic list of Polygon instances and want to see if a point p—perhaps the location of a mouse click—is in any of them, then we want to traverse the list, sending each object $\mathcal{P}$ in the list the message contains?(p). Dynamic binding ensures that the method associated with the class of $\mathcal{P}$ is invoked. For example, if $\mathcal{P}$ is of class Rectangle, the more efficient implementation associated with rectangles is invoked and not the method associated with either the class Quadrilateral or the class Polygon.

WHY USE THESE TECHNIQUES?

In this section, we briefly examine some of the reasons for using object-oriented design and implementation techniques. At times this text will sound like an advertisement because we do believe that these techniques are improvements over existing technology. However, we have made every effort to present a realistic view of the role of object-oriented methods in software development. Following are some reasons to use object-oriented technology.

- *Promotes reusability.* Object-oriented techniques yield structures that are more readily reused than other design techniques. Later chapters and examples will illustrate that reuse comes in many forms:

    1. There is reuse by using an instance. For example, an application might use many instances of class Quadrilateral.

    2. There is reuse by using an instance in a definition. For example, the Quadrilateral uses instances of class Point.

    3. There is reuse by evolution. For example, class Quadrilateral is used to define class Rectangle.

    The support for data abstraction in object-oriented methods promotes these types of reuse. Designers view object-oriented techniques from different perspectives. Those currently using languages such as C will see the additional potential for reuse provided by classes. Those using languages such as Ada or Modula will see packages and modules as providing the first two types of reuse. What they will not have seen is the third type of reuse.

- *Facilitates maintenance.* The information-hiding supported by most object-oriented programming languages facilitates maintenance. The interface of a class defines the set of operations on the data of an instance of that class. If a change is made to the representation of data defined in the class, then those operations defined in the class that interact with the changed data need to be modified. There is no need for users to modify their references to instances of the class unless the signature of one of the operations has been changed. The impact of this and many other maintenance activities is localized.

    For example, consider an implementation of the class Rectangle in which we wish to use two points to define it instead of four points. [Note that if we require a rectangle to be aligned with the x and y axes, then we can define it in terms of its upper-left vertex and its lower-right vertex.

Many microcomputer systems provide facilities to draw rectangles in terms of these two points.] The methods draw, move, contains?, and referencePoint would have to be reimplemented to determine the other two points if they are needed. These changes would be localized to the code of the methods of the Rectangle class.

- *Exploits commonality.* Object-oriented techniques exploit commonality in two ways. First, there is commonality across applications. Software development firms tend to develop applications that address a common domain such as communications or graphics. By developing units that are easily reused, object-oriented design exploits the commonality within a company's applications. Second, there is commonality across system components. For example, a graphics system defines numerous shapes such as lines, triangles, circles, and rectangles. These components are different shapes, but they have many common attributes. Object-oriented design develops a structure that factors out these common elements into a class, which can then be the basis for defining each of the individual shape classes.

- *Reduces complexity.* This is where the advertisement starts because we have little more than anecdotal evidence to support this claim. A recent paper by Rosson and Gold[83] does provide some evidence in support of the claim. Existing procedural techniques require that the designer have a solution in mind before beginning the design process. This requires the designer to be an expert problem solver because the design technique only supports the computerization of a solution rather than the problem-solving process. This further implies that the designer cannot begin the system design until a complete problem solution is known. With today's complex systems, this is often a severe limitation.

  Object-oriented techniques begin the development process in the problem domain rather than in the solution domain. This relieves the designer from developing a complete solution before beginning any design work. Thus, the designer is able to handle more complex problems because of the support provided by the design techniques.

WHEN SHOULD THESE TECHNIQUES BE USED?

This is a difficult question to answer because any design paradigm can be used to produce some solution to any problem. A designer should wish to select the technique that will lead to an effective solution. As we will see later there are a number of paradigms, each with particular value for certain types of problems. The following characterize some situations in which the object-oriented paradigm is appropriate.

- *When multiple instances of complex entities are part of the solution.* The use of objects in design leads to an architecture that is characterized by discrete structures that communicate with each other. The encapsulation of functionality means that otherwise lengthy and complex flows of control are decomposed into shorter, simpler segments hidden within the individual objects. Consider a window management system. The functionality needed to save the underlying screen, display a variety of information, and interact with the user must be provided for each window that is created. For some applications, users may have the power to create an almost unlimited number of windows. Having each instance of a window contain the functionality that it needs results in an architecture that distributes responsibility. Such a system easily handles multiple occurrences of complex entities.

- *When solutions will evolve over time.* The use of inheritance to evolve new definitions from existing ones supports the solution of complex problems. Areas in which solutions evolve over time rather than being obvious at the outset require many changes as an application is developed. Developing subclasses from existing classes allows the designer to modify the behavior of classes incrementally as new information about a solution becomes available. These changes can be made without disturbing existing software components, which depend on the classes that are to be modified.

- *When prototyping leads to quick development of module interfaces.* The encapsulation of representation characteristic of objects supports the prototyping of systems. Once the module interfaces are developed, the underlying representations of classes can be modified without impacting the modules that use the services of the changing module. Quickly developing the format of a window can be followed by detailed implementation that provides sufficient speed of response while using acceptable space. Strictly speaking, this is a characteristic of data abstraction that is an integral part of object-orientation.

- *When a number of related applications will be developed over time.* The object-oriented paradigm encourages the development of an inventory of reusable software components. By making an investment in the development and testing of components, a company can gain momentum with every new project. As the inventory builds, each new application goes out with less and less original code and more and more previously written and tested code.

- *When large development teams and large applications require partitioning of the system.* The development of large systems requires independent work done in parallel. The encapsulation of objects provides a natural partitioning of the system. Early agreement on class interfaces leads to few major changes to the architecture of the application.

SOFTWARE DESIGN

The design of a software application involves a number of facets. The high-level design specifies a system architecture that is a network of modules. The process of designing the application requires that the system developer identify the modules. The designer

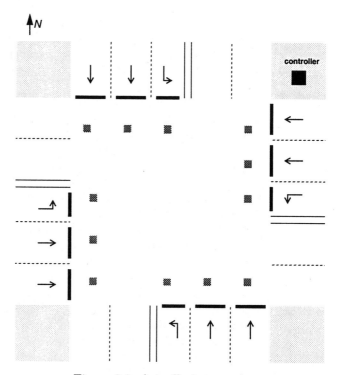

Figure 2.5: A traffic intersection.

must follow some guiding principle in decomposing the problem into modules. The choice of this guiding principle has a profound impact on the architecture of the resulting application.

Once the modules are identified, the internals of each must be specified. Again, there must be guidelines to direct the designer in this specification process. These guidelines should develop modules that are appropriate abstractions. The guiding principles for the identification of modules and for the design of these modules are termed a *design paradigm*.

Each design paradigm presents a different viewpoint on system development. The procedural paradigm utilizes functional decomposition to represent the solution of a problem. A solution is viewed as a sequence of tasks. The object-oriented paradigm uses a modeling approach to represent the problem environment. The solution is then crafted from elements in the model. The differences between the two paradigms can best be illustrated by applying each to a single problem.

Example: Traffic Intersection

Consider the development of a software system that will control the traffic at the intersection shown in Figure 2.5 by controlling the traffic lights based on inputs from various sensors. The requirements for the software system are described below.

Requirements

Software running in a microprocessor-based control box shall control the traffic at an intersection by controlling the traffic lights based on inputs from sensors placed in each of the traffic lanes at the intersection. When a vehicle drives (or stops) over a sensor, that sensor sets a bit in a memory location in the control box. This memory location (byte address) is unique for each sensor. Either mechanical or electronic sensors may be used, but both types interact with the controller in the same manner. The controller can reset the bit for a given sensor, then detect the presence of a vehicle by polling the corresponding bit until it becomes set. If a bit is reset and a vehicle is either stopped or moving directly over the sensor, then the bit is again set—that is, a sensor write takes precedence over a processor write to the same bit.

The control box also contains a clock that can be read to determine the current date and time of day and a timer that can be set for up to 1024 seconds. When the timer counts down to zero, it generates an interrupt to the processor.

The intersection contains two types of traffic signal. One type is the standard signal with a red, amber, and green light. The other type is a standard signal with an additional green arrow that points left. The first is used to control traffic in straight and/or right turn lanes. The second is used in each of the left turn lanes to indicate a protected left turn—that is, a green arrow indicates that vehicles in that lane may turn left without yielding to oncoming traffic—while a circular green light indicates that a left turn is allowed, but oncoming traffic has the right of way. The lights are controlled via memory-mapped output. Each signal has an associated byte in memory, and a separate bit in each byte controls a light in a signal. Setting a bit causes the associated light to turn on, and resetting that bit causes the light to turn off. A separate bit can be set to put the signal in flashing mode in which each light whose bit is set will blink on and off. The mapping of bits in a byte depends on the signal type.

The controller's responsibility is to sequence the signals in such a way that traffic flow is maintained through the intersection in a safe and fair manner. For traffic in opposing directions (that is, north/south and east/west), if a vehicle is in a left turn lane, then the controlling signal should provide a left turn arrow for either T_L seconds or until the sensor in that turn lane indicates no more vehicles, at which time the signal should be circular green until traffic in the adjacent straight lane is stopped with a red light. When a protected turn light ends, the signals for the traffic in the oncoming direction should indicate circular green for a duration of T_S seconds. This duration should be extended if the signal in the opposite direction has not yet been green for a full T_S seconds. Note: If no traffic in either direction is sensed for a duration of T_X seconds, then all signals should be sequenced to amber and then red if there is any traffic sensed in the cross direction.

If no traffic is sensed in any lane, then the lights should sequence every T_N seconds. In this sequence there are no left turns—that is, the signals in left turn lanes show red lights in all directions.

The controller supports three interrupts other than the timer interrupt:

- A *power on/start* interrupt, which is used to initialize the controller. Initialization should start traffic moving in the north/south direction.

- A *test* interrupt which is used to check all the signals by sequencing them rapidly through all possible states—that is, assuming that all sensors have been tripped and that T_S and T_L have values of 10 and 5 seconds, respectively.

- A *hold* interrupt which is used to control the intersection while a new program is being loaded into the controller. In the hold mode, the all signals flash red except the signals for the two right lanes in both the northbound and southbound directions, which flash amber.

Any one of these interrupts can be used to set the system mode. The mode remains selected until another interrupt arrives.

Traffic volume at this intersection is projected to double over the next two years. Traffic control may need modification to incorporate factors such as time of day and current volume into the control algorithms. These considerations will be determined based on measurements made periodically over the next 18 months.

Analysis of the Traffic Intersection Domain

The analysis phase is divided into two parts: domain analysis and application analysis. For this example, the domain analysis would require that we study the domain of traffic intersections and software systems for their control. There are many sources for such an analysis, but for this example we will use our everyday knowledge of traffic intersections. The hardware for an intersection includes a set of sensors, the traffic lights, and the control box. The software will coordinate the indications from sensors about vehicles present in the intersection and the pattern of red and green traffic lights. In addition, the system is to have other capabilities such as a test option, which cycles the lights through the set of configurations. The system can also be set to a default state, which might be flashing yellow in one direction and red in the other.

Twenty-five objects can readily be identified from the statement of requirements: 12 traffic lights, 12 sensors, and 1 controller. These specific objects can be abstracted into three classes: Traffic Light, Sensor, and Controller. This preliminary analysis can be refined as more information becomes available.

A Traffic Light establishes permissions for each direction of traffic flow. Typically one direction will have one or two—in the case of a turn arrow—lights lit. Which lights to illuminate will be determined by the controller. Different traffic signals will have differing numbers of lights depending upon their responsibility.

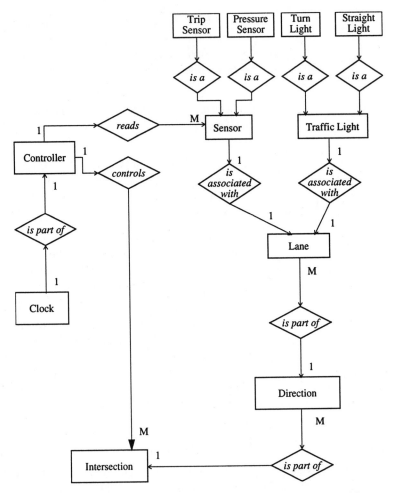

Figure 2.6: An ER diagram for the traffic intersection problem.

A Sensor indicates the presence (or absence) of a vehicle in a particular lane. There are several kinds of sensors, such as electromagnetic and pressure; each works differently internally. All the sensors, however, set a bit whenever the sensor is tripped. After the decision to change the state of the intersection, every sensor is presumably reset by the controller.

The Controller physically contains the switches for the lights, the data stores for the sensors, and a clock for timing the start of the poll/decision cycle.

These entities are described by defining classes and by defining the relationships between the classes. Figure 2.6 shows an entity-relationship diagram that illustrates the relationships between the classes. The *is a* relationship shown in the diagram is the inheritance relationship. The general class Traffic Light provides the basic functionality to two specializations: Straight Light and Turn Light.

This particular intersection uses two kinds of traffic signal. One is the standard

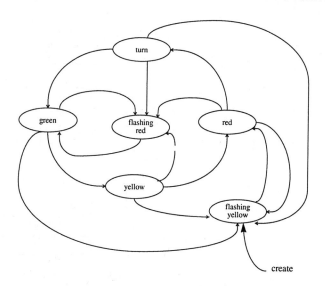

Figure 2.7: State transitions for a left-turn signal.

three-color signal for the go-straight lanes. The other is a four-light signal: red, amber, circular green, and green turn arrow. Each signal has a current state, a set of valid next states, and a default state. The states and valid transitions for one kind of traffic signal is shown in Figure 2.7. In practice, state diagrams would be developed for each entity in the ER diagram as part of the analysis process.

The application analysis considers those parts of the general domain that apply to the current problem. The ER diagram, for example, contains two kinds of sensors. In an application for one intersection there probably will be only one kind of sensor included in the application analysis.

Design

In this section we will compare the structured and object-oriented approaches to design. We are more interested in the perspective of the person doing the design than in the particular products from each phase.

Structured Design

A number of design techniques have been developed for the procedural paradigm. Structured design applies a functional decomposition to a proposed solution of a problem to arrive at a sequence of tasks. Controlling the traffic intersection is then viewed in structured design as a sequence of actions: Wait for a clock interrupt, poll the sensors, determine the next state, send the signals to change the lights, and reset the clock. Figure 2.8 shows a structure chart that provides one possible decomposition. Much more detail could be included, but this figure provides the basic idea of the sequence of events that would be carried out. Once the tasks are determined, the

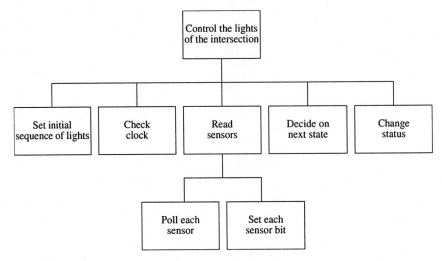

Figure 2.8: A structure chart for the traffic intersection problem.

design of each one includes the definition of the data structures needed to support it.

Figure 2.8 illustrates the basic kind of information developed in the procedural paradigm. Extensions to the paradigm have recognized the importance of data in the development process. Data flow diagrams provide one means of capturing information about data, although much of the information concerns the flow of data rather than a description of the data itself. Figure 2.9 provides a partial data flow diagram for this system.

The viewpoint of the paradigm is clearly task-oriented. Procedural abstraction takes priority over data abstraction. The diagrams provided here illustrate that the procedural paradigm works mainly with a proposed solution to the problem. This does not provide much help in actually solving the problem, nor do structured analysis techniques that aid in defining the problem but not in determining its actual solution.

Object-Oriented Design

The development of an object-oriented design for an application has two main components: class design and application design. The design process builds a model of the problem environment by describing the individual entities present in the environment. This modeling process is bottom up in that we first describe the individual entities (by defining classes) and then coordinate these classes to provide a complete application. However, the best way to understand the process is to first examine the application perspective before considering class design.

The application design includes a model of the problem environment. The model will be built by declaring instances of the appropriate classes. The instances are connected in a configuration that models the interaction of the entities in the real world. The solution to the target problem is obtained by adding *computer artifacts*

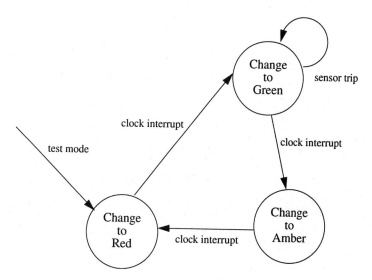

Figure 2.9: A partial data flow diagram for the traffic light problem.

such as user interfaces to the model of the real world. The design of the application depends upon the existence of the appropriate classes.

Class design takes the modeling approach of the application design and narrows its focus. A class definition is going to be a model of some concept. The concept may be a physical entity such as a digital switch or a more abstract entity such as the role of window manager. Each class will provide some portion of the final application through its instances.

Figure 2.6 presents a set of classes, represented by boxes, that were identified for the traffic intersection problem. A number of relationships, represented by diamonds, exist between the classes. We will discuss the meaning of several of these relationships in later chapters. The *controls* relationship is application-specific because it directly corresponds to information from the problem domain. The *is a* relationship is the inheritance relationship and is independent of the application.

The actual application will be developed by creating instances of the various classes to model the problem. There will be 12 traffic lights in the application. However, two types of traffic lights are needed. The two types will have much in common, but they will be different in some aspects. Figure 2.10 shows that this is handled in the design phase by using inheritance. A general traffic light class is created and two subclasses are defined by specializing the general definition into two more specific classes using the inheritance relation.

The application would also include 12 instances of one of the sensor classes. Each sensor instance is associated with a traffic light instance by including one instance of each as a component in an instance of the lane class. The *is part of* relationship between the Clock and Controller classes expresses the idea of one class being used as part of the implementation of another class.

<u>class</u> Traffic Light
    <u>data</u>
        current state
        set of valid states
    <u>operators</u>
        test
        flash yellow
        flash red
        next state

<u>class</u> Straight Light *is a* Traffic Light
    <u>data</u>
      current state
      set of valid states
    <u>operators</u>
      test
      flash yellow
      flash red
      next state

<u>class</u> Turn Light *is a* Traffic Light
    <u>data</u>
      current state
      set of valid states
    <u>operators</u>
      test
      flash yellow
      flash red
      next state

Figure 2.10: Hierarchy of traffic light classes.

Final Notes

The object-oriented analysis and design appears to be much larger and more complex than the procedural design. This is partly because the object-oriented design provides both a view of the solution as well as the problem in one entity-relationship diagram. The result is a description of the problem domain that includes pieces that are much more general and reusable than the pieces that are developed as part of the solution to a specific problem as viewed in the procedural paradigm. While both techniques result in a workable solution, the object-oriented technique will build for the future and satisfy the situation at hand.

SUMMARY

Object-oriented techniques include the use of three devices: objects, classes, and inheritance. We have presented intuitive definitions for each of these concepts. We have also considered why and when to use object-oriented technology. With a small example we have illustrated the object-oriented approach to design and compared it to the approach in the procedural paradigm.

Much of this book will be devoted to specifying, explaining, and illustrating the guidelines that constitute the object-oriented paradigm. The text will include language-independent examples. Additionally, C++ based examples will be used to illustrate implementation considerations.

FURTHER READING

Several overviews of the object-oriented paradigm are available. You may wish to consult one of them for different examples or a new perspective. These include an overview by Korson and McGregor[60] that introduces a special issue of *Communications of the ACM* on object-oriented design, Brad Cox's book[23], and Bertrand Meyer's book[73]. A blend of structured and object-oriented approaches is considered by Wasserman[94].

3

The Development Process

Software engineers use the concept of a life cycle to organize and manage the development process. Certain tasks are assigned to each stage in the life cycle. Experience with many projects using basically the same life cycle model provides a basis for estimating the amount of time to allocate to each stage. Changes in development methodology will change the life cycle. New stages may be added to the model or old ones deleted and the amount of time spent in a particular phase may change.

The object-oriented approach improves the interfaces between the various phases of the life cycle. This is because the "pieces" developed at each level in the life cycle are the same, namely classes. Each stage in the object-oriented life cycle refines the information known about each class. The class is the primitive unit for analysis, design, and implementation. The importance of this fact is that the output of the analysis phase is—albeit in a slightly modified form—a syntactic unit in the language of implementation!

There is not always complete agreement on which activities belong to which phase of the life cycle. The fact that the same unit—the class—is used throughout the object-oriented life cycle makes this less a concern but, at the same time, makes it a more difficult question to answer. We will place activities in the phases in which experience has shown us they belong, but our methodology does not rigidly require that the user follow this blindly.

This chapter considers the traditional application development life cycle and proposes modifications to it that emphasize reuse and support the object-oriented paradigm. The steps in the life cycle are presented in a sequential fashion, but this in no way is intended to mean that their application is linear. Indeed, the analysis, design, and implementation activities are each iterative internally; as a complete life cycle the phases are iterative as well. The chapter outlines a step-by-step application development process that carries through the use of object technology. Succeeding chapters will examine the various phases in detail. In addition to development issues, this text will also address some of the "process" issues related to object-oriented software development. Issues in the testing of object-oriented software, project team organization, and the implications of reuse will be addressed.

CONFLICTING GOALS

Application designers often work with conflicting goals when developing software. The application should be developed quickly and within budget. The software components should be carefully designed to be complete abstractions that will be reusable. Both sides of this issue were presented when we discussed reasons to use object-oriented techniques, but there are obviously no simple answers. Companies will be making difficult decisions about how to best utilize their limited resources.

This text will make much mention of reuse because we believe it to be a core theme for software engineering in the 1990s. The reusability issue is analogous to the problem of long-term investment that American industry has been facing recently. There is a desire among managers to make the bottom line look as good as possible as quickly as possible without regard to the long-term implications for the company. Likewise, there is a "get it out the door" mentality in many software development organizations. There are good ways to accomplish these goals and those that are not so good. One company has implemented a "half the interval" program to develop revisions of existing applications in half the time. With the first application they met their goal—because the developers worked twice as many hours per week. Developing libraries of high-quality components that can be used in many parts of a system and using appropriate automation of the development process are good ways to "cut the interval," but these techniques do not work overnight. Omitting necessary testing procedures and expecting professionals to simply work longer hours will produce a given system more rapidly, but are not appropriate techniques that produce long-term benefit to the company. On the contrary, software developed in such an environment is likely to barely meet requirements and to be next to impossible to maintain and enhance.

Object-oriented techniques support rapid prototypical development of software, another technique for reducing the development time for an application. The encapsulation and information hiding properties of objects allow for a quick implementation that later can be improved upon without interfering with other parts of the system. Quick prototyping will also be supported by having a complete toolkit of high-quality reusable parts that can be used to develop a new system. The material in this chapter will include techniques for supporting the development of reusable components.

THE APPLICATION LIFE CYCLE

Software engineers utilize the life cycle approach to manage a company's application inventory. The life cycle shown in Figure 3.1 is a high-level view of a standard life cycle widely used in procedurally oriented projects. This particular model is termed the *waterfall model*[33]. Each of the phases in this model is elaborated into a number

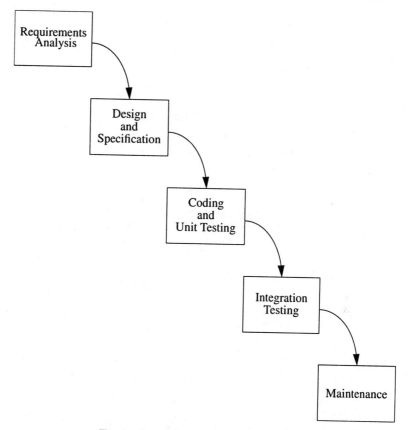

Figure 3.1: The waterfall life cycle.

of subprocesses in practice. These phases take an application from its beginnings in analysis into the maturity of maintenance. Since this life cycle is intended to model the entire application development process, we will term it an *application life cycle*. Other models, many of which more closely represent the true complexity of the development process, have been proposed, most notably the *spiral model*[10] and the *fountain model*[46].

Application life cycles have been widely used as a basis for structuring software development projects. We will assume that you are familiar with this general form of life cycle or one of its variants, and we will discuss only the modifications needed to support the philosophy of development described in Chapter 1. The application life cycle guides project planning and monitoring. It is also a good way to consider the overall development process and the resources used to produce the system. We will use an application life cycle as a structuring agent for our discussion in this text. The model we will use is introduced in Figure 3.2.

The figure is linear, but the development process is not. No figure can do justice to the complex interactions between phases in the object-oriented development process. Boehm's spiral model and Henderson-Sellers' fountain model still do not account for

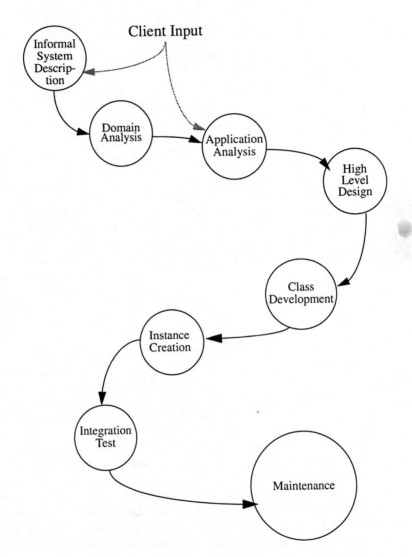

Figure 3.2: A proposed application life cycle.

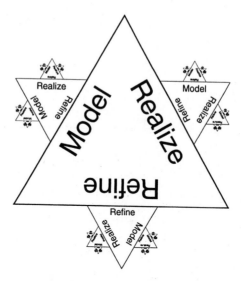

Figure 3.3: The fractal software development process

all possible behavior. Some portion of the analysis may be carried out before the design begins, but portions of the analysis may proceed in parallel with the design and implementation of other portions of the system. In fact, the interactions are more complex than even this description. Speaking at an OOPSLA '91 research workshop on reuse, Brian Foote from the University of Illinois proposed a "fractal model" of the software life cycle. We have coupled this concept with the philosophy described in the first chapter to produce the model shown in Figure 3.3. The self-similar nature of a fractal fits well with the idea that a class is often the starting point for new classes that are needed to provided services to the originating class. This continues recursively in a self-similar manner. It also fits well with our concept of *modeling* the problem domain, *realizing* classes in a sound engineering manner, and *refining* and reusing the resulting products. We will continue to use the more detailed diagram in Figure 3.2 as a guide to our discussion. The model in Figure 3.3 will serve as a visualization of the overall process.

One difficulty with an application life cycle such as the waterfall model, from our perspective, is that it does not look beyond an individual project, nor does it consider any "product" smaller than the entire application. The economics of software development now require an emphasis on reusing software components. This goal will not be reached without refocusing managers' attention and developers' efforts. Explicit attention should be paid in the software development process to developing reusable components as part of the application development process. Object-orientation provides the class as a natural unit. The next section considers a separate class life cycle that operates independently of the application life cycle. This life cycle integrates with the application life cycle at the class development phase shown in Figure 3.2. After discussing the class life cycle we will return to the application life cycle.

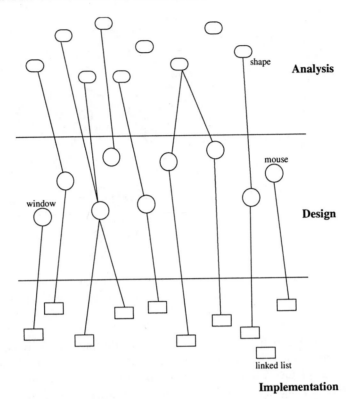

Figure 3.4: Mapping of objects from phase to phase during system development.

CLASS LIFE CYCLE

For reuse to play a major role in software development, program components must have a life independent of the application for which they were originally developed. Individual components are identified and incorporated into the system at every stage in the application life cycle as illustrated in Figure 3.4. Component development addresses the design and implementation of pieces that can aid in the solution of the current problem but that are sufficiently general to be of use in future projects. Locating the appropriate pieces that will be generally useful is a difficult and time-consuming process. Application development can be thought of as the coordination of these individual components to produce the solution to a specific problem or the development of a particular product. Since the class is the unit that we wish to reuse beyond the current application, Figure 3.5 presents a *class life cycle*. Henderson-Sellers and Edwards[46] have also presented two separate life cycles that vary from those presented here in only a few details. The pictures that they use probably give a better representation of the complexity of the life cycle than our simple figure.

This life cycle should be thought of as orthogonal to the application life cycle—that is, the identification of classes is part of the application life cycle, but the steps of

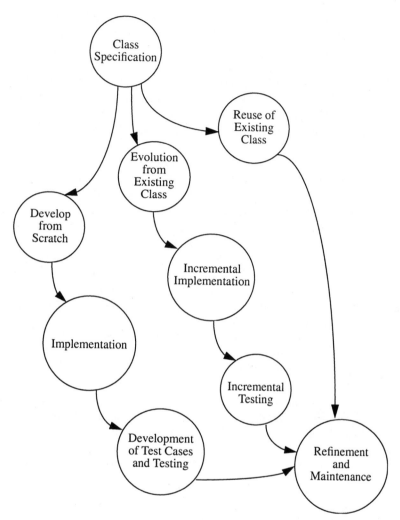

Figure 3.5: The class life cycle.

the class life cycle are independent of the development of any particular application. This independence is intended to support the *complete* description on an underlying entity without regard to the current system being developed. Additional classes are encountered at every level of development. Figure 3.4 illustrates this by considering the three major levels of system development. At each of these levels, new classes are identified. Classes identified at the analysis level will be problem-specific, while classes identified at the implementation level will provide primitive data structures that apply to many applications. With the identification of each new class, the class life cycle guides its development through each stage.

Consider an application in which a need for a graphic display device has been identified. If such a class does not exist, the development of one begins. Very few applications would require the use of all conceivable operations on a display. Viewed as part of the development of a particular application, only those operations needed by the system at hand would be identified and implemented. By considering the component independent of the application, the need to develop beyond the requirements of the immediate use in one application becomes apparent. This independence should produce a class that is as complete a model of the concept being represented as possible and one that is more likely to be reused in other systems. For this approach to be successful, management must take an "investment" view of the development process. That is, decisions must be made that extend beyond individual projects. As we enter the 1990s, a components industry is emerging in which the development of components rather than systems is the goal. In this case, the investment decision is which libraries to purchase and how to allocate their cost to the various projects that use the library functionality.

In a purely object-oriented system development an application program *is* a class. All of the elements needed to solve a problem are gathered together in one class definition and the problem is solved by an instance of that class. Thus the class and traditional application life cycles share many common characteristics. However, we distinguish between an application life cycle and a class life cycle because the application life cycle should also include many "product" considerations such as publications that accompany the actual software, installation considerations, and even training users to use the product. Primitive classes such as a list class would not be considered an application, but instances of primitive classes are aggregated into other class definitions. These, in turn, are aggregated into more complex class definitions and eventually we encounter a class that would be considered the complete application. A switching system includes several queues that provide buffering of incoming messages. These queues might be implemented by creating an instance of a linked list within the definition of the queue class.

Each phase of the class life cycle is summarized briefly below to provide an overview. A more complete discussion will follow in later chapters.

Class Specification

Once a class has been identified, a specification is developed that includes the operations that objects of the class can perform along with their data representation. These specifications are developed based on the notion of modeling the concept to be represented by the class. The guide for including functionality in the interface of the class is whether objects that belong to this class can be thought of as having this behavior. Because this is the interface available to other classes, this list of behaviors should be carefully considered. Changes to the public interface of a class will have a major impact on other classes that rely on its functionality.

Specifications will be developed for every class no matter at what level of the development process it is identified. The specification of a class that interfaces the application to a database would include behaviors to search the database and to add information to the database. The interface of a hash table class should contain functions to store an item and to retrieve an item. Should the hash function that determines the placement of an item in the table be a part of this interface? It is certainly part of the behavior of the table. It is not, however, behavior that a *user* of the hash table needs to be able to access directly. This function can be part of the implementation rather than the public interface. The public interface lists the "responsibilities" of the class rather than a complete list of its functionality. For example, objects that were intended to be placed in the hash table should have a getName or getKey method to provide the input to the hashing function. Given a choice, we will always make the public interface as small as possible while still providing all the behavior needed by a user of the class.

The class specification defines the set of operations on the data store of the object. These operations should be "inward looking"—that is, they should operate on the data store that is encapsulated within the object or return information about the state of the object. Even the names of the operations should reflect this operation-on-self perspective. For example, a class that encapsulates a data value, x, might have an operation that returns the value of x to an inquiring object. The name for such an operation should be something similar to x() or get_x() as opposed to read(). Even though the internals of the operation probably would not change from one name to the other, the name conveys the idea that object A will ask object B to provide B's value of x. Note that these names only make sense if x is a widely used term in this domain and not simply an implementation-dependent variable name. It is appropriate for a class Point to have a method named x since this is a standard way of referring to the first component of an ordered pair. On the other hand, it is not appropriate for a class Rectangle to have a method named x.

The specification of the class must be sufficiently complete to allow it to be compared to the specifications of classes in the resource base of classes available for reuse. The specific techniques to best execute this search are still being researched, but progress has been made. We will address these issues in Chapter 10.

Class Design and Implementation

The class specification guides the search of the software base for existing classes that might be used to provide the necessary functionality for the current application. Figure 3.5 shows three possible directions that the development process may take depending upon the results of that search.

Reuse of an Existing Class

Our preference, obviously, is to reuse existing classes whenever possible. In order to do this the developer must be able to find the classes that are likely candidates for providing the required behavior. Occasionally applications will solve problems that are so closely related to previous problems that application-specific classes can be reused. However, most often, "as-is" reuse will be limited to the lower-level primitives such as basic data structures or to very general structures that use parameters during instantiation to customize their behavior.

The classes in this resource base are assumed to be stable, mature implementations that have been thoroughly tested. No further implementation is required and no testing of the class is required. There will be a need to test the integration of instances of this class with others, but that is a part of the application development process rather than class development.

Evolution from an Existing Class

The most likely reuse situation is that a class will exist that provides behavior *similar* to that specified for the new class. The developer will use that existing class as the starting point in defining the needed class. The new class will be incrementally evolved from the existing class. With less effort than would be required to develop a new class, we are able to reuse many of the supporting products from one class in the development of the new one. Evolution may be either horizontal or vertical. Horizontal evolution results in new versions of existing classes while vertical evolution results in new classes that are derived from the existing classes. We will concentrate here on the vertical incremental development of classes and briefly discuss versioning later.

- *Incremental design.* Incremental design is design of a specialization of the existing class. By determining the intended membership in this new class, the designer can determine what additional behaviors can be added to the class and which existing behaviors should be reimplemented.
- *Incremental implementation.* Much of the implementation will be inherited from the existing class; however, some of this inherited implementation will be overridden by providing an alternate implementation in the new class. This new implementation will more closely fit the specialized definition and may even be a more efficient implementation because it will not need to account for as many different possible situations. In some cases it will be possible to implement a method in such a manner that it makes use of the existing class's implementation with only a small amount of new code that must be written as a preamble or a conclusion for the older method. We will consider how this is accomplished and its impact on implementation. Those behaviors that are added in the incremental design phase must also be implemented. Their implementation will be "from scratch."
- *Incremental testing.* The effort of testing the newly developed class can be greatly reduced in incremental testing. One of the time-consuming tasks in testing is the generation of test cases. Many of the test cases for the new class can be obtained from the existing class's test suite. Some portions of the new class will not need to be tested because of the previous testing in the existing class.

Develop from Scratch

This branch of the life cycle is used only as a last resort; however, until an extensive software base is developed, this is how most initial development will occur. Any class that is developed without evolving from an existing class will be considered to be the start of a new inheritance structure. We will explore the implications of this statement in Chapter 6, but briefly it means that we will create two classes in this process: an abstract class to embody the concept being represented and a concrete class to implement the concept.

- *Design.* The design phase takes the interface produced during the analysis phase of the application life cycle as input and determines the other attributes of the class. Although it is often difficult to know where analysis ends and design begins, the attributes identified in analysis are those that have to do with the problem domain. Attributes identified in the design phase are those needed to implement the concept as a computer-based entity. The design provides all of the details of the class. The form may be informal and low-level using the syntax of an implementation language, or it may be higher-level and more formal, using a representation such as the Object-Z specification language. The output of this phase is sufficient detail about the classes' attributes to support their implementation.

    The design of individual classes includes structuring the data store that is the center of the class definition. This internal representation is made up of primitive objects, such as integers and reals, and composite objects—objects that are made up of other objects. The values of these data attributes constitute the state of the object. The internal representation may also include private functions that implement pieces of the public operations.

    The low-level design of individual classes involves important relationships such as inheritance and composition. Both of these relationships involve an important principle: *Don't do any work you don't absolutely have to!* The object-oriented paradigm facilitates the reuse of existing definitions as a basis for new definitions. While the composition—or *is part of*—relationship is available in other paradigms, it is the inheritance relation that makes object-oriented design unique.

    There are two important relationships between classes: *is part of* and *is a.*

    is part of. The *is part of* relationship is available in many paradigms. The relationship indicates that some portion of the representation of an entity can be provided by the other entity. In the case of the object-oriented paradigm, the definition of a class can include an instance of another class. The behavior of the existing class is then available to be used by the implementation of the new class. For example, consider a classDisplayable Shape class to be developed. Every shape is to have a reference point that is its "handle" in the system. A portion of the representation of the Displayable Shape class could be provided by an instance of the Point class. Point is said to be a *part of* the representation of the shape class. The relationship established by defining the instance is stated as "class Point *is part of* class Displayable Shape."

    There is a fine line between a class's representation and its implementation. The *is part of* relationship represents an implementation-level association between classes but still does not totally constrain its implementation. At the design level, we are concerned with the required functionality that the class can provide. At the implementation level we will be concerned about how to provide the instance of the required class.

is a. In Chapter 7 we will discuss the differences between *object-based* and *object-oriented*, but much of what is presented here applies equally to both. An essential difference between the two is support for the inheritance—*is a*—relationship. This relationship uses an existing definition of a class as part of the definition of a new class, as does the *is part of* relationship. The inheritance relationship provides the designer with an additional and very powerful tool for system design. The *is a* relationship between two classes signifies that one class is a special case of the other.

This relationship maps an existing class definition and a partial definition of a new class into a complete class definition. Each language provides a variety of mappings that determine how the pieces of the existing class are incorporated into the resulting class definition. Rather than only bringing a part of the implementation of the new class, an inherited class contributes to the specification of the new class. Later we will consider a number of examples of this relationship.

Consider the need for a triangle class in a graphics system. We could design this class from scratch, but this would be a waste of effort. We have already seen some of the behavior we need for Triangle. It is part of the class Displayable Shape. The definition for Triangle can begin by adding in the public specification of the class Displayable Shape to the new class's specification. In this way, for example, Triangle inherits a reference point attribute. This establishes the relationship that Triangle *is a* Displayable Shape.

The *is a* and *is part of* relationships provide the designer with powerful tools for the development of new software components from existing ones. By viewing these techniques as mathematical relations, we will be able later in the text to more formally discuss the various relationships in the object-oriented paradigm.

- *Implement.* The desired behavior and state of a class are implemented through the declaration of variables, the implementation of the interface operators, and the implementation of functions to support the interface operators. The data to be stored in the variables are usually instances of other classes that provide services needed by the class being developed. For example, the services provided by the Point class are useful for some of the operations in our Displayable Shape class. These class instances form a second layer of implementation. Each of the classes identified at this level in developing the implementation are designed by recursively applying this class life cycle.

The representation of the hash table class might include an instance of an array class as the holder of the hashed items, an integer variable that records the number of items currently in the table, and the hash function discussed above. Finally, the representation includes the implementation of each of the interface operators such as storeItem and retrieveItem.

Obviously, many aspects of the representation are language-dependent. A good object-oriented language will provide the separation between the public interface and the representation we have described here, although it is possible to follow good practice even without language support. Provision for separate compilation of the interface and the representation is useful. In Chapter 7 we will consider important characteristics of object-oriented languages.

- *Test.* Individual classes provide a natural unit for testing. The narrow, well defined interface provided by a well designed class makes exhaustive testing a realistic approach. By beginning the testing of classes at the most abstract level and proceeding down an inheritance relationship, new classes can more easily be completely tested by not retesting those pieces already tested.

Refinement and Maintenance

This is an important part and, according to many studies, the most time-consuming part of any software life cycle. The traditional maintenance activity has been directed toward applications. The refinement process will be directed toward classes and the structures that link them together. Since we are developing with abstractions, part of maintenance is to modify these abstractions over time. As our experience base grows, we will be able to identify abstractions of our abstractions so that inheritance structures will often have levels added through generalization—that is, by adding levels above the existing root classes.

Recent research[47] supports the hypothesis that object-oriented design develops structures that are easier to maintain. The encapsulation of concept and the hiding of implementation make classes much more independent than the "pieces" in other paradigms. Over time, a number of operations will be added to the interface of the class and the implementation will be modified to improve performance. New applications that use the class will lead to new services that were not included in the original design. Later, we will see a number of ways in which these new services can be provided. The isolation of the specification from the implementation will facilitate the tuning of the class.

As classes are used and reused by other class definitions, a number of interdependencies are created. Most modifications of the public interface of a class do not affect the classes that utilize it. Adding methods to the public interface does not require changes in existing software. We will see later that deleting methods or changing the signature of a method are the two alterations that require system-wide attention.

PUTTING IT ALL TOGETHER

In this section we put together the application life cycle with the class life cycle to present an object-oriented application development process. Figure 3.2 lists the steps in the technique. The development procedure begins in the problem domain and provides a natural progression from the problem to a solution. Because of this rearrangement and the problem-centered nature of the development process, some of the activities traditionally assigned to the design phase have been moved into the analysis phase. The following discussion illuminates those steps in the process that will change significantly from the traditional life cycle.

Analysis Phase

The analysis phase includes two stages: domain analysis and application analysis. Both of these involve the identification of abstractions in the problem domain. Specific objects are located and grouped into sets based on common characteristics until finally an abstraction about the problem can be identified.

An important result of the analysis phase is the identification of relationships between the abstractions. The objects identified in the analysis step are not isolated items. Most, if not all, of them interact with other objects in the problem environment. These interactions are the relationships among the objects that constitute the structure of the application. These relationships most often are represented in the application system as messages between objects. These messages are requests by one object that another object perform some action on itself. The flow of control in an object-oriented application consists of two parts: the flow of control within each individual operation plus the pattern of messages between the objects.

Domain Analysis

Domain analysis develops a model of the domain in which the application is being developed. Domain analysis should be performed prior to application analysis because we should not constrain the problem before we understand it. In fact, we should never constrain a problem until it is absolutely necessary. The client may change the requirements (a not unheard-of situation) or the problem environment may change. Domain analysis examines a wide area within a problem domain. By examining this broad perspective, the analysis covers more than just the immediate problem to be solved.

Abstractions are not easily recognized in a problem space, although individual objects are often easy to identify. An abstraction is best identified by considering many related concepts and identifying common characteristics. By identifying a wide range of concepts in the problem domain, domain analysis supports the abstraction process. The important abstractions may not even be identified until after the first application has been developed.

Domain analysis is a long-term investment. It may be of more immediate benefit if, during the initial development, the requirements are altered; it may also pay off quickly on very large projects. The greatest value will be the development of abstractions that represent the essential concepts in a problem domain. These abstractions will form a software base that will support the development of a number of applications.

Classes are identified by recognizing groups of objects that share common characteristics. These groups can often be partitioned in a variety of ways. For example, consider the following list:

> A gasoline delivery truck
> A station wagon
> A convertible
> A school bus
> A dump truck

Depending upon the developer's ability to recognize abstract relationships, classes such as Car, Truck, and Bus might be identified or all these examples might be grouped into a single Vehicle class. We will see later that both the very general classes, such as Vehicle, and the more specific classes such as Car and Truck *should* be identified to develop a complete set of reusable abstractions.

Application Analysis

Application—or systems—analysis refines information developed during the domain analysis phase and focuses on the precise problem to be solved. Figure 3.4 shows classes in the analysis level that do not map to any class in the design level. These classes represent information that falls outside of the application analysis. Our contention is that better abstractions will be developed due to our experience with the broader domain. Traditional methodologies artificially separate systems analysis from the design process. This segregates the system's designers and developers from those that understand the problem best! Furthermore, the real-world entities identified by the applications analysis often are not visible in the final application. This makes the system harder to understand since it does not correspond to reality.

The application analysis phase of the object-oriented methodology is an iterative process. The analysis phase includes identifying entities that are in the problem domain. Grady Booch[11] suggested using the nouns in a problem statement as the objects. We will discuss more specific techniques in Chapter 4. The objects are relatively easy to identify because the problem domain is easily accessible. It is physically available or represented in some type of model that can be accessed.

If each object identified at the application level had to be designed and implemented individually by the system designers, there would be very little benefit to the paradigm. The power of the paradigm is realized by developing abstract descriptions of sets of objects that share a common behavior. These descriptions—classes—are then used to create multiple instances that are the workhorses of the application.

Many times the differences between systems analysis and high-level design become blurred. The analyst often looks at a problem domain and, rather than seeing individual objects, sees the abstract concept. It is sometimes even impossible to see each individual object anyway. For example, in an air traffic control system, it is impossible and undesirable for the analyst to identify each individual flight that will be handled by the system. It is necessary that the concept of a flight be recognized as being an important abstraction in that problem domain.

High-Level Design

Although system design and class design are often the same process in a pure object-oriented environment, we will separate the system concerns from the techniques for designing a class. In the high-level design phase, the top-level view of the application is designed. In a purely object-oriented design this amounts to the development of the interface of a class that represents the system. "Executing" the system will be accomplished by creating an instance of the application class and sending it a message.

Class Development

The application design phase is essentially class development since an application often is represented by a single class and, even when it is not, it is an aggregate of several class instances. The high-level design phase will have identified the need for numerous classes and will have provided a start on the class specification. This phase will proceed through the life cycle for each of these classes. The result will be a set of classes that have been developed independent from, but in support of, the desired application. Our discussion in the previous subsection of this life cycle will be sufficient for this chapter.

Instance Creation

It is finally time to return to solving the original problem! The last several steps have focused on developing the classes that would be needed to represent the pieces of the solution. Here we create instances of classes that correspond to the entities that were identified in the first step.

The relationships identified in domain analysis are the application-level relationships. These relationships will, for the most part, be represented by messages from one instance to another. Part of developing the final application system is establishing the communication channels between the instances. These channels may be established by passing references from one object to another.

Integration Testing

The final development stage is to test the system as a complete application. The encapsulation of each object and the completeness of class testing reduces the time needed for integration testing. The interface of an object-oriented application is usually as well defined as that of the individual objects. The individual operations are sufficiently well insulated that the combinatorial effects of varying the order of operations can often be reduced to a manageable number of cases that have to be tested.

Application Maintenance

As with the rest of the development process, maintenance impacts both the application and the individual classes. The inheritance relationship provides a great deal of support for extending the existing application to include new features or even changing the way some features work. The information hiding makes debugging a process of improving code in a single class rather than chasing ripples across many classes in the system.

Application maintenance includes locating faults in the operation of the system as well as adding new features to an existing system. Some bugs will result from faulty connections between class instances—that is, bad messages. In most cases, however, application maintenance will reduce to locating the class instance responsible for the difficulty and either modifying its class's implementation or changing the role of that particular object in the application by changing the message or order of messages that it receives. New features will most often be implemented by defining new classes and creating instances.

Most of the maintenance activity will occur at the class level. The separation of the class's implementation from its specification will isolate the effects of most changes. Few if any changes to the interface of a class will be needed to correct problems. However, occasionally changes in the interface will be required to add features to a system.

SYSTEM ARCHITECTURE

The architecture of an object-oriented system is determined by its component objects and the relationships between objects. This architecture also reflects the problem domain since it consists mainly of objects from the problem domain. However, orthogonal concerns of performance, compiler limitations, and hardware constraints are realities that must be accommodated in an application. These concerns complicate the architecture of the application, but they should not be allowed to adversely affect the development of classes that provide the component instances of the application. Figure 3.6 shows the interaction of the object and process architectures for a system. A few of the lines are drawn from the software base to the individual processes to show that the internals of the process consist of instances of several different classes and that a single class may provide instances to several of the processes.

Applications are divided into processes for many different reasons. Only on rare occasions is the process architecture designed to model the problem domain. Most often the reason is performance and size of the application. This implies that the process architecture may change if the underlying hardware, compiler, or operating system changes. This is indeed a cost of porting or upgrading to a new environment. On the other hand, the object architecture is intended to model the problem and thus is a relatively stable design, discounting errors made in the design process.

We would like our development process to separate these concerns for the problem domain from those concerns that are environment-dependent. Figure 3.6 illustrates this by indicating that the software base of classes is independent of the process architecture. Instances of a single class may appear in several different processes or in only one process.

In the design process, one architecture is predominant at any time. In those cases where the process architecture is imposed for performance, it seems logical that this element of the design should come late in the design process—after the classes have been determined. Otherwise, how can we know the constraints that arise because of

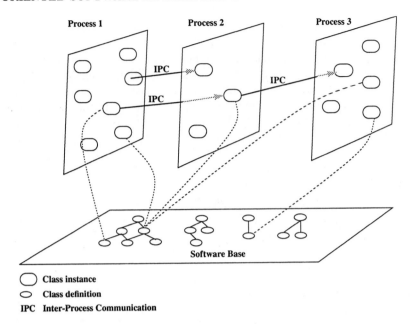

Figure 3.6: The interaction of process and object architectures for a system.

the size or efficiency of objects? It is also logical that the more stable architecture be the first developed and the foundation upon which the application is based. The classes in the software base shown in Figure 3.6 will be used for this as well as other applications, so their structure and definition should not be based on concerns about one particular application. The "object architecture" of a system is independent of any other architecture that may be defined on the system. This includes concurrency models or process architectures. The modularity of the objects and the abstract nature of the classes allow them to coexist with other structures imposed for performance or other reasons.

The abstract nature of classes provides a modular architecture. By separating the implementation of a class from its interface, the behavior of a system can be radically altered with relative ease. For example, the user interface of an application can be exchanged for a different one by creating an instance of one user interface class as opposed to another. Different scheduling algorithms or storage patterns can be provided by introducing instances of different classes.

The architecture is largely reflective of the messages sent between objects. As a result it is very flexible because many of the messages are not bound until run time. Client-server models are easily implemented and modified—dynamically, in fact. Reconfiguring to meet changes in the problem domain is facilitated by maintaining a model of it in the architecture of the program.

COMPARING LIFE CYCLES

In the previous sections we have provided an overview of the life cycle for object-oriented system development. We would now like to compare the life cycle for the procedural paradigm to the new life cycle. In particular, we are interested in the relative amounts of time spent in each phase. One study using data collected from a number of companies and giving rough comparisons between the two life cycles has been published[91].

As should be apparent from our emphasis on abstraction and modeling the problem domain, the methodology we are proposing requires that more time be spent in the analysis and design phases than in the traditional model. The time is well spent because the product of the analysis phase is a better set of abstractions upon which to base the design of more specific components. The design phase also produces a more robust and more factored design. It is more robust because the interfaces of the components produced are separated from the implementation of the components. It is more factored because inheritance allows us to design in layers and blend these together: *Functionality can be defined at its most general level and then inherited into lower-level components.*

What may not be apparent from the methodology being proposed here is that the implementation phase will actually take much less time in an object-oriented system. This is a logical result of the last statement in the previous paragraph. If functionality is defined at its most general level and then inherited into the classes defined at the lower, more specific levels, then there is less duplication of code. Inheritance allows the designer to model classification by creating subclasses of a class, but it also recognizes commonality by allowing information common to all the subclasses to be defined once in the parent class. The deeper—that is, the more levels—the inheritance hierarchy is, the more commonality can be recognized and the smaller the implementation for all components will be.

The smaller implementation of the components will have further impact in the testing activities. A number of techniques will be discussed in Chapter 9 that exploit the hierarchical layered design of classes. These techniques will reduce the time needed to test a class by recording what has already been tested and by not retesting certain portions of that information in the subclass definitions. The information hiding resulting from the separation of the class specification and the class implementation also contributes to the reduction in testing effort.

The maintenance phase of the life cycle presents the most convincing comparison between the procedural and object-oriented life cycles. With each new version of an application, faults are fixed and/or new features are added. In the procedural approach, these modifications require that many, if not most, of the modules in the system be "opened" and modified. Each of these must then be retested to be certain that the new features work correctly and that no new faults have been introduced into the original code. The practicalities of deadlines force many compromises and "hacks" in the development of a new version of a system. These not only affect the version being produced, they become a legacy for future versions because of the "open" nature of the procedural architecture. A study by Henry and Humphrey[47] further substantiates this last statement.

The encapsulated nature of the object-oriented architecture focuses the maintenance efforts on fewer modules. Mancl and Havanas[69] presented statistical information for a project at AT&T Bell Labs that supported this assertion. Their data showed that information hiding of a class also narrows the scope of maintenance activity. Modifying the implementation of a class but not changing the interface should have no effect outside that class. These characteristics prevent changes in one class from causing changes in another class, unlike the procedural approach in which a modification of one procedure often causes changes in several other procedures.

PROJECT ORGANIZATION

The life cycle for object-oriented system development has implications for the organization of the project. Four factors influence the activities of the team in our methodology:

- *Agreement on Basic Concepts.* A set of basic classes will be identified as the fundamental concepts of the problem domain. These will be used in many parts of the system and thus will have a heavy influence on the entire system. The team should agree on this basic model of the problem.
- *Agreement on Interfaces.* During the analysis and design phases, the project team will need to agree on at least a minimal interface for each class—especially the basic classes from the previous item—that will be used throughout the system. These interfaces will become an important and early part of the project documentation.
- *Emphasis on Reuse.* The saying goes, "You can't use it if you can't find it." As the collection of classes becomes larger, formal techniques will be needed to index, annotate, and classify the classes. Some of these techniques exist now in the configuration management of modules under the procedural paradigm. However, the object-oriented approach results in many more "pieces"—namely, classes—to track. The project will need to devote personnel and resources devoted to the reuse of components. These expenditures are offset by the savings in implementation and testing.
- *Emphasis on the Problem.* The problem-centered nature of this methodology requires more knowledge of the problem during development. The team must have ready access to a domain expert. This may be a team member or simply a liaison assigned by the client. The commonality among the applications developed by many companies means that the developers become domain experts after experience with several projects.

These factors imply a team structure that includes specialities such as domain knowledge, data modeling, and information storage and retrieval. The domain specialist will be the resource for the domain analysis. In a focused company, the developers may serve as the day-to-day domain experts; however, there should still be interaction with the client if the product is being developed under contract. The support function may be performed by developers as well. These functions include managing and maintaining component libraries and developing supporting documentation, including formalizing the analysis, design, and implementation documents.

The project staff must be organized in ways that facilitate communication. There is a need for agreement on many items that are of interest to all members of the team. Tools such as dynamic, on-line documentation can provide part of this support; however, discussion on the various aspects of a concept needed by different portions of a system require interaction. In the traditional approach, many projects organize into teams that are assigned subsystems to develop. In the object-oriented approach, projects organize into teams to develop a hierarchy of related classes. A team proposes an interface for the classes in the hierarchy for which it is responsible and other members of the project agree to this interface.

Project management must be oriented toward the success of the project at hand. Higher management should have a longer-term view that can influence the conduct of a project but can also achieve long-term objectives for the company. The development of significant libraries requires either a very large project or a higher-level plan that will justify the investment in the libraries for the company and facilitate their dissemination to a number of projects. This higher-level plan might be to become a library vendor of classes in their industry or within the company. The evaluation of progress on the project will have to take into account the differences in relative amounts of time in the various phases of the life cycle. Management must also provide incentives to the teams to design reusable classes. These incentives can range from extended schedules for the initial development to monetary rewards based on the amounts of reuse a class actually receives.

SUMMARY

In this chapter we have started examining an object-oriented software development process. We presented the idea of a separate life cycle for classes to be used in addition to the standard application life cycle. These two life cycles were blended together into a series of steps that provide a comprehensive methodology. In succeeding chapters we will consider many of these steps in greater detail and with a number of examples. One important idea pointed out in this chapter is the separation between classes and the applications that use instances of these classes. While we will use several complete applications as examples, much of the discussion will be focused on classes and their design.

We have only touched on many of the process issues involved in the development of an object-oriented system. We will discuss many aspects of reuse in this text, but we will not extensively address such issues as software depositories or other general process issues. We will discuss some aspects of project organization, tools, and issues in testing that are process concerns. We will argue that many process techniques from the procedural world can be reused if we consider the implications of hierarchy, encapsulation, and dynamic binding introduced by the object-oriented approach.

FURTHER READING

The articles by Boehm[10, 9] provide extensive discussions of the intentions of life cycle models. The article by Henderson-Sellers and Edwards[46] provides a substantial account of their view on the life cycles for object-oriented systems. This includes both application and component life cycles. Booch[11] provides an overview of several phases, but does not take a life cycle-guided view of the development process.

4

Analysis and High-Level Design

In this chapter we consider the analysis and high-level design phases of the object-oriented application development process. The analysis process is divided into domain analysis and application analysis. Domain analysis establishes the broad context within which the system will be built. Application analysis focuses the domain analysis using the requirements for the specific application.

This chapter includes guidelines for identifying objects in the problem space. It identifies sources that can aid in the search for appropriate objects and the classes they represent. The application-level relationships between these classes[1] are considered part of the design phase. The chapter also provides techniques for capturing these relationships in an easily understood form.

ANALYSIS

Analysis is the problem-definition phase in application development. The output from this phase is a clear and concise definition of the problem. Traditional "systems" analysis produces a procedurally oriented document that specifies the functionality of the desired system. Object-oriented analysis will produce a more comprehensive document that describes the functionality of the system and a basic characterization of the problem space.

The language of the analysis should be the *user's* language. That is, the system requirements should be stated in terms that the user can understand and validate. There is extensive interaction between the system users and an analyst to arrive at an accurate and comprehensive statement. This statement usually includes a brief description of the problem preceding the specification of the proposed solution, and

---

[1]We will use the terms class and entity interchangeably because we see "class" as the unifying thread through the entire life cycle for each concept included in an application.

provides the basis for the high-level design of the system.

Let's turn our attention to how traditional analysis documents might change in the object-oriented environment. The purpose of the document has not changed, nor has the orientation of the language. However, two aspects of the document should change—the focus and the point of view.

The object-oriented development process provides an opportunity to model the problem. Requirement documents normally emphasize the functionality of the desired end product. This description comes from the user. Unfortunately, it has been well proven that users cannot anticipate how their needs may change once the application is available. Consequently, software applications often do not have the impact they should have.

The analysis documents from an object-oriented development effort should provide a more in-depth description of the problem domain. By considering a larger portion of the problem space rather than just the portion relevant to the immediate problem, the concepts identified in the analysis will be higher-level abstractions than those ordinarily developed during an analysis effort. These abstractions are the basic building blocks for flexible and extensible software. By using abstractions as its foundation, the resulting software can more easily accommodate changes in requirements. These abstractions can help the users to better understand the problem and the potential solutions.

The point of view of an object-oriented analysis document should be different from that of a procedural analysis document. Traditional documents are functionally oriented. This point of view perceives the system as providing a set of services. The object-oriented analysis documents should give priority to describing the entities in the problem domain. It should present the problem as a set of entities that interact and address the relationships between these entities. This point of view considers the system to be a model that can be manipulated in controlled ways.

After developing this description, the analyst is better able to build the system specification for a specific application. The specification can be written in terms that the client for the system can understand. The object-oriented approach will provide a natural path from this description of concepts into the design phase.

DOMAIN ANALYSIS

Domain analysis provides an essential ingredient in our software development approach. In this section we provide an overview of the process. For more detailed information see [81] and [85]. Domain analysis provides a set of abstractions that are a high-level representation of a domain of knowledge. The representation is used as a reference during the development of specific system requirements. Because the analysis often explores areas that are beyond the scope of the current application, this technique is only practical in an environment that exploits the information for reuse in expanding the current system or in building future systems.

Domain analysis is a study of the broad areas of knowledge that encompass the problem that is the focus of the application to be developed. The boundaries on a domain are fuzzy. They are defined more by experience and practical considerations—

such as available resources—than by formal definitions or limits. The intent is to analyze a sufficiently wide area so that related concepts are identified; these may influence the development of our understanding of the concepts central to the application. This broad area is also insurance. As users change their minds about the requirements for a system, the broad scope of the analysis will likely have anticipated these changes and further analysis will not be needed.

The analysis is performed by a team that includes people with skills in fields such as knowledge representation, analysis, and the domain of interest. The domain experts are chosen for broad experience with a variety of pieces of the domain. The domain engineer is responsible for developing a representation of the problem. The interaction between the domain experts and the domain engineer closely resembles the process of knowledge acquisition for an expert system. The techniques of that discipline can be very useful in guiding the domain analysis phase of software engineering.

The goal of the analysis is to identify the basic concepts that characterize the domain. These concepts must be integrated into a coordinated model of the domain. In the section below, *Modeling the Problem*, we discuss techniques for building the model. One of the basic requirements is that the model must include information about the *relationships* between concepts as well as complete information about each of the individual concepts. This information provides the glue that binds the concepts together into a comprehensive view of the domain. As knowledge within the domain evolves, so must the model.

It is important to note that domain analysis is an ongoing activity that may be reconsidered at any time during the development of an application, but it is a process that should continue well beyond the active development of any particular application. The abstractions and relationships must be updated as the domain changes. The results of analysis also evolves as we achieve more experience with the domain and refine our abstractions.

The purpose of performing domain analysis is to provide a foundation for system development that is more deeply rooted in domain-specific knowledge than in a functional decomposition of a problem solution that requires the designer to arbitrarily decide on the division between modules. Traditional analysis techniques provide locally optimal problem statements that are very sensitive to changes in user requirements. By not taking into account a larger body of information about the problem, key generalizations may be missed and, along with that, opportunities to broaden the applicability of the system may be missed too.

The benefit of using domain abstractions as the foundation for system development is adaptability. Applications based on domain information will more readily adapt to changes in knowledge within the field as well as changes in user requirements.

Modeling the Problem

The output of the domain analysis phase and the input to the application analysis and high-level design phases is a model of the problem domain. A number of modeling techniques are available for this purpose. One family of techniques that seems particularly appropriate is the semantic data models. This section examines semantic data models and the contributions they make to system development.

Table 4.1: Semantic data model and the object-oriented view.

Semantic Data Model	Brief Characterization	Object-Oriented Design
external	user's view of the data	class specification
conceptual	meanings of entities and the relationships between them	application relationships between classes
internal	the physical model of the data	class implementation

Semantic Data Models

A number of data models have been developed since Codd first proposed the relational data model[20]. Several of these models were developed to extend and generalize Codd's original concept. The term *semantic* is used because the extensions provide the modeler greater capability to express the *meaning* of the problem domain. The extensions are intended to provide the capability to represent complex objects and to more faithfully represent the relationships between entities. Peckham and Maryanski[78] present a survey of several of the new semantic models.

There is still no consensus on one particular model. Rather than select one, we will utilize elements from several to illustrate their use in object-oriented analysis.

Although semantic data models as well as the relational data model were originally intended for database design, broadening their scope to system development is relatively straightforward. The ANSI/SPARC proposal for database architecture standardization considers three levels of modeling: external, conceptual, and internal. These three levels can be mapped onto three levels for object-oriented design, as shown in Table 4.1. The external and conceptual levels correspond to the high-level design phase discussed in this chapter.

- *External level.* The external level is the view from *outside* the application. It reflects the user's perception of the problem rather than that of the implementor. The classes developed at this level have specifications that provide the operations corresponding to the user's actions.

  For example, a system to process orders for financial products would include an external level containing operations that directly manipulate the financial products. Classes such as Common Stock, Preferred Stock, Municipal Bond, and Option, would provide entities familiar to the stockbrokers, financial planners, and backroom personnel. Each financial instrument would be represented by a separate class. The operations on these classes would include recognizable financial transactions such as buy and sell.

- *Conceptual level.* At the conceptual level we are concerned with the relationships between the entities identified at the external level. These relationships are the directly observable interactions that were discussed above. At this level the relationships can be recognized and understood by the users of the system.

In our financial system, we have already identified classes for such instruments as Common Stock and Option. At the conceptual level there is a relationship between common stock and the options written in that common stock. The relationship could be expressed as *on* — that is, a person may take an option *on* a particular stock. This relation is understandable to the financial professionals using the system.

An important attribute of any relationship is its *cardinality*. The *cardinality* of a relationship is the number of instances of one entity that correspond to the instances of the other entity in the relationship. For the relationship between the Option and Common Stock entities, one option is related to one stock, but it is possible for there to be many options on any one stock. This relationship is termed *many-to-one*. As in database design, this relationship will be implemented by including in the option class an attribute that provides the identification of the particular stock for a particular option. In the next chapter we will consider this issue in greater detail and will provide a discussion of other cardinality values.

- *Internal level.* In the internal level, we consider the physical model of the entities. This is the class design phase of our life cycle. The physical model includes the two types of attributes: data and methods. Method attributes model the behavior of the entity, while the data attributes model the state of the entity. Our model includes a separation between the methods that we wish to use to provide a public interface and the remainder of the attributes, which are private.

  During the analysis phases, the attributes that are identified will be descriptive. That is, they will provide the descriptions of the behavior and the state of the entity. During the detailed class design phase, additional attributes will be added that assist the descriptive attributes in providing an implementation of the entity. These additional attributes will become part of the implementation of the class definition and will not be available for public access. This provides us with the flexibility to change the implementation without affecting users of the class. What is much more difficult to change is the public interface of the class since other classes may have incorporated references to those public attributes in their definitions. This implies that the public interface should be *minimal*—that is, the interface includes only those items that are necessary. It also implies that the interface should be carefully developed and critiqued by others in the development team before it is published.

Relations in Semantic Data Models

Peckham and Maryanski[78] discuss several general relationships that are represented in many of the semantic data models. Table 4.2 provides a list of them. Several

Table 4.2: Types of relationships in semantic data models.

Relationship	Description
Generalization	One entity represents a generalization of the concept behind several other classes.
Aggregation	One entity comprises instances of several other entities.
Classification	One entity is an instance of another entity.
Association	One entity is a container for other entities.

of these relationships play a central role in object-oriented design. They provide a representation for such concepts as inheritance and instantiation.

The relationships shown in Table 4.2 differ from those at the conceptual level, which are described in terms of the problem. The relationships identified in Table 4.2 provide support for implementation. These tools for the designer provide assistance in implementing the interactions between classes:

- *Generalization.* The generalization relationship and its inverse, specialization, allow abstractions to be defined in layers of increasing specificity. Abstractions in a lower layer represent the more specialized cases of the abstractions in higher layers, to which they are related. This hierarchy of abstractions provides a structuring element when we attempt to model a domain. As higher-level abstractions are identified, the applicability of our model widens. Abstractions may be added at any level at any time by simply relating them to those above and below them in the layered model.

  The generalization relationship informs readers of the model about the level of specificity of each abstraction in relation to other abstractions in the model. The generalization relationship is recognized and incorporated into analysis techniques that support the procedural approach to software development as well. The difference here is that in the object-oriented approach we have design- and implementation-level devices that exploit this relationship directly. The inheritance relationship, present in object-oriented languages, provides a direct mapping of the generalization relationships into our system's implementation.

  Generalizations are usually formed by viewing a set of ideas and identifying the common elements that characterize the set. Cars, trucks, and buses can be subsumed by the more general idea of vehicles. This broader abstraction may be able to also aid in the definition of other more specific abstractions such as race car, van, and tractor.

- *Aggregation.* This relationship supports the development of the representation of an abstraction from several smaller and presumably simpler elements. It roughly corresponds to the declaration of components within a record. For example, a queue might be considered to have three attributes: space for the elements that are being stored in it, its capacity, and the current number of items in it. The queue class would then have an aggregation relationship with the classes that represent space, capacity, and current size attributes. The actual instances of these attributes will eventually provide the state of the instances of the larger abstraction.

- *Classification.* Classification relates an abstraction to the instantiations of that abstraction. We do not often design a system at the level of instances. However, this relationship can be useful in cases where the design of the system includes the sharing of information among the instances of a class. In an interpreted language environment such as Smalltalk or the Common LISP Object System (CLOS), each instance of a class includes its class as an attribute. This provides the possibility of developing inter-instance communication via a "blackboard" system in which an instance may write to the blackboard and any instance may read from the blackboard. Other objects in the system would have no access to this attribute, which would be visible only to the instances of the class.

  During development, we are faced with the question of whether to develop subclasses to represent the differences between some of the concepts. For example, given a Person class, should we make subclasses for male and female? This is certainly an important "specialization" of person! This should be used only if it is an important characteristic in our domain—if we are developing medical software and wish to model physiological information, for example. Otherwise, this can be handled using aggregation by a single gender attribute.

- *Association.* The association relationship indicates that one abstraction serves as a holder of instances of other abstractions. The difference between association and aggregation is the intention of the grouping of entities. The aggregation indicates a set of entities used to provide the component parts of a class while association indicates the grouping of entities because they are somehow related. This grouping makes its components individually available to the remainder of the system. For example, a department contains people, so a department class associates people who are assigned to the department.

One of the semantic models, the entity-relationship model[18], provides support at both the external and conceptual levels. It does so for identifying and describing entities that are representative of the user's views of the data. In addition, ER modeling can provide the mapping from these views to the actual data structures—that is, the internal level. Of the current semantic data models, we consider it the simplest and most useful. It will be discussed in greater detail later in this chapter.

Identifying Objects and Classes

During the analysis phases, the objects that are identified are application-level objects. That is, they correspond to the user's view of the application domain. These lead to classes that model the user's point of view rather than the physical data structures.

Consider the design of a microcomputer-based application. One object is the computer's display screen, which presents part of the user interface. This would be abstracted into a class Display Screen, reflecting the user's perspective. An implementation-level class that would be identified later might be a special bitmap memory structure that is scanned to determine what is displayed on the screen. A Bitmap class would be used as part of the implementation of the Display Screen class.

Identifying Objects

One of the more difficult tasks in object-oriented design is identifying the correct objects and abstracting from them the appropriate classes. Tsichritzis[92] lists five categories of objects:

> Physical objects
> Roles
> Incidents
> Interactions
> Specifications

This list does not imply that every application has objects from each of the categories, nor does it imply that we must spend time classifying objects into one of five categories. The list simply provides a stimulus for the designer as the application domain is analyzed.

Physical Objects

Physical objects are the easiest and most obvious entities to recognize. They can usually be directly observed in the problem domain and their attributes can be identified and measured. Information about this type of object is usually available from several sources. Owner's manuals, blueprints, and equipment lists can provide information for the object descriptions. An application should be designed to include software objects that represent each of the physical devices with which the system is interfaced. This software object handles protocols, buffering, and any other special functions associated with a particular device.

Examples: An implementation of the game of chess would include objects to represent the various pieces as well as the playing board.

A system for course registration at a university would contain objects that represent the students who enroll in the courses.

A network management system would include objects corresponding to the various physical resources of the network: switches, CPUs, and printers.

Roles

The role of an entity can often be abstracted to the point that it can be recognized as an object separate from the entity that fulfills that role. The role itself is characterized by the object. The operations of the object are the skills provided by the role.

Roles are objects that will often be attributes of other objects, but they will also be "modifiable" attributes. A class may take on several roles at one time. For example, a retired doctor is in the roles of retiree and physician. Retiree may be a role that applies to a very wide range of classes while physician is a very specialized role.

Examples: Object-oriented systems often have "manager" objects that perform the role of coordinator for a group of resources. Windowing systems, for example, usually have window managers that coordinate mouse clicks and other operations on windows.

An object-oriented operating system would have a scheduler object responsible for managing the CPU resources and coordinating the multiple processes.

A person working in a factory might fulfill the role of a foreman or a machine operator.

Incidents

An incident is an occurrence of some activity. An incident object is usually a data-intensive entity that manages the information of importance about the occurrence. The operations of an incident object are used primarily for providing access to the data. The incident has a duration, but the objects that represent the activity may have a longer life to provide a system history.

Examples: In the context of an air traffic control system, an example of an incident would be a flight. This incident object would maintain data such as the flight number, destination, number of passengers, and information about the aircraft being flown.

An automated security system might produce an "alarm" object whenever a security incident occurs. The alarm object would contain information such as the sensor that has been tripped and the time at which it was tripped.

Interactions

Interactions represent a relationship between two objects. This type of object is analogous to the associational entity that is used in database design. Such an entity is required when the relationship is between many instances of one class and many instances of another class. The interaction object relates one particular instance of the first class to one particular instance of the second class. The data of the interaction object includes information used to locate the two instances being related. It also includes data that characterizes the relationship.

Examples: The cardinality of the relationship between students and courses being offered at a university is many-to-many—that is, one student registers for multiple courses while each course accommodates multiple students. A registration system would contain many instances of course registration objects. These objects would relate an individual student to an individual course and might itself contain data to designate the semester.

Specifications

Specification objects represent requirements for some entity. Operations on a specification object might provide views of selected pieces of a structure or support merging simple entities into more complex objects. Specifications usually reference other objects. Part of the data for a specification object will be identifiers for these other objects.

Examples: An automated hardware testing system would include objects that represent the schematics of various pieces of circuitry. These objects would be accessed as references during the development of test plans for a circuit as well as during the actual tests themselves.

A recipe object specifies the ingredients and their amounts as well as the order and ways in which they are to be combined.

A color object might specify the levels of red, green, and blue needed to create that color on a color monitor.

Identifying Relationships

In the analysis phases, the relationships that are to be identified are application-specific. These relationships involve interactions between entities in the problem domain.

Application-level relationships are represented in the design in one of two ways:

- *As a message.* The relationship between two objects may be represented as a message between the two objects. When a student wishes to enroll in a course, a student object would send a message to the registration system object requesting a course and section number.
- *As an interaction object.* The relationship between two objects may be represented by an interaction object independent of either of the two entities. In the university registration system, the relationship between an instance of the student class and an instance of the course class would be handled with an interaction entity. This interaction entity would be termed *course registration.*

APPLICATION ANALYSIS

The application analysis phase takes the model of the problem domain created during the domain analysis and focuses it to the application currently being built. The client's requirements for the system are used as the constraints that narrow the amount of domain information that will be part of the active design process. At this point, the information that is retained has been influenced by the broader view of the domain analysis. The application will have a structure that is more robust than it would have been if a narrowly focused analysis had been conducted.

The domain analysis has produced a model that represents the important concepts of the domain with no assumptions about the representation being used in a computer-based system. The application analysis phase imposes the conditions that accompany being part of a computer-based system. Response time requirements, user interface issues, and special requirements such as security of the data processed by the application are factored into the process at this level.

A number of authors have proposed analysis methodologies that blend various parts of what we have described. Many of the models recognize the need for more than one view of the application. Most consider the two areas we have stressed: the application view and the class view. The specification and operation of each class must be detailed. The interactions between classes that form the architecture of the application also must be represented.

Rumbaugh et al[84] presents the Object Modeling Technique(OMT), which structures the information gathered during analysis into three types of models:

Object Model
Functional Models
Dynamic Models

Rumbaugh does not provide sufficient linking between the three models. Hayes and Coleman provide a formal approach to blending these three models[44]; however, this linkage relies on formal methods that few are willing to adopt.

Other models include Shlaer and Mellor[85], Coad and Yourdon[19], and Page-Jones and Weiss[77]. We will mention Shlaer and Mellor again shortly. We believe that Coad's approach does not adequately recognize the differences between the procedural and object-oriented approach. The result is a technique that does not adequate tap the power of objects. Page-Jones' technique is not sufficiently developed at this time to be a comprehensive methodology.

CAPTURING THE INFORMATION

The information concerning the entities and the relationships between these entities must be captured to communicate both the analysis and design information to others. As stated above, Shlaer and Mellor[85] consider three complementary sets of information that provide comprehensive coverage of the information needed to totally describe the entities and their relationships. Their technique includes representing information on the attributes of the entities, the states that are possible given the previously defined attributes, and the sequence of transitions between states. Although there have been attempts to capture all of this information in a single technique, the results have been very complex figures that are difficult to read. Other diagramming techniques such as Booch diagrams[11] require the user to learn a new syntax almost as involved as a programming language.

CRC Cards

An informal technique that is sometimes useful in capturing information is CRC cards. The acronym stands for Class, Responsibility, and Collaborators. This technique was developed by Beck and Cunningham[6] for use in team sessions where entities were being identified and behaviors were being specified for interfaces. Figure 4.1 shows a

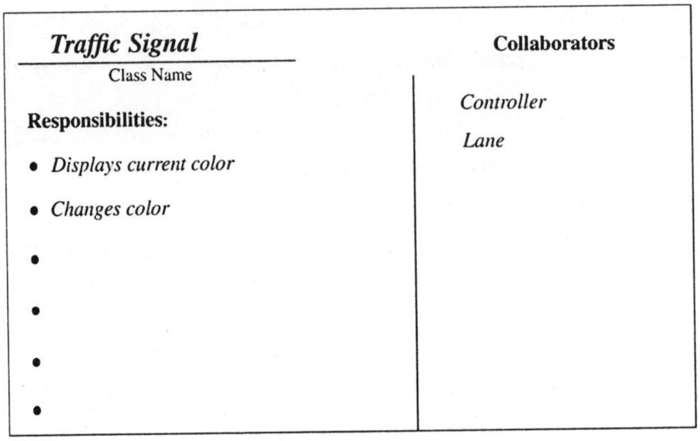

Figure 4.1: A sample CRC card.

CRC card that illustrates one of the examples from Chapter 2. An entity is given a descriptive name, in this case "traffic signal." The responsibilities—or behaviors—of a traffic signal are then listed. This is a preliminary interface for the class. Finally, the other entities that will know about traffic signals, or with which the traffic signal will interact, will be listed as collaborators.

This is a useful tool for the initial stages of system development. The cards can be handwritten, passed around for comments, and easily replaced as the analysis and design are refined. Although there is no indication on the card of inheritance or other specific relationships, Beck and Cunningham report arranging the cards in an order of most general on top, with the layers of cards underneath representing layers of inheritance. Once the classes are well established, the information can be represented using a more formal technique.

The CRC cards are particularly suited to the initial phases in which the architecture group may brainstorm about the overall structure of the system. CRC cards can be used to group the classes needed within each subsystem. This design is easy to modify and shows the relationships in a simple manner.

Entity-Relationship Diagrams

A diagramming technique must provide a notation for representing all of the important information gathered during analysis. A variety of useful techniques have been developed to represent the information resulting from the analysis phase. In this section we describe some techniques that we have found to be useful.

The entity-relationship (ER) diagram provides a simple notation that can represent the essential details of entities and the relationships between them. In addition, the ER diagram provides a notation for the attributes of an entity and for the cardinality of a relationship. The cardinality of a relationship will be fully defined in the next chapter, but for now consider the cardinality of a relationship between entity x and entity y as the number of x's associated with a single y and the number of y's associated with each x. In Figure 4.2 we see the symbols used to represent entities and their attributes, and relationships and their cardinalities.

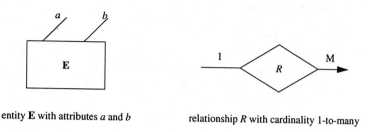

entity **E** with attributes *a* and *b*   relationship *R* with cardinality 1-to-many

Figure 4.2: Syntax of Entity-Relationship diagrams.

These few items are all that are required to represent the rich models available in the semantic data model domain. The simplicity of the ER diagram is one of its strengths. The other strength comes from its generality. No limitations placed on the types of entities or relationships that can be represented. The infinite variety of problem-centered relationships that will be defined can be handled as naturally as the inheritance relationship that will be present in virtually every development effort.

Figure 4.3 provides a fragment of an ER diagram. The Student and Course entities are related in a many-to-many relationship. That is, many students will register for one particular course and each student will register for multiple courses. The notation *0:M* indicates that although there may be many students registering for a course there may not be any registrants. The notation *1:M* would be used if there was a requirement that there always be at least one instance on that side of the relationship. The Course Registration entity is an associational entity used to

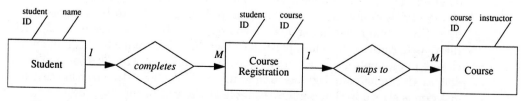

Figure 4.3: Resolving a *many-to-many* relationship using an associational entity.

replace the many-to-many relationship between Student and Course, because a many-to-many relationship is difficult to maintain properly. The cardinality of the resulting relationship between Student and Course Registration is one-to-many, as is the one between Course and Course Registration. The relational data model requires that all many-to-many relationships be decomposed. The object-oriented data model can accept the many-to-many relationship shown in the first part of this figure and thus presents a simpler data model that is more flexible than the relational model.

The ER diagram does not provide a technique for representing the transitions between states for an entity. A simple technique for this is the finite state diagram. Again, a simple diagramming technique can be used to produce a very flexible representation involving any states and any transitions. The diagram is for a single class and is associated with that class. This eliminates the problem of diagrams becoming larger as the system becomes larger, but it still represents a management problem of tracking the large number of diagrams for individual entities.

Additional Techniques

The ER diagram gives an overview of the relationships between all of the entities in the system. This does not scale up very well. An extremely large project would produce an ER diagram that would fill the walls of a large room. Recently, a technique has been developed for clustering groups of entities in the ER diagram and creating a new higher-level ER diagram that replaces that cluster with a new single entity[28]. This produces a hierarchy of ER diagrams with the root of the hierarchy being a single, very high-level representation of the entire system. By traveling down through levels, the appropriate amount of detail can be reached as general entities are replaced by a diagram involving several more specific entities.

OMT uses a notation that includes a specialized form of the ER diagram. A sample is found in Figure 4.4. The symbols provided by this technique meet the requirements of some who want a total notation that requires little or no text other than names in the diagram. Others prefer a technique, such as that presented in the previous section, that is easy to learn but requires extensive annotations. We will continue to use the simpler but potentially more cluttered diagrams.

The ER diagrams capture the relationships among classes but do not provide extensive information about any particular class itself. We have already mentioned the state diagram as a commonly used technique. One shortcoming of this simple approach is that it fails to provide a means for expressing conditions on the transitions. Kappel[54] has used a variation of petri nets as an alternative to the finite state diagram. This provides a means for expressing conditional transitions and a representation that is easily checked automatically. It is intended to be a portion of a complete ER diagram that illustrates the complete system, hence the name Behaviorally-Integrated Entity Relationship(BIER) diagram. The complete diagram showing all classes in an application is too cumbersome to manage without tool support, so we will use the individual diagrams to show information about state transitions. A sample diagram is shown in the graphics example at the end of this chapter.

Coleman et al[22] have used the statechart language of Harel[41] to develop *objectcharts*. These charts provide a formal syntax for treating a class as a finite state

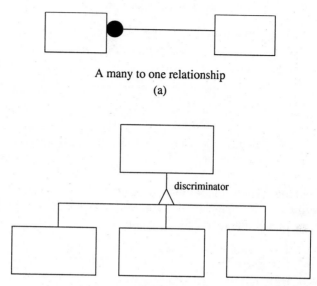

A many to one relationship
(a)

An inheritance relationship that differentiates between subclasses
(b)

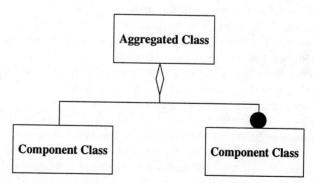

Components of a class with a one-to-one and one-to-many relation
(c)

Figure 4.4: A selection of symbols from the OMT notation.

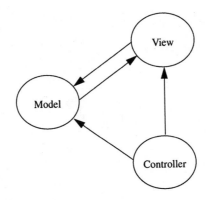

Figure 4.5: The Model/View/Controller framework structure.

machine. These diagrams supplement the inter-class interactions shown on ER diagrams with intra-class information. This notation includes the same information
shown on Kappel's BIER diagrams.

HIGH-LEVEL DESIGN

There is a close relationship between the analysis and high-level design phases in
the object-oriented approach. The analysis processes are problem-centered, with the
high-level design phase bringing in the "practical" considerations of being a computer
system. This includes developing those parts of the solution that represent the "computer artifact" portion of the solution, such as the user interface. The low-level design
phase concentrates on the detailed design of classes. We will consider application
design here, and Chapter 6 will provide guidelines on the design of individual classes.

The high-level design phase should develop the system architecture—that is, the
overall model that will be used to structure the application. This system-level decision
affects the distribution of responsibilities into subsystems of the application. The
system architecture does not affect the structures of individual classes.

The client-server model is a system architecture that has been used in procedural
systems and is applicable to object-oriented systems as well. The perspective of this
model is that one portion of the system provides a well defined set of services to
another portion of the system. The objects that request service are grouped together
into the client subsystem. The X-window system for user interface design uses the
client-server approach to structure its graphical interactions. The central "engine"
of an application is often the client of a number of server subsystems such as a user
interface, a print server, and a database server.

An architecture that has been used successfully in Smalltalk is the Model/View/-
Controller (MVC)[35, 62] (see Figure 4.5). In this architecture, a model is an application object that operates independently of any user interface. The view manages
the output portion of the user interface while the controller handles the input por-

tion. Input events cause messages to be sent to the model. As the model changes its state, it notifies the view through a dependency mechanism, which causes the view to update the display. This dependency mechanism defines a relation between a model and any view that allows the model to function the same way independently of the view associated with it at any time. Similarly, the controller performs operations on the view and the model upon the occurrence of an input event.

A number of other configurations have been used successfully. Many of these arrangements of classes represent the architecture of a subsystem rather than an overall system. The term *framework*[26] has been applied to these arrangements. These are sets of abstract classes that collaborate in well defined, well documented ways that provide the general design for an application. An application is constructed by defining new subclasses of these abstract classes and instantiating them to implement the specific behavior needed. For MVC, an application is created by developing a subclass of Model to perform the processing associated with the application. A user interface is created by defining subclasses of View and Controller, of which many reusable subclasses such as buttons and dialog boxes already exist in most Smalltalk systems. The result is a new subsystem created with a fraction of the effort normally associated with such a project.

The appropriate architecture for an application can be developed using a few simple criteria:

- *Minimize communication between pieces.* The subsystems should be formed to minimize the amount of communication between the various high-level pieces. A user interface should be able to handle interaction, error correction, and hardware control without bothering the main application. Only when a request is entered via the interface should it be forwarded to the remainder of the application.
- *Hide complexity.* The subsystems should bind together those groupings of classes that exhibit a high degree of coupling. A framework, for example, will have a high degree of interaction among its classes. It may in fact be a subsystem by itself.
- *Group functionality logically.* Even though the input and output devices may not communicate with each other very much, it is logical to group them together into a subsystem that handles IO. This provides a unit that is easy to recognize and locate in the event of problems.

These criteria sound very much like those for classes and with good reason: Classes are similar to subsystems with their encapsulation of concept. In fact, each subsystem could be implemented as a class that aggregates its components to provide a set of services. Like the process architecture referred to earlier, the classes and the subsystem architecture are orthogonal. Instances of a single class may be part of more than one subsystem. Unlike the process architecture, the instances of these classes will usually be used to provide low-level implementation details.

The high-level design phase augments the list of required classes by identifying those concepts that are required to make the solution work in a computer environment. These classes will include classes needed to interface the application to the world outside of the system. These interfaces include those to other software systems such as a database management system, mice and keyboards, or to hardware devices that the application uses for data collection or that the system is responsible for controlling. The output from this phase is a more complete specification of the classes needed for the application, the relationships between the classes, and a subsystem view of the application.

High-level design can be characterized as a process of module identification and specification. The modules may be individual classes or they may be groupings of classes into subsystems. The specification process is responsibility-driven[100]. The term *contract* has been used by both Wirfs-Brock et al[101] and Helm et al[45] to describe the agreement on class interfaces. The contract analogy is appropriate because both of the objects must fulfill the terms of the contract. The requester must not request services unless they are on the agreed-upon list and the provider must provide each of the agreed-upon services.

The two phases of design—high-level and class—are very closely related if the designer follows the paradigm completely. In that case, everything in the application is an object, including the application itself! From this perspective the two phases are combined. The design of the application becomes the design of a large class. This type of class design examines the behavior expected from the application and uses this to form the interface of the application class.

The application class will be designed internally using instances of classes that provide the behaviors that correspond to the subsystems identified in the high-level design. The component instances interact with each other according to the interfaces defined for each class. Each of these classes will in turn be designed internally to provide the services specified in the class interface.

EXAMPLE: A SIMPLE DRAWING SYSTEM

We will use many examples in the text but this simple graphics system will be a continuing example that will be considered in each of the phases of the object-oriented software development process. The system will be taken from the analysis and design phases to the implementation and testing phases.

Requirements

The requirements statement for a simple draw program is given below. The statement includes both functional requirements as well as a description of the objects in the domain:

> The requirement is for a sketching program that allows the user to draw a picture using a set of figures. The user shall be able to select from a set of standard shapes and "draw" the shape in the picture, move existing shapes, and remove individual shapes from the drawing. The principal input device shall be a mouse for selecting and positioning shapes, although the system must provide support for entering text. Data attributes that have associated numeric input shall use an on-screen device to provide this capability. The output shall be in color.

The shapes to be included in the system are dot, line, circle, rectangle, triangle, and spline. Each figure drawn on the screen shall have a reference point that can be used to select that figure. When the mouse is activated sufficiently close to a particular figure, the figure shall be highlighted on the display. The mouse may be used to drag the figure around the screen by placing its cursor on the figure and activating the pick. Each figure will have an associated color, which the user may select from a list of available colors, or the user may allow the system to default to the current drawing color.

The user interface shall have a separate area for each of its functions. It shall provide reasonably fast response to a user's commands. The interface shall use menus that have a consistent "look and feel."

The system shall be extensible—that is, it shall be easy to add additional standard figures and new type fonts, accommodate a new type of input or output device, or add additional operations such as duplicating a figure. The system shall also conform to existing standards so that it may interact with other graphics systems.

We said it was a simple system! This statement has two components: the required functionality and the objects to be represented in the system. The document provides the functionality required by listing the commands that shall be available to the user of the system. The requirements for input and output also provide additional description of functionality.

The document also provides a description of the objects in the problem domain. In this case the most prominent objects are the shapes to be provided by the system. A more elaborate system might allow alteration of the types and thicknesses of the lines used in drawing the figures. The user interface is also described briefly.

Is the description of these objects an addition to the requirements document? Partially. Some information about the shapes would have been included in any requirements document. However, the information is rearranged and enlarged in the object-oriented document. A more complete description of the objects emphasizes the object-oriented point of view. By including these descriptions in the requirements document the designers and implementers have an expanded basis of information close at hand.

Analysis

Domain Analysis

The analysis phase for the graphics system begins with a domain analysis of computer graphics in general and "drawing" programs specifically. We will not attempt to list all the information that might be developed here but we will center on a couple of standard sources. First are standards documents. These documents provide a broad consensus on some target domain. The Graphics Kernel System (GKS)[49], for example, was an early graphical standard that defined a large number of terms and provided a system architecture for graphical systems.

By reading the GKS documents, a large number of entities can be identified and

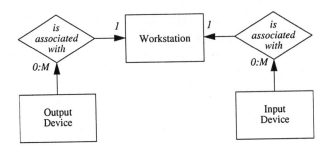

Figure 4.6: Components of a workstation.

characterized. Three major entities are: workstation, input device, and output device. According to the GKS standard, several input and/or output devices may be associated with a workstation, but it is not required to have both input and output devices in order to be considered a workstation. That requirement can be modeled as shown in Figure 4.6. The 0:M indicates that there may be 0 or more occurrences of this entity in the relationship. The relationship is listed as *is associated with* since this is the language used in the standards document. This relationship will be made more specific during the design phase.

The GKS standard provides many details about input and output devices. For input devices, the standard describes six categories:

> *Locator*—enters a position in the coordinate system
> *Pick*—identifies an item on the display
> *Choice*—selects from a set of choices
> *Valuator*—inputs a value
> *String*—inputs a text string
> *Stroke*—inputs a sequence of coordinate positions

Each of these special types of input devices can be represented using our diagramming convention for the relationship between a class and its subclasses.

These are specializations of the more general concept of an input device. Figure 4.7 shows the ER diagram for this relationship. As a convention, we will not use the diamond-shaped relation indicator on those diagrams where it is obvious that the only relationship is specialization. With the large number of specialization diagrams used in object-oriented development it is simply easier to omit the relationship box.

Figure 4.6 includes three abstract classes. Each of these classes would be the root of an inheritance hierarchy of more concrete classes that specialize the concept represented in the abstract class. Figure 4.7 shows a second level of abstract classes that represent a classification of input devices as stated in the GKS standard. Eventually there will be classes that are even more specific, such as a mouse or keyboard. Adding all of these entities to the original diagram as in Figure 4.8 would make it

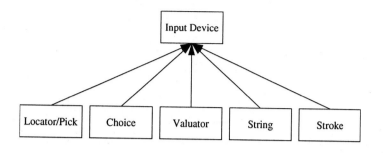

Figure 4.7: GKS types of input devices.

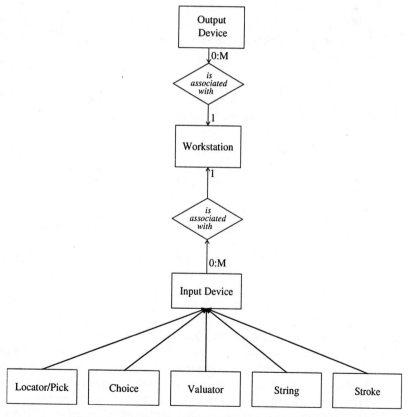

Figure 4.8: Input device cluster (expanded).

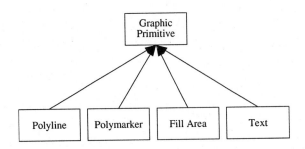

Figure 4.9: GKS graphic primitive entities.

cluttered and difficult to understand. A clustering technique can be used in which the abstract class represents a cluster of classes in a high-level diagram and a second lower-level diagram can contain the more specific classes. This layering of diagrams can be supported by a tool that allows the user to traverse the hierarchy of diagrams.

A number of other entities can be identified from the GKS standard. This list is not complete but will give us some additional entities to work with:

- *Segment*—A set of graphic objects that are part of the drawing
- *Polyline*—A single, or several connected, straight line segments
- *Polymarker*—Symbols to differentiate between multiple lines in the same picture
- *Fill area*—An enclosed area that is all set to one color
- *Text*—A string of characters
- *World coordinates*—Coordinates from the problem space such as feet or miles
- *Normalized device coordinates*—Coordinates that have been scaled to be between 0 and 1 with 0 being the lower limit of the device and 1 being the upper limit
- *Window*—A region of the display that is the destination of a particular set of output instances

The polyline, polymarker, fill area, and text entities listed here are the four output primitives defined by GKS. This relationship is shown in Figure 4.9. This basic structure will allow us to build a large set of standard shapes for our system.

A second source of domain analysis information would be other draw and paint programs and their documentation. Since a draw program does not represent the real world as such, using existing programs as a source of entities is a useful approach. Obviously we will only be able to identify those characteristics that are apparent to the user unless we have more detailed information, perhaps from an article written by the system developers.

By looking at similar—possibly competing—applications we can identify shapes

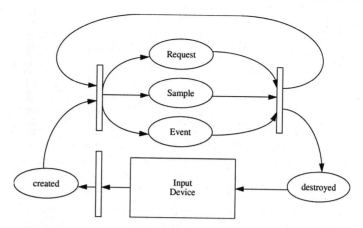

Figure 4.10: State diagram for the input device entity.

that should be included in the domain analysis results and that may be a part of the final system. We can also experience modes of interaction that may be useful. Each of these ideas that are identified should be captured as entities, relationships, or actions on entities and added to the collection of diagrams being built.

Additional information is needed for each of these entities. It should be collected and recorded during this phase. We mentioned three types of information earlier: data and state models, relationship models, and system models. So far, we have been identifying entities and the relationships between them. A simple listing of the attributes for each entity should also be made. For the general entity, input device, three data attributes can be identified from the GKS standard:

- *Mode*—request, sample, and event modes
- *Status*—accepting data or finished
- *Value*—current value to be sent to the application

A third type of information concerns the state transitions that the entity may undergo. In Figure 4.10, we consider the Input Device entity. The diagram shown there is a modification of the BIER approach of Kappel and the usual finite state machine representation. The state transitions that are of interest to us concern the mode of the input device. The GKS standard states that a device may be in only one of the three modes: *request, sample,* or *event at a time*. Each vertical box in the diagram indicates an action that causes the state transition. (These will become methods in the class that represents the entity.)

This is an initial cut at the domain analysis. It will be revisited and revised over time. The abstractions will be refined, more clearly defined, and made more abstract— perhaps by the addition of more layers of abstract classes—as the development of this system and others gives us a broader experience base in this domain.

Application Analysis

We are finally ready to move to the application analysis phase. The purpose of this phase is to focus and filter the information from the domain analysis based on the requirements of the specific system to be developed. Some of the information that we gathered during the domain analysis phase will not be used in the design of the current system. That effort will not be wasted in the long run, however, if we are a company that will be building many graphical systems or if the clients change their minds about the system requirements during or after development. The information will be used in the design of future products. The effort will not be wasted even for the current project because, by looking at a larger piece of a domain than our system embraces, we will develop abstractions that are more general and thus more powerful than those that would have been identified by looking only at the requirements for the current system. This development of powerful abstractions is a key ingredient to the approach we are presenting.

A comparison of the domain analysis information and our system requirements will determine those entities that are needed for the current system. These can be targeted for further development. Figure 4.11 presents an expanded ER diagram that includes the major entities that will be needed for the draw program's initial development. Each of these high-level entities will be exploded into more detail in lower-level diagrams. The input device hierarchy from the GKS standard will not be totally implemented for this simple system; but, Figure 4.12 shows those pieces that will be added to satisfy specific requirements. Note that the diagram in Figure 4.12 is actually an explosion of the Input Device entity in Figure 4.11.

High-Level Design

The high-level design phase continues the work begun in the application analysis phase. The first step in the high-level design of an application is the identification of objects that will be needed in the application. These are the objects that can be found by considering the entities identified in the problem domain. These objects will be represented in the design by classes from which the objects will be created. Each of the entities that were identified and specified by the application analysis phase will be classes in the design phase.

A set of additional classes that would be identified during analysis as application-level classes are:

Circle	Polyline
Display	Rectangle
Dot	Triangle
Line	Spline
Mouse	Square

These classes were identified from the requirements document. They are the "things" that the document discusses. This is the easy part! These are also the application-level classes. Some of them are shown in Figure 4.13. This hierarchy of classes combines our application classes and the classes we have identified from our analysis of GKS primitives. We have made the shapes required for the draw application into

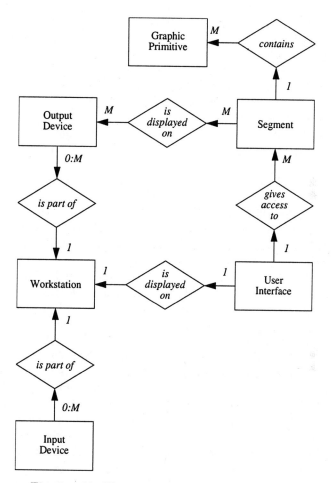

Figure 4.11: Elements of the graphics system.

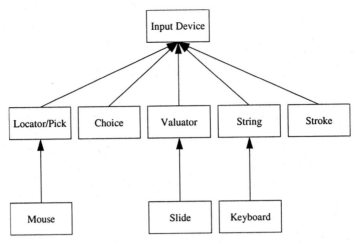

Figure 4.12: Specific input device entities.

specializations of a polyline. We have classified circles and polygons together under a more general notion of a "closed line."

We will identify more classes when we move to the class design and implementation levels. The Mouse and Display classes both represent physical entities. The shape classes can be considered representations of incident-type entities in the graphics system.

An important note here: The items listed above are mostly classes rather than objects. That is, Dot refers to the general class of dots rather than one specific dot on the screen. We cannot point to one shape and call it *the dot*. Rather, we immediately identify it in a more general form, a class rather than an instance. Whether we first identify instances or go directly to the class, the result is the identification of classes. In fact, with an interactive graphics system there is no way to know how many dots the user will create. There may be many, one, or none in any given execution of the system. The mouse object, on the other hand, refers to one actual object that will always be in the system. This mouse object will be an instance of a Mouse class.

In the high-level design phase some of the classes identified will be instantiated as single objects. Most systems have some fixed resources such as input and output devices or the user interface. In these cases the entities identified are actual objects that will be a part of the application. Classes must then be identified to serve as a source of these objects. The mouse object and class illustrate this.

In the high-level design phase the system architecture is laid out. In a simple system such as this draw program we would have only a few subsystems. Figure 4.14 shows three subsystems: a user interface, the graphics engine, and the persistent store. The user interface handles all interaction with the user. It may be an event-driven system that responds to clicks of the mouse or presses on keys, or it may be a simple polled system. Either approach should have no impact on the design of the other two subsystems. The graphics engine is responsible for producing the graphic objects utilizing information from the user regarding size and location of the object. The

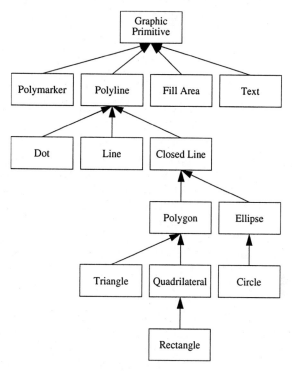

Figure 4.13: GKS graphic primitive entities (expanded).

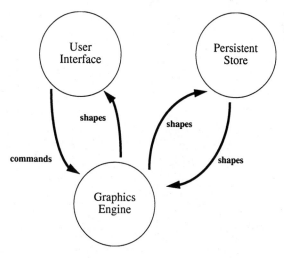

Figure 4.14: The subsystem architecture of the draw program.

graphics engine could also be used to provide geometric information about objects in a more sophisticated system. Finally, the persistence system stores the graphical objects on persistent storage.

SUMMARY

In this chapter we have begun an in-depth look at the object-oriented software development process. The two analysis phases, domain and application analysis, provide problem-centered information. These phases take a different point of view about organizing the information that will be the foundation for the architecture of the application. The analysis process produces an entity-relationship diagram that captures the relationships between the entities in the problem. This phase also records information about each individual entity. State diagrams and annotations can be used to capture this information. Abstract data type specifications can also be used to describe the attributes of an entity. The high-level design phase produces a subsystem-level view of the desired application. The design is accomplished by considering the application and each subsystem to be entities that have a specified behavior and a hidden implementation. The application can then be designed as any other class.

A draw program example was introduced. The simple draw program will be used through several chapters to illustrate subsequent phases of the development process. The analysis phases of this project produced many classes and a number of relationships between them. These classes have been organized into inheritance structures that are abstractly represented in high-level diagrams and more specifically represented in expanded diagrams. Figure 4.13 illustrates this by expanding upon the basic primitives of GKS. A subsystem architecture has also been proposed for the draw program. As we move from the high-level design into design of individual classes, we will be increasingly interested in the design of the interfaces of each class. There is not enough space to do a complete design of all pieces of the system, but in Chapter 6 we will provide additional details of each class in the application.

FURTHER READING

Several books and articles have addressed the topics covered in this chapter. The entire September, 1990 issue of the *Communications of the ACM* was devoted to object-oriented design. The Object Modeling Technique that covers both the analysis and design phases is detailed in [84]. Shlaer and Mellor[85] provide a methodology for object-oriented analysis. Rebecca Wirfs-Brock provides both system design and class design information in [101].

5

Relationships and Structures

Object-oriented analysis and design centers around the identification of entities in the problem domain and the representation of the relationships between these entities. In this chapter we consider several mechanisms for modeling the relationships between entities. The relationships are important for several purposes: as representations in the data modeling phase, for guiding the process of locating faults in the implementation, and for automated tools that assist in the development effort. A unifying principle underlying each of these techniques is the mathematical notion of a relation. By viewing the relationships between entities as relations, we gain the power of existing knowledge about the behavior of relations. The relational data model[20] provides a modeling methodology based on relations. We will not limit ourselves by the constraints imposed by the relational model, but will use the concept of a relation to provide a basis for making inferences about relationships between classes.

After considering the general idea of a relation, we will discuss in detail several of the more common relationships. The use of these relationships will be considered as will their implementation. Relationships play a major role in the object-oriented paradigm. Therefore, a number of examples of less well known relationships between entities will be considered to provide a view of how these relationships are treated in general.

RELATIONS

Informally, a relation may be viewed as a correspondence between the members of two sets. The basis of the relation is some rule that relates members of one set to members of the other set. More formally, Liu[68] defines a *relation* from set A to set B as a subset of the Cartesian product $A \times B$, where the Cartesian product is the set of all ordered pairs (a,b) such that $a \in A$ and $b \in B$.[1] If R is a relation from set A to set A, that is, from A to itself, then R is said to be a relation *on* A. A relation R on A can be formally written as

$$R = \{(a,b)| \ a,b \in A\}$$

Four properties of a relation, R, will be of use to us:

- *Reflexive*—if $a \in A$ then $(a, a) \in R$
- *Symmetric*—if $a, b \in A$ and $(a, b) \in R$ then $(b, a) \in R$
- *Antisymmetric*—if $a, b \in A$ and $(a, b) \in R$ then $(b, a) \notin R$
- *Transitive*—if $a, b, c \in A$ and $(a, b), (b, c) \in R$ then $(a, c) \in R$

A relation may have zero, one, two, or three of these properties.

Types of Relations

These properties can be used to define several general types of relations. Two of these categories will be useful in our subsequent discussions. By classifying a relation into one of these categories, we can infer several characteristics of its behavior.

An *equivalence relation* is a relation that is reflexive, symmetric, and transitive. The concept of belonging to a family can be viewed as an equivalence relation. Trivially, I belong to the same family as myself. Symmetrically, if Bill belongs to the family that I am a part of, then I am a part of the same family as Bill. Finally, if Bill belongs to the same family as Thelma and Thelma belongs to the same family to which I belong, then Bill belongs to the same family as I do. [Note: this is true for a biological family, but not for families by marriage.]

A *partial ordering relation* is a relation that is reflexive and transitive, but is antisymmetric rather than symmetric. The boss/subordinate relation is a partial ordering relation. Everyone may be considered their own boss. If Joan is Stan's boss and Stan is my boss, then Joan is my boss. But if I am Terri's boss, Terri cannot be my boss and thus the relation is antisymmetric. This is termed a partial ordering because Stan may have several subordinates other than myself, but there is no ordering of this group relative to each other.

Equivalence relations have the effect of partitioning a set of items into disjoint subsets of items that represent some natural grouping under the defining rule of the relation. Every item in the relation is at the same relative level—that is, no element "comes before" any other. The partial ordering relation, as the name implies, creates a layered set of items. It is a partial order in that several items may be related to a single item and thus be at the same level. Joan may be the boss of several people among whom there is no boss/subordinate relationship. We will see examples of these relations in this chapter.

We will be considering the relationships between classes and the relations that represent these relationships. Typically the set on which our relations will be based is the set of all classes in the software base. Because of their complex structure, classes

---

[1]The notation $x \in S$ is read as "x is an element of set S" or "x belongs to S." We will also use the expression "x is an instance of S" in contexts where S designates the set of instances of a class.

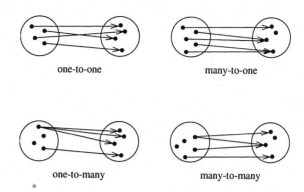

one-to-one   many-to-one

one-to-many   many-to-many

Figure 5.1: Cardinalities of relationships.

will usually be involved in several different relationships with many other classes. The *rule* that defines a particular relation must be well defined so that it is clear for each relation exactly how membership is determined.

Cardinality

There is one attribute of relations that will be of particular use to us. The *cardinality* of a relation represents the number of instances in one set that are related to a specific instance in the other set. Rather than count these values for each member of the first set, four categories are used to characterize the general types of cardinality. Figure 5.1 illustrates the categories.

In a *one-to-one* relationship, one instance in a set is related to only one instance in the other set. The relationship *currently married to* on the set of married people is a one-to-one relationship by law. In the relational data model, this type of relation is easily modeled by including the identification of one instance in the representation of the other instance. Thus each married person needs a single-valued slot to record the identification of the person to whom he or she is currently married.

A relationship with *many-to-one* cardinality models relations in which an instance from set A is related to one instance from set B, but each instance in set B is related to one or more instances in set A. A *one-to-many* relationship simply reverses these roles. In certain religions it is permissible for husbands to have multiple wives, but each wife is allowed only one husband. This can be handled in the rules of the relational data model by having each wife instance contain a slot that records the husband's identification. A more general data model might also support a list of wife identifiers in the husband instance.

In a *many-to-many* relationship, an instance in set A can be related to many instances in set B and an instance in set B can be related to many instances in set A. The relation *has been married to* is a many-to-many relation. A person may have been married to several people. Each of those people may have been married to several people, including this original person. By the rules of the relational model, this type of relationship is modeled by introducing an instance of a third entity that is termed an *associational entity*. This third entity might be termed a marriage certificate in our example. It serves as a correlation entity by listing the participants in each particular marriage. This third entity is necessary to maintain the integrity constraints of the relational model.

The object-oriented data model relaxes some of the restrictions of the relational model by allowing individual data items within a class specification to have a more complex structure than that permitted by the relational model. The relational data model requires that individual data values within an entity be instances of atomic data types—for example, dates, numbers, or strings of characters. The object-oriented model would allow each person instance to have a *list* of former spouses. This eliminates the need for the third entity type in the mapping of the *has been married to* relation. We will see other examples of the flexibility of the object-oriented data model.

APPLICATION VERSUS CLASS RELATIONSHIPS

In the object-oriented design process, two levels of relationships can be identified: application-level and class-level. These two levels provide a natural division between high-level and low-level design. The application-level relationships are intended to aid in modeling the problem while the class-level relationships are intended to support the implementation of the individual classes.

Application-Level Relationships

In the object-oriented development process, the analysis and high-level design phases include modeling the problem environment. The classes identified and developed at this level correspond to real-world entities. The relationships between these classes are also identifiable in the real world.

For example, in the design of a resource management system for an airline, aircraft and pilot classes would be among the classes identified. One relationship between these two classes would be *assigned to*—that is, a pilot is assigned to an aircraft for a particular flight. The classes and the relationship are named using the terminology of the problem domain. During a typical career with an airline, a pilot flies many aircraft and each aircraft will be flown by many pilots. This results in a many-to-many relationship. The object-oriented data model would allow this relationship to be modeled by lists in each class. However, an associational class provides a simpler data representation in this case because in maintaining two lists we have to be certain to keep them "in sync." Instances of a flight class could be used to associate a pilot and a plane on one particular flight. A pilot instance could maintain a list of the flights he flew and from that determine the planes that he flew. Similarly, a plane instance could keep a list of the flights in which it was used, or we could compute either association by examining the flight instances.

Although there are an infinite number of possible relationships in problem domains, experience with object-oriented data modeling and other types of data mod-

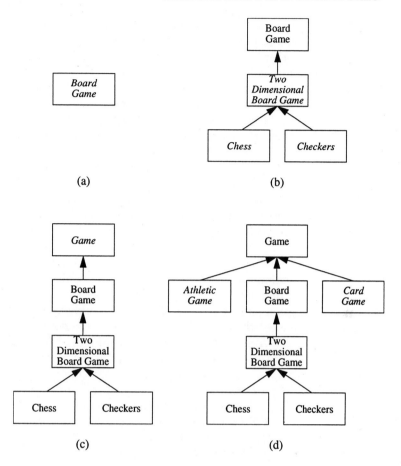

Figure 5.2: Specialization hierarchy evolution.

eling indicates a few general relationships that are useful in the modeling of problem domains. These general relationships, described as application-level relationships, will be very similar to class-level relationships. The difference is in the use of the relationship rather than the definition. An application-level relationship is part of the modeling of the domain, whereas class-level relationships are oriented to the implementation of individual classes. A brief characterization of each of the application-level relationships will help explain their role.

- *Specialization/Generalization.* This key relationship develops a layered model that begins with an abstract concept (see Figure 5.2(a)) and, in successive lower layers, defines entities that are increasingly specific (see Figure 5.2(b)). The entities in a lower layer can be viewed as special cases of the entity in a higher layer. This relationship is termed "specialization/generalization" because we may find a concept that is more abstract than some concept in the hierarchy (see Figure 5.2(c)). In this case, the new abstraction creates a new level in the hierarchy. The recognition of this new abstraction will often lead to the identification of other abstractions that will be special cases of the new abstraction (see Figure 5.2(d)). In the case shown in Figure 5.2(c), the new abstraction becomes the new root of the hierarchy. However, a new abstraction may appear at any level in the hierarchy.

The specialization relationship is often referred to as the *is a* relationship. This relationship is a partial ordering relation. The concepts defined in this manner form layers in which a set of entities is dependent upon a more general definition. The mapping of this relation associates an entity with its more general "parent" entity. This explains the arrows in Figure 5.2 pointing from the more specific to the more general. Recognizing this relation as a partial ordering eliminates the possibility of cycles in the specialization structure and facilitates tool building.

The effect of building this layered structure is to classify entities based on being a special case of a concept. Figure 5.3 shows a classification that begins with the very general concept of a graphic primitive from GKS. In successive layers we define increasingly specific kinds of geometric shapes. This structure takes known geometric shapes, "classifies" them, and builds a model of the domain.

A new class is introduced in Figure 5.3. Displayable Shape is added between Polyline and the rest of the hierarchy. This class is added to provide some additional attributes that are not part of the GKS definition of primitives but that are useful in the remainder of the shape classes. In particular, Displayable Shape defines a reference point for each shape. We will provide more details on Displayable Shape in the next chapter.

An entity may be a specialization of more than one general concept. Displayable Shape provides a link between being a Graphic Primitive and being a specific shape on a graphics display. Figure 5.4 shows that a Displayable Shape could be defined as a specialization of two concepts, Geometric Shape and Graphic Primitive.[2] This figure illustrates that there is often more than one "dimension" of interest for a particular entity. Here objects are being viewed as shapes and also as capable of being displayed on a computer graphics device. These different views on an object can be thought of as classifying the object based on separate criteria for each view. Consider the general concept of a person. One possible classification dimension might be sex. A simple variable with a boolean value might suffice to represent this concept in many applications. However, an application that will include extensive biological information might require sufficient behaviors that varied between the two sexes to develop two separate specializations, one for males and one for females. At the same time, we might wish to "view" persons from the standpoint of their careers. This dimension has nothing to do with

---

[2]Since our draw program would inherit little of value from Geometric Shape, we will use single inheritance for most of our examples and only occasionally refer to possible uses of multiple inheritance.

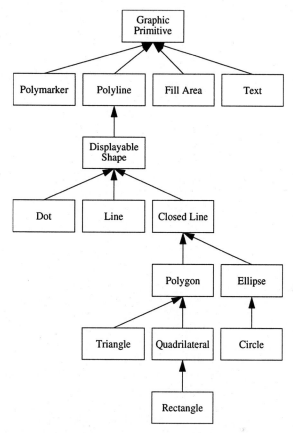

Figure 5.3: Specialization hierarchy of shapes.

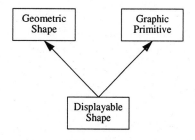

Figure 5.4: Multiple classification hierarchy.

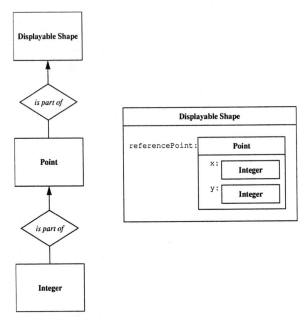

Figure 5.5: An example of aggregation.

the classification by sex. We will discuss later some of the complications these multiple classifications can introduce into the implementation of systems.

- *Aggregation.* This data modeling relationship produces a nested arrangement. New entities are defined as parts of other entities. This is modeling by developing a collection of parts. Figure 5.5 shows several entities. The object of Displayable Shape uses a reference point of class Point, which in turn is made up of two Integer values. This produces a hierarchy of classes all related via aggregation. This hierarchy differs from the generalization/specialization hierarchy in the meaning of the relationship that is giving structure to the hierarchy. Many of the properties of the generalization/specialization hierarchy are present in the aggregation hierarchy—for example, the aggregation relationship defines a partial order on a set of classes.

    The interface of a class being defined by aggregation is a model of that concept and does not include direct references to the instances defined within the class. This preserves the information hiding of the abstraction. The implementation of the methods of the class will forward messages to these internal instances as appropriate. Consider a car class that is constructed of parts such as an engine, transmission, tires, and other pieces. The interface of the car class would have methods to start the car, speed it up, and stop it. The application designer and future users of the abstraction should not be sending messages directly to the brakes instances nor the engine at the application level. A refueling operator, for example, would be provided by a car that would then direct the fuel to its fuel tank component.

- *Association.* The associational relationship relates two entities where one of the entities will hold instances of the other. This relationship has been extensively represented in object-oriented environments through the "container" or "collection" classes available in many object-oriented libraries. A container class does no modification to the instances it holds, but often passes messages to the instances that it is holding. These classes include implementations of the data structures from "Data Structures 101." What is important about these classes is a common protocol for receiving, storing, and returning the instances they hold.

  At the application level, an entity may be developed to hold other application-level entities and coordinate services for them. For example, a window manager is a container for windows. The window manager routes messages from "outside" to the appropriate window. One issue in the design of these classes is the visibility of the instances. Can an outside object send a message directly to a window that is being held by the window manager? It is not a violation of information hiding to send this message directly because the instances being held are not part of the implementation of the container class. The class's implementation has to do with how to maintain a set of items. Trying to modify the value representing the number of items in the set without adding or deleting an item from the set would be a violation of the information hiding. This is because the size of the set is a part of the implementation of the container class.

  The difference between aggregation and association is important to understand. Aggregation is a relationship between a class and the *parts* of its representation. A car class would be represented as an aggregation of instances of an engine class, seat class, tire class, and others. Association is a relationship between a class and the "pieces" that take advantage of its service. A car and a person in the role of a passenger are related by association. Blake and Cook[7] distinguish between a *collection* and a *structured whole*. The modeling of a collection is carried out by the association relationship while the structured whole is modeled by aggregation.

  The example in Chapter 2 of controlling the traffic at an intersection includes examples of the association relationship. The Intersection class associates instances of the Direction class. An instance of Intersection will hold as many instances of Direction as are needed to model the particular intersection. On the other hand, a Traffic Signal is an aggregation of Traffic Light instances.

The interaction of two of the application-level relationships provides one of the powerful features of object-oriented system design. The specialization relationship creates a lattice of entity descriptions. Because each class in the lattice is a special-

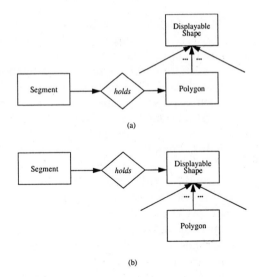

Figure 5.6: Polymorphism of relationships.

ization of those classes higher in the lattice, the class includes in its interface all of the behaviors that are present in the interface of the higher-level classes. Polymorphic substitution supports an associational relationship between two classes that is actually a relationship between a class and a complete hierarchy of classes. Figure 5.6 illustrates this concept using the **Segment** class from our design of the GKS standard and some of the shape classes. In Figure 5.6(a) a segment can hold any instance of a **Polygon** whereas in Figure 5.6(b) a segment can hold any instance of **Displayable Shape**—dots, lines, splines, and circles as well as polygons. This supports a style of design in which a container's usefulness is expanded as the number of classes in the associated hierarchy increases. The usefulness is expanded without any modifications to the container class.

CLASS-LEVEL RELATIONS

The class-level relationships arise as we design the implementation of a class. Often the implementation of one class depends in some way on instances of other classes. Class-level relationships may be the implementation of application-level relationships or they may be the implementation of attributes within the class. The ways that one class can contribute to the implementation of another are quite limited and therefore are easy to enumerate and discuss. We will consider three relations:

messaging
composition
inheritance

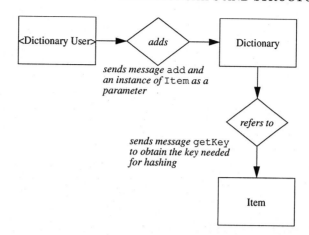

Figure 5.7: Some relationships surrounding class Dictionary.

In this section we will use the design of a dictionary class to illustrate the relationships. For our purposes, a dictionary is a component that holds objects. The objects are ordered and retrieved based on the value of a "key." For the instances of a class to be storable in a dictionary, the class must provide a method to furnish the value of the key. Some of these relationships are shown in Figure 5.7.

Messaging

Most application-level relationships will be realized in the application as messages between instances of the two classes involved. The message must correspond to one of the behaviors specified in the public interface of the class whose instance will be the receiver of the message. The message may also provide information to the receiver in the form of parameters. In a procedural system, the parameters would simply be data that the receiving procedure would either modify and return or use for decision making. The objects passed as parameters in a message will be the recipient of messages within the implementation of the behavior to which they are passed and/or be used as parameters in subsequent messages. The results of these messages will be much more complex than the results of passing data to a procedure.

The relationship between a class and the classes whose instances are passed to it as parameters is termed *refers to*. The graph formed by the patterns of messages forms the heart of the structure of an object-oriented system. As discussed above in the section on the association relationship, this relationship is between the class that receives the message and all possible parameter values, including the subclasses of the originally specified formal parameter.

The Dictionary class has an add method. That method takes as a parameter an object that is to be entered into the dictionary. We will refer to this object as item and its class as Item. The add method sends a message to the parameter object to find out the value of its key. The Dictionary class *refers to* the class of any object that can be added to the dictionary. This requires that there be agreement between the

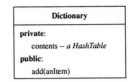

Figure 5.8: A partial definition for class Dictionary.

dictionary class and those classes whose instances it may contain. During the design phase, the establishment of a messaging relationship between these two classes will require that the designers of the appropriate classes coordinate the definitions of the interfaces of the classes.

Composition

The composition relationship has been widely referred to in the literature using an array of aliases such as "client," "component," and "is part of." This is the implementation relationship that corresponds to the aggregation application-level relationship. The hidden implementation of a class is provided by creating instances of one or more classes. Both composition and messaging are relationships between classes in which an instance of one class is being used as part of the implementation of the other.

Consider the implementation of the Dictionary class. One basic data store that could be used to hold the items in the dictionary is a hash table. The low-level design of the dictionary class would show an *is part of* relation between the Dictionary and Hash Table classes (see Figure 5.8). During implementation, an instance of Hash Table would be declared within the definition of class Dictionary. Notice that while the relationship is between two classes, it is realized by using an instance of one class within the definition of the other class.

Inheritance

Inheritance is perhaps the single-most distinguishing feature of object-oriented programming languages. A number of issues are all bound up into this term. Some we will use with the term and some we will not. These issues include:

> Subclassing
> Subtyping
> Hierarchy

We will treat some of these issues now and defer some until later. There are differing views on inheritance and its use. We will try to present these and give our view and its justification.

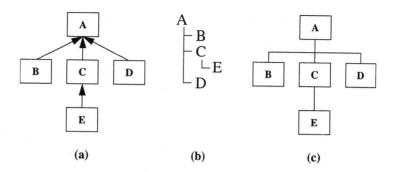

Figure 5.9: Inheritance diagrams.

From one perspective, inheritance is a technique for allowing new classes to be defined in terms of existing ones. A new class B that inherits from an existing class A is termed a *subclass* of the existing class. This implies that B includes some of the previously defined behavior of A as well as defining some additional behavior of its own. Figure 5.9 shows three notations used in the literature for this concept. Diagram (a) is the general and widely used diagram for inheritance. Diagram (b) is a textual rendering of inheritance with indentation used to indicate subclasses. Diagram (c) is part of an extended notation for ER diagrams that indicates that lower boxes represent special cases of the concept in the higher-level box to which they are connected.

There are almost as many different realizations of inheritance as there are object-oriented languages. These different realizations result in different possible styles of design. We will consider several of these models in the chapter on languages. There are also differences in the ways that inheritance can be used: inheritance for *implementation* and inheritance for *specialization*.

Inheritance for Implementation

The establishment of an inheritance relationship between two classes "for implementation" means that the internal representation of the existing class is used to provide part of the internal representation of the class being defined. We do not recommend this use of inheritance because it is orthogonal to our use of inheritance for specialization in a model of a domain. Most object-oriented programming languages make no distinction between the two uses for inheritance.

Consider, for example, the use of inheritance for the implementation of a Circle class given the availability of a Point class as shown in Figure 5.10. It is easy to see that a Point class provides part of the implementation of a Circle class. To define a circle, we need only a point to define the center and a value to define the length of the radius. As a subclass of Point, class Circle not only gets the location of its center as provided by x and y, but it gets a method to move the circle "for free." Unfortunately, we lose several things. First, we lose abstraction. It is difficult to argue that a circle

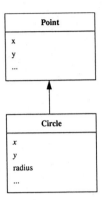

Figure 5.10: The use of inheritance for implementation.

is a point with a radius greater than zero. Second, we have lost the identity of the circle's center as a point—it is a point, but its class is Circle. A method to answer an instance's center has to answer itself! But, of course, this "point"—the center point—is different from other points in that it behaves as a circle as well. We can send a message to this point to answer its radius, for example. Finally, a Circle instance can respond to messages that make sense for points but not for circles—for example, answering its polar coordinates.

Inheritance for implementation is commonly used in prototyping developments, but this use of inheritance clashes with our goal of developing reusable classes that model domain abstractions and not their implementation.

Inheritance for Specialization

The use of inheritance that most naturally fits the relationship provided by most object-oriented programming languages is for the implementation of the generalization/specialization relationship. This use of inheritance is referred to as the *is a* relationship. In Figure 5.9, this states that an instance of B *is a* instance of A. In this use, the most important result of the inheritance is that the interface of the existing class becomes part of the interface of the new class. This means that the new class possesses all of the behaviors of its parent class. This produces a "plug-compatible" component that may be used in place of the original class. The result of this use of inheritance is a powerful, extensible design that takes maximum advantage of polymorphism.

To define our Dictionary class, we could begin by looking for existing abstractions of which it is a special case. A dictionary *is an* ordered list, but with additional operations such as looking up entries using a key. An existing Ordered List class provides some of the behaviors that we need for Dictionary, but not all. Our only real concern in this type of inheritance will be whether there are behaviors in Ordered List that we do not want in Dictionary. If there are, we may wish to reorganize the hierarchy or develop some additional abstractions, or simply look for other classes from which to inherit.

Return to the graphics system example. As part of its high-level design, we identified two generalization relations. One involved the shape entity and the entities such as rectangle, circle, and so on. This generalization relation should be implemented by a Displayable Shape class that is inherited by each of the classes Circle, Rectangle, and so on. Classes such as Circle would have an interface that includes the interface of Displayable Shape as a subset. This might be a proper subset. For example, Circle might have a method termed radius, which certainly would not be part of the Displayable Shape abstraction.

This use of inheritance appears to parallel subtyping. We expect that operators in a subtype will behave *exactly* the same as the same operator in the supertype. In a subclass, an operator may have exactly the same signature but may behave differently from the same operator in the superclass. There are differences between subtyping and subclassing[3]. We will provide one particular example of these differences here. Often when a class is defined using inheritance, even though the interface is inherited, the implementations of the inherited methods are overridden. In the high-level design of the graphics system, the shape entity had a draw method defined as part of its interface. This method would be inherited by each of the specialized shape classes. The draw method of Displayable Shape would not be able to do anything specific, so it might just print an error message. The draw method inherited by the Circle class would be modified to draw a circular shape.

A second variety of inheritance is termed *is kind of*. This type of inheritance allows the new definition being created to selectively include attributes from the existing class(es). This means that we could model entities in terms of exceptions. For example, a bird class might have an attribute about flying. A subclass modeling an ostrich would choose not to inherit that attribute since ostriches cannot fly. The ostrich is *a kind of* bird that does not have exactly the same attributes as a bird. The power to cancel attributes is useful in small prototyping environments, but it is not suited to building large, robust structures of reusable components. The *is a* form of inheritance is sometimes referred to as *strict* inheritance while *is kind of* and some other varieties are referred to as *non-strict* inheritance. In the case of ostriches, it is more appropriate to make a class Ostrich a subclass of a Flightless Bird class, which is in turn a subclass of a Bird class.

USING RELATIONS

In the previous chapter we considered application-level classes and relations. The relations between these classes are stated in terms of the interactions found in the problem domain. The *is part of* and *refers to* relations are most often implementation-level relations—that is, they relate a class to the classes that provide its internal representation and operations.

Consider the design of a simple simulation model for a checkout line in a store. The high-level design of this model would identify classes for customers, a waiting line, and a server—a checker and a cash register. Operations on the model include the arrival of a customer and reporting statistics such as the average length of the waiting line and the amount of time the server is idle. At a lower level of design, the problem of how to implement the waiting line must be addressed. The existence of a Queue

Longevity	Accessibility	
	EXCLUSIVE	SHARED
DEPENDENT	*is part of*	public data
INDEPENDENT	not enforceable	*refers to*

Table 5.1: Longevity versus accessibility.

container class would make implementation straightforward as it provides exactly the behavior we expect in a waiting line if we assume that customers don't exit the line except after being served.

The use of an instance of Queue by our Simulation Model class has created a dependency between the two classes. The instance of Queue is dependent on the existence of an instance of a Simulation Model and we have an *is part of* relationship. However, since a waiting line is an abstraction in the application domain, should the queue be available to other classes—that is, should the relationship be messaging— *refers to*—rather than component?

If we were to make the Queue instance independent of Simulation Model, then at least two undesirable circumstances arise. First, access to the queue outside of Simulation Model means that it can be manipulated directly. If a customer is added to the queue directly, then the simulation model would miss performing important functions such as recording that customer's arrival time. Second, independence provides the queue with "a life of its own" and the simulation model that is responsible for its creation cannot be responsible for its destruction. This is a concern primarily for implementations in which there is no garbage collection and storage management is under program control. Who will be responsible for the queue's destruction?

In this example, the Queue and Simulation Model classes are clearly best matched in an *is part of* relationship. We now describe how appropriate relationships can be identified.

Messaging Versus Composition

Kim *et al*[58] present a detailed analysis of the *refers to* and *is part of* relationships. They consider two characteristics of the relations between the class and the instance object used within it. One characteristic is the accessibility of the instance object—that is, is the instance used exclusively by the class defining it or is it shared? The other characteristic is longevity—whether an instance of a class depends on an instance of another for its existence. Table 5.1 summarizes the four possible combinations of the two characteristics.

The Dependent/Exclusive entry in the table corresponds to the *is part of* relation. This entry indicates that the existence of the instance being used to implement the class is dependent on the existence of an instance of that class. The dependent instance has no use other than that provided by its association with the instance of the class on which it is dependent. This usually means that the declaration of the instance is within the definition of the class. It also indicates that the instance is hidden in the definition of the class it is helping to implement. Some may take the position that *is part of* does not require the Exclusive access rights. However, proper style—which we will discuss later—requires that all attributes be hidden from outside access. The Shared characteristic of the Dependent entry should be viewed as a violation of good style and therefore off limits.

The Independent/Shared entry in the table corresponds to the *refers to* relation. The Independent characteristic indicates that the declaration of the instance is external to the definition of the class. The Shared characteristic indicates that other objects have access to the instance. This relation is usually implemented either by declaring a pointer to an instance as a part of the class definition (in languages that support pointers) or by receiving the instance as a parameter in a message.

The Independent/Exclusive entry would be a possible, but clumsy, way of implementing a relation between two classes. How would the instance get created if it was outside the class definition? Possibilities include declaring the instance as a global or to add it to some global container instance. In either case, this could lead to the developer forgetting to provide the required external instance. In either case, we could not guarantee that only the creating instance of a class had access to the instance being used to implement it. This is simply not a desirable possibility as it violates our notion of encapsulation.

The design of the Dictionary class provides illustrations of the *is part of* and *refers to* relationships. The declaration of the instance of the Hash Table class inside the Dictionary class is an example of the Dependent/Exclusive relation. When an instance of Dictionary is created, an instance of Hash Table is automatically created. The existence of the Hash Table instance is dependent upon the existence of the instance of Dictionary. The Hash Table instance should not be visible to users of the dictionary. The behaviors exhibited by the dictionary should not include those of the hash table used in its implementation. This implies that the hash table is used exclusively by the Dictionary instance. The development environment will require access to the definition of the Hash Table class when compiling the Dictionary class.

The Dictionary class add method illustrates the *refers to* relationship. The parameter of the method is an instance of some Item class. The implementation of add will include sending messages to the actual parameter that is passed during a message. For example, the method would send a message to the instance to obtain the value of its key. This requires that the Dictionary class know something about the Item class. This establishes a dependency that must be represented in the development environment. The existence of an instance of Item does not depend upon the existence of an instance of the Dictionary class. Nor is the instance of Dictionary the only object that knows of the existence of the instance of Item. In this case we have an Independent/Shared relationship. The Dictionary class is independent of the Item class even though a dictionary contains instances of Item. The add method for Dictionary creates a *refers to* relationship between the two classes.

is a Versus *is part of*

The *is a* relationship is often used when the appropriate relationship is *is part of*. A simple guideline is that *is a* is used when the interface of the existing class is to become a subset of the new class's interface. *All* of the attributes of the existing class should become attributes of the new class. When it is desired that a behavior is needed to help the new class carry out its purpose rather than be part of its purpose, *is part of* should be selected. As we saw, it is not the case that a circle *is a* point. A Circle class needs a Point instance to carry out its modeling, but it should not have the same interface as a point, nor should the interface of a Point be a subset of its interface.

Consider the Simulation Model class. We discussed previously using an instance of a Queue in the class implementation. Assume another entity is identified—say, a printer server for an operating system that queues print requests and sends them to the printer. We wish to implement the print server by using a queue. One approach is that the new class could inherit from the simulation server class in order to gain access to its queue. We do not want the operators of the server class, such as arrive(aCustomer), to become part of the interface of the new Printer Server class. Some languages provide sufficient flexibility in the inheritance mechanism to allow the inherited operators to become public members of the interface or private members of the implementation.

The problem above should have been solved in the same way as we built the simulation model. Instead of inheriting to get the queue, a queue object should have been declared as an attribute of the new class. Although the inheritance solution can be implemented and compiled, the structure that results is not easy to understand. It is not developed in a logical fashion, but only an opportunistic one. It is impossible to see intuitively how a printer server "*is a*" simulation model. This makes it very difficult for components to be located for reuse.

In our opinion, inheritance should be used when the behavior (defined by the set of operators) is to become part of the interface of the new class. When the service of a class is needed for implementation but not as part of the interface, then the *is part of* relation should be used. These two techniques provide diverse alternatives for system design.

FRIENDS AND RELATIONS

The *friend* relation is less well known than the relations discussed above, but it is a useful one nonetheless. The *friend* relationship signifies that the "friend class" needs to have special access to the representation of the class that it is befriending. Classes that work closely together may be implemented to provide more information to those classes that are assisting in the representation of a concept. A single concept is sometimes implemented by more than one class. For example, Stroustrup[88] implemented the linked list concept using three classes:

- The list
- The links
- A list iterator (or cursor)

Since all of these classes are needed to provide a single concept, the three work together very closely, particularly to provide an efficient implementation. This usually requires that each class have access to what would otherwise be private implementation details in the other two classes. There are two choices. The implementation details can be made available to any object in the application—that is, made public—perhaps with a caveat not to use certain methods. The second alternative is to provide special access privileges so that these three classes can access information that is not available to other objects in the system. C++ provides the "friend" keyword for this purpose. It allows the designer to provide these special access privileges where necessary. In particular, a friend has access to the private data of the class.

Although the name for this relation comes from the C++ realization of it, the relation is a design concept that may be useful in any language. The relation would be used whenever a single concept is to be realized in more than one class. For the above example, the list class accesses the representation of the data inside the individual links. The separation of the list from the list iterator allows for multiple simultaneous iterators—that is, pointers into a list—for a single list. The use of special access to the representation of one class by another violates the intent of data encapsulation, but provides an important special case that should be used with extreme caution. Automated tools that assist with system development must provide ways for recognizing these linkages between classes.

STILL MORE RELATIONS

Other relations have been investigated and are beginning to be recognized as useful. Relations termed the *family* and *community* have been defined in the literature. These are used for system development and management purposes rather than implementation purposes. A *family* is the set of classes in a single inheritance structure. In our approach, these are all related by the specialization/generalization relationship.

The *community* is the set of classes that are used for a single application. This relation is not explicitly supported in any object-oriented language that we know of. It is a very useful relationship to consider when building tools for software development. Figure 5.11 illustrates that applications are developed by selecting appropriate classes and creating instances of them. These classes will come from many different inheritance families, so traversing the inheritance relationships is not sufficient. When the software base of classes holds several thousand classes, there must be some way of grouping together those classes being used in a single application. Obviously this is not a design relationship, but one that should be maintained by the development environment. It is also useful in considering the structure of libraries of reusable classes. This relationship would play an important role in automatically developing the internal documentation for an application that is constructed largely from instances of existing classes.

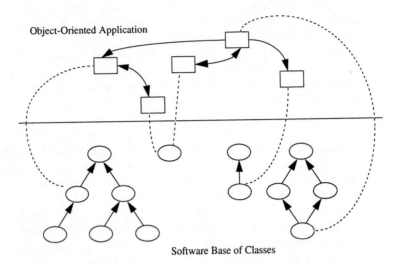

Figure 5.11: Application construction.

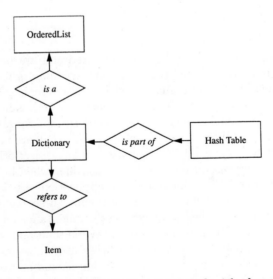

Figure 5.12: Dependency structure associated with class Dictionary.

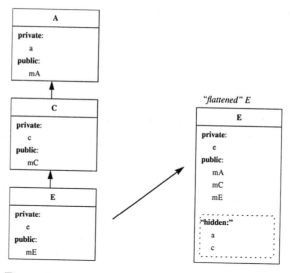

Figure 5.13: Building a complete class interface.

STRUCTURES

Taken together, all the relationships between classes develop a complex set of dependencies. These dependencies form structures that can be utilized for a number of purposes. Figure 5.12 shows the kinds of dependencies, even for the simple cases considered in this chapter. We will discuss the use of relations and their resulting structures as the basis for development environments in Chapter 13. The dependencies also serve as primary input into the processes of configuration management, version control, and automated documentation.

Both the *is a* and *is part of* relations result in directed acyclic graph structures. These structures are directed because these two relations are partial ordering relations. The antisymmetric attribute of these relations is reflected in the acyclic property of the graph. The graphs provide a basis for navigating the inheritance relationships between classes. Inheritance supports the incremental development of definitions but, when a designer is considering using an instance of a particular class, the complete interface of that class must be available. Consider the inheritance structure shown in Figure 5.9 in which E is a subclass of C, which is a subclass of A. The user of instances of class E must be able to see the complete interface of E, which is the combination of the interfaces of classes C and A as well as E. Inheritance is generally specified in programming languages in pieces or increments. The specification for class E would include specifications for any new methods being added to the interface, methods that are being redefined, and an inheritance link to class C. The inheritance lattice provides a structure that is represented in the syntax and that could be used to "flatten" the hierarchy and produce an interface composed from the interfaces of the parent classes following the rules of the inheritance model of the particular implementation language. Figure 5.13 illustrates the product resulting from this process. Design tools should make this process transparent to the user but could provide the option of indicating where the attribute is actually first defined.

Paper-based documentation systems must either provide separate information about each class or face the inefficiency of redundancy and the danger of obsolescence or inconsistency. A hypertext tool could easily use the inheritance dependencies to collect and present in one document the information about class E dynamically. Changes to class A would be immediately available and included in the next request for documentation that included class A. More will be presented about this when we discuss tools.

Another important use of these dependencies is to provide structure to the *software base*[92]. This repository of reusable components will have a very complex set of interdependencies. They are based on the use of instances to define both the interfaces and implementations of other classes, their common association with a given software project, or other user-defined relationships. The encapsulation and information-hiding properties of objects will control the complexity of these relationships so that modifications to one element in the lattice does not cause an excessive amount of difficulty for other elements. A successful object-oriented software development support system will require a relationship traversal facility that is capable of manipulating various forms of relationships.

MORE GRAPHICS: CLASS RELATIONSHIPS

In this section we consider the role of relations in our continuing graphics example. First, we will discuss the use of the application-level relationships: aggregation and association in the graphics application. The class-level relations, *refers to*, *is a*, and *is part of*, will also be discussed in the context of the system. The application-level relationships will relate a class to a set of classes, while the class-level relationships express the relationship between two classes.

Application-Level Relationships

Aggregation Relationship

The user interface for the draw program is shown in Figure 5.14. There are several graphical features of this User Interface class. The large drawing area and the boxes that form the menu are rectangles and can be provided by instances of Rectangle or its subclasses. These objects are created as part of the implementation of the interface class and thus are private to the class. Even though a window manager might know of the existence of these rectangles—if each represented a different window—as far as the rest of the application is concerned all messages are addressed to a User Interface object. We would say that the User Interface is, at least in part, an *aggregation* of Rectangles.

Association Relationship

The segment concept in the GKS standard is a container for instances of Graphic Primitive and its subclasses. The instances that are held by one instance of segment as

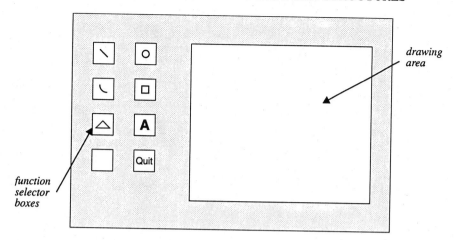

Figure 5.14: Draw program user interface.

opposed to those held by another are grouped via some logic on the part of the system user. In a CAD system, various subsystems—electrical, plumbing, mechanical—might each constitute a segment. There is an association relationship between the class Segment and the class Graphic Primitive and its subclasses. We would say that a Segment *associates* a set of instances of Graphic Primitives. As an application-level relationship, this association models the idea that a segment contains any shapes that are drawn by the user. Unlike the example of the aggregation relationship, the instances of Graphic Primitive are not part of the implementation of Segment.

Class-Level Relationships

is a Relationship

As seen above, classes are often designed in groups rather than as isolated individuals. Several families of classes can be identified in the graphics system being developed. Figure 5.15 shows the set of classes that represent the shapes that the system is capable of drawing.

The top-level class of the structure shown here, Graphic Primitive, serves two purposes. First, it provides a set of functionality that is common to any shape that might be created. This factored set avoids the duplication of functions in a number of classes. The inheritance relation between the Graphic Primitive class and the specific subclasses supports the inclusion of functions from the root class in the subclasses. Shapes—whether triangles, circles, or whatever—can all be moved by erasing the current figure from the screen, moving the figure's reference point to the new location, and redrawing the figure. This can be implemented at the root class level and then used, without modification, by each of the subclasses.

The second purpose of the root class is to provide the basis for a set of interchangeable classes in a typesafe environment. Routines can be written to expect instances of the root class as arguments. Instances of any of the subclasses can then be used

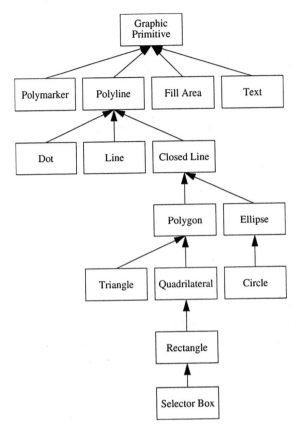

Figure 5.15: Graphic Primitive specialization hierarchy.

in place of, or in addition to, instances of the root class. In the graphics system, there is a need for a list of all of the figures that have been drawn by the user. The list is defined as a list of instances of Graphic Primitive. As a user creates triangles, rectangles, and so on, these instances may be added to the list. This polymorphic behavior is used in strongly typed object-oriented languages to recognize the special dependency between a class and its subclasses.

The family of shape classes also illustrates the "plug compatibility" that gives software engineers some of the same flexibility that hardware engineers have enjoyed for some time. Any one instance of a shape subclass can be replaced by any instances of the other subclasses. Adding a new shape class to the family does not require any reworking of existing code for those objects that handle shapes. It merely requires the writing of code for the new subclass, and much of that is inherited from the existing classes.

The importance of this compatibility can be seen in the family of display devices shown in Figure 5.16. The common interface provided by the root class allows one type of display to be easily replaced by another. All that is required is the substitution of an instance of one subclass for an instance of another. The common interface that

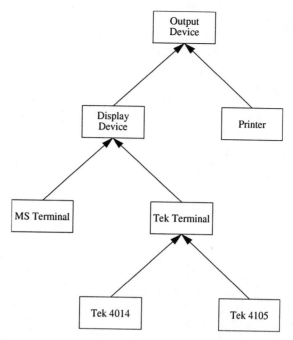

Figure 5.16: Output device specialization hierarchy.

masks implementation differences supports the development of very portable systems.

is part of Relation

The second relation to be illustrated here is *is part of*. The user interface of the graphics system includes a number of occurrences of this relation. The interface shown in Figure 5.14 is typical of most draw programs. The small boxes in the interface represent the functions that the user may select using the mouse. Each box is an instance of the Selector Box class. The User Interface class declares these instances as part of its definition. There is an *is part of* relationship between the User Interface and the Selector Box classes.

Each Selector Box instance is a region of the screen that represents a particular shape or action and is *selectable*. The user moves the mouse cursor into the box that represents the desired choice. When the mouse button is pressed, each Selector Box instance, in the list maintained by the User Interface instance, is queried to determine whether the press occurred within its boundaries. The responsibility for comparing boundaries with the location of the press rests with each instance. The box that was the object of the mouse button press activates the action associated with that box.

Comparing Two Relations

The use of the *is part of* relation is the appropriate technique for providing the functionality of the Selector Box class to the User Interface class. If the *is a* relation were used, then the capabilities of the Selector Box class would be inherited by the User Interface class. The functionality present in the interface of the Selector Box becomes part of the interface of the User Interface class. But an instance of the User Interface class is *not* a Selector Box. In fact, each independent Selector Box must know its own unique boundaries in order to implement the User Interface.

The comparison of the two relations can be summarized as follows: The *is a* relation is appropriate when the new class is a special case of an existing class. Through this relationship the public interface of the existing class becomes a part of the interface of the new class. The *is part of* relation is appropriate when the functionality provided by the interface of the existing class is needed as part of the functionality of the new class.

SUMMARY

This chapter has presented several relations that are used in the design of object-oriented applications and classes. These relations provide structure to the space of reusable classes. They also determine the architecture of an application. Some of the relationships provide the means for capturing the relationships that exist in the problem domain while others provide the links between concepts and their implementations.

The inheritance relationship is actually a family of possible models that have somewhat differing purposes. Their realization in different object-oriented programming languages further complicates the understanding of inheritance as a unitary concept. We have presented what we believe to be the inheritance model that is most productive given the current language landscape—namely, inheritance for specialization. This use of inheritance provides a close parallel to the typing structure of many of the object-oriented languages and provides a mechanism for modeling the problem domain as part of the application development process.

FURTHER READING

Wegner and Zdonik[96] provides a look at inheritance from several perspectives. Cardelli and Wegner[13] provides a more abstract view of the subclassing mechanism. Chen[18] considers a general semantic data model in which relationships are placed on the same level as the entities they relate. Pintado and Tsichritzis[80] discuss the use of fuzzy relationships and affinity links to represent some of the relationships between classes.

6

Class Design

In this chapter we will consider the design of classes. An individual class can often be designed and implemented independently of the application for which it is intended. It should not, however, be developed independently of other similar classes that have already been defined. This chapter provides basic guidelines and some practical tips for the design of classes.

The obvious first step in class design is the identification of a concept that is needed for an application. In a previous chapter several categories of classes were discussed. The application analysis process includes identifying the need for classes that model the problem domain; however, these will not be the only classes present in the final application. The class design process can also lead to the identification of additional classes, as we will see in this chapter.

CLASS LIFE CYCLE

Classes are encapsulated models of a concept and provide a natural unit for reuse. The encapsulated nature of the class means that a single syntactic unit can be used to provide the behavior of the concept to an application. The information-hiding characteristic of a class means that the class is easier to integrate with others.

The class life cycle was presented in Chapter 3. It is intended to call attention to the need to explicitly recognize and manage these reusable components. Chapter 4 presented numerous ideas for the identification of classes. Although classes are identified as part of the application analysis and design processes, if a class is to be reused then it must be recognized outside of the specific application in which it was first identified. Figure 6.1 illustrates that the application life cycle and the class life cycle should be thought of as integrated at one level yet separate at another. This implies that the development of the class should be as independent as possible of the

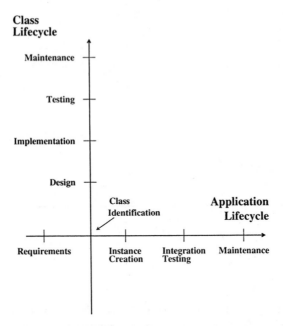

Figure 6.1: Class and application life cycles.

application for which it is immediately intended.

This independence has an important impact on the initial development of a class. The class should be developed as completely as is economically possible. By *complete* we mean development that includes all the appropriate attributes in the initial design of the class. It is easy to spend time only on those attributes that will be used in the current application. Complete development becomes both a design and a management issue.

The management issue is how to account for time spent on development of functionality that will not be used by the project paying for the designer's time. The alternative is to leave out methods not needed and to add them at a later time. If this sounds like maintenance to you, you are correct. The cost of maintenance design and implementation can be as much as ten times that of original design. It is a sound decision for a company to invest in complete development of each class initially since design costs will easily be recouped during maintenance, but a modification of the management environment at most companies will be necessary to support this.

The design issue is whether to "throw in the kitchen sink" with respect to a class definition or to include only those methods needed in the current application—or do something in between. Our answer is to provide a complete model of a concept—but only one concept. It is not reasonable to design a queue that has an add and a delete method but no isEmpty just because it is not needed for the current application. It is also not useful to develop a list class that has add, delete, addRear, and deleteRear methods and then only use a few of the methods because we really needed a queue and not the generality of a list. The designer strikes a compromise between these two positions by specifying an interface that provides all of the behavior of a queue—but no more.

The benefit of this approach is the development of abstractions that are sufficiently specific to be useful but sufficiently general to support the full meaning of a concept.

GOALS FOR CLASS DESIGN

Our primary goal is to design each class so that it has the following characteristics:

- A faithful model of a single concept
- A reusable, "plug-compatible" component
- A robust, well designed software component
- An integrable, extensible component

Model of a Single Concept

Often, when a "concept" is identified during the analysis and high-level design phases, it will need to be represented by more than one class. Following a basic software engineering principle, one module should represent one concept. We will view a class as the module in the object-oriented paradigm. Our design strategies will have to decompose an idea into an appropriate set of classes to represent this idea.

The individual class should represent one very well defined idea. The designer can evaluate the public interface developed for a class and make judgements about whether the methods listed in the interface can be divided into groups. If there are natural divisions among the methods, each grouping of methods represents potentially separate modules. Guidelines in the software engineering literature about developing modules apply with little translation to the development of classes.

The purpose of a class should be clearly identified and explicitly stated in a design document. The public interface of the class should be specified using the signatures of the methods[1] and preconditions and postconditions. This complete specification will provide sufficient detail for the specification-based testing we will discuss in Chapter 9.

Reusable Components

We are developing components that we hope will be used in future applications. Each of the previously mentioned characteristics contribute to the reusability of the class. However, additional characteristics are desirable. For example, we will utilize design techniques that stress the standardization of the interface among *related* sets of classes. This will promote the "plug compatibility" of the classes within a set. Further discussion of this topic can be found in Chapter 10.

Reliable Components

Computer systems must be reliable, but the system is only as reliable as its least reliable component. Each component should be thoroughly tested. Components often

---

[1]The *signature* of a function is the name of the function and the types of each of the parameters.

are not tested as completely as they should be due to the cost. However, if we want to build reusable classes—and we do—guaranteeing the reliability of the components through testing is absolutely necessary.

The flexibility of object-oriented systems will make testing and quality assurance more difficult. Our design techniques must provide maximum testability. The clear specification, discussed above, will assist in this goal. Making each method as small and focused as possible will also contribute to testability. We will present techniques for testing classes in Chapter 9.

Integrable Components

We want to be able to use instances of classes in the development of other classes and applications. This requires that the interface of a class be as small as possible and that no pieces of data or methods required by the representation of the class be defined outside the class definition. Our design procedures should minimize the chances of naming conflicts. The messaging syntax of most object-oriented languages will also reduce the possible naming conflicts by qualifying the name of each method with the name of the instance to which it belongs.

The encapsulation provided by the class structure makes the integration of a concept into an application much easier. This is because only a single syntactic piece is needed to add the concept to an application. The encapsulation property assures that all of a concept is bound together under one interface while the information-hiding property ensures that implementation-level names will not interfere with those of other classes.

DESIGNING THROUGH REUSE

Our second goal is to accomplish the first goal with as little effort as possible! There are four ways to design a class from existing classes[92]:

- Selection
- Decomposition
- Configuration
- Evolution

This is where much of the power of the object-oriented technology is found. The increased reuse of the classes is a powerful competitive advantage for a company. Much of our class design will be based on the reuse of existing classes.

Selection

The easiest way to design a class is to not design it! Wouldn't it be nice to be able to have the software component you need by simply selecting it from the components that already exist? That is the purpose of developing a software base. In Chapter 13, we will discuss techniques for constructing object-oriented libraries to make the existing classes readily accessible.

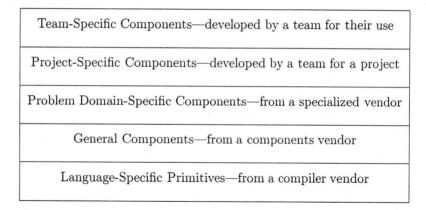

| Team-Specific Components—developed by a team for their use |
| Project-Specific Components—developed by a team for a project |
| Problem Domain-Specific Components—from a specialized vendor |
| General Components—from a components vendor |
| Language-Specific Primitives—from a compiler vendor |

Figure 6.2: Layers of an object-oriented components library.

An object-oriented development environment should provide a library of often-used components that is layered from a conceptual viewpoint. Most language environments come with a library of primitive components—such as integer, real, and character—that provide a foundation layer for all other functionality. Every library of basic components—"Data Structures 101" components—should build on that layer of primitives. These are classes that are easy to make very general and reusable—for example, lists, sets, stacks, queues, and so on. This layer also includes a set of general classes that provide other services that cut across application domains, such as windowing systems and graphics primitives. Figure 6.2 shows that on top of these layers are built domain-specific libraries. The lowest-level domain library is a broad domain library that includes the fundamental concepts of the problem domain and that support the development of a wide range of applications. Project and team-specific libraries include domain libraries that contain information specialized to the appropriate levels.

Just being a class does not automatically imply a reusable component. A poorly designed class will not be reused any more than a poorly designed procedure. The design qualities presented in the previous section are necessary for a class to be widely used. Particularly, a class must provide the full range of operations associated with the real world entity that it models. If the required operation is not present, most developers will simply write a completely new module rather than build on the existing one, or they might use inheritance for implementation.

Decomposition

Often what we originally identify as a class is actually a combination of several concepts. As we begin the design process, the methods that are identified can be seen to fall into disjoint categories. Or, we may find that the data attributes may be divided into sets that model disjoint concepts. This leads us to decompose what was to be one class into several. The design process now begins on the newly identified classes. Our hope, obviously, is that the newly identified classes will be easier to design than the original, larger class, or they may already exist. In fact, perhaps the set of new classes will include some that exist already.

How can the designer identify a multiconcept class? There are two guidelines:

- *Does a specified operation make use of the data of the class?* Operators that do not use or modify the data in the instance of the class do not belong with the class. By considering the purpose of this operation, a new class may be identified. While it is unusual to have a class with little or no data, certain interface classes routinely do not have much, if any, data.
- *Would some applications use only one subset of the class methods while other applications use a disjoint subset of methods?* It is certainly the case that not every application makes use of every operator of a class. However, a little reflection can often identify a subset of methods that perhaps are useful only in a special case. In that instance, the decomposition results in two classes with one a subclass of the other.

Configuration

During the design of a class, we may encounter the need for features of that class that can be provided by instances of existing classes. The new class is configured by declaring instances of the appropriate classes as attributes of the new class. This is similar to declaring local variables in the procedural paradigm. However, the power and flexibility of an instance of a class provides much more power than that local variable.

For example, the server in a simulation may be required to use a timer to keep track of service times. Rather than develop the data and operations needed for this behavior, the designer should seek out a timer class and declare an instance of it within the definition of the server class. This server would also need a storage manager to hold the customers as they arrive and wait for service. An instance of a queue class would serve this purpose. The time to serve each customer would be determined by a known probability distribution. An instance of a class that represents a random variable having a Poisson distribution or a random variable having a uniform distribution could be used.

Evolution

The new class we need to develop may be very similar to an existing ine, but not exactly the same. In this case, selection is not an appropriate method. However, it may be possible to evolve the new class from an existing one. The inheritance mechanism may be used to represent the generalization/specialization relationship. The specialization process can be used in one of three possible ways as illustrated in the left portions of Figure 6.3.

If the new concept is a special case of a concept represented by an existing class, the specialization operator can be used to produce the beginnings of the new class from the existing class's definition. This is the typical use of class inheritance. The existing data structures and operations become part of the new class, as shown in

(a) Objects in new class B are a *specialization* of those in class A.

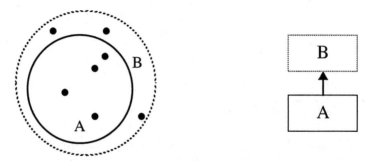

(b) Objects in new class B are a *generalization* of those in class A.

(c) Objects in new class B and in A share some attributes in common.

Figure 6.3: Uses of specialization in evolving class A into class B.

Figure 6.3(a). The public methods of the existing class become part of the public interface of the new class.

If the new concept may be more general than those in the software base, the new class, B, will not have all of the characteristics of the existing class, A. The generalization operator can be used to move those characteristics that the two classes have in common to a new, higher level class. The higher level class is B, which we are trying to design. The original class A becomes a subclass of class B as shown in Figure 6.3(b).

Finally, we may find an existing class A that shares a portion of the conceptual basis of the new class we wish to design. The common portion of the two concepts forms the basis for a new class, which becomes the superclass for both the existing and the new class that was our current design target, as shown in Figure 6.3(c).

The last two of these three design possibilities involve the modification of an existing class. In both cases, operations or data defined in the existing class is moved to a new class. If information-hiding and data-abstraction principles have been followed, these movements should have no impact on existing applications that use those classes. The interface of the classes remains the same even though some of the methods are now reaching the class via inheritance rather than definition in the class. We will discuss the management of change in object-oriented design below.

DOING IT THE HARD WAY

Ultimately, classes must be developed from scratch. The design of a class is a blend of data modeling, function specification, and ADT definition. The class is a data model of some concept. The data attributes of a class are the model. The methods of the class are the operations that are allowed on that data model. It is not possible to determine which of these two is determined first, nor should we be concerned about it. The two processes are complementary.

Classes have been identified in the literature as passive or active[92]. *Passive classes* are data-centered. They modify their encapsulated data models in response to messages sent from other objects in the system. *Active classes* provide some essential piece of the action that a system must carry out. Like instances of passive classes (passive objects), instances of active classes (active objects) receive messages, but these objects are responsible for sending additional messages and controlling some piece of the application. In a windowing environment, a window object is a passive object. The window has contents that are displayed based on messages that come to the window. The window manager is an active object that is responsible for a variety of operations on the windows that it controls.

There is no clear-cut difference between designing a passive class and an active class. In the design of a passive class, the data model takes priority and methods are determined later. In the active class, the services to be provided by the class are translated into methods. The data needed to support these services are designed after the services are identified. Many classes are a blend of these two extremes.

Interfaces

The interface of a class defines its interactions with other classes nd presents the formal specification of the class. The interface includes the signatures of each method with its preconditions and postconditions. The signature of a method includes its name and the classes to which the parameters belong.

Naming Methods

The naming of methods may seem like a small matter, but it is indicative of the point of view that the designer should adopt. The purpose of a method is to operate on an instance of the class on which the method is defined or to provide information about the state of that instance. In other words, a method is inward-looking. The name of the method should reflect that orientation. A Point class would have methods to provide access to its x and y coordinates. One of these methods might be called readX, but this implies that it is being read from a device. Naming the method getX or just x would be more descriptive.

The information passed to a method constitutes the remainder of its signature. The inward-looking nature of methods means that fewer pieces of data need to be passed. The method will include sending messages to those objects provided as parameters. Thus a method may cause other objects to modify their state as well as the state of its own object.

Not only should names of methods present an inward-looking orientation, but they should be chosen to standardize the class interfaces in an inheritance lattice. Traditionally, standard data structures have had certain names that occur in every implementation. A first-in, first-out queue has two operators, "enqueue" and "dequeue," which add elements to and remove elements from the queue, respectively. Similar operations on a priority queue have been termed *insert* and *deletemin*. One of the goals of our approach is to develop "plug-compatible" components that can be switched with very little, if any, alterations. This becomes impossible if many of the messages sent to a component must be renamed. This is particularly troublesome if there is no real reason for the names to be different.[2] The names for the methods mentioned above would work just as well if they were *add* and *delete*. In fact, an entire range of collection classes could be standardized to have methods by these names.

The topmost class in an inheritance structure may be used to establish a standard interface. As part of this standardization, the specification of several methods can establish a number of standard names for them. A Collection class, as the abstract class at the top of an inheritance lattice, could specify a standard interface that includes operations add, delete, isEmpty, and isFull. The use of abstract classes in design allows the specification of protocols without a need to immediately consider implementation details. For example, by using a collection abstraction, we can decide later whether to use a linked list or an array to actually implement the collection.

Where feasible, the naming of methods should conform to the standard language

---

[2]The use of different names has resulted primarily from requirements of procedural programming languages that subprogram names be unique within a given program. Thus, for example, "insert" could be used for only one data structure. The polymorphism provided by object-oriented programming languages eliminates the need to use different names for similar operations.

of the domain. For example, our Point class has components named x and y because "x" and "y" are commonly used in geometry and computer graphics domains. Using names such as a and b would not be as clear to users of the class.

Levels of Interface

Classes have three separate and well-defined audiences; in some, but not all, languages there are three distinct levels of access in the class definition. These constitute "contracts" with each audience. The class agrees that messages of the form listed in the appropriate interface will be answered and acted upon. Classes in the audience agree not to send messages that are not part of the contract.

- *Public.* The audience of the public interface of class A is the set of all objects defined within the lexical scope of an instance of class A. This interface is the major listing of methods for the class. The public interface includes methods for the usual arithmetic operators as well as input and output functions.
- *Private.* The private interface of the class are those methods that are for use only by other methods of the class. These are implementation-dependent; they further hide the details of implementation from the outside (public) world. Not all object-oriented programming languages provide support for private attributes, but the concept is useful for design. Large public methods can be decomposed into smaller public methods that in turn call private methods.
- *Subclass.* The subclass interface of class A is the set of methods that are accessible to instances of subclasses of A. The instances of the subclass may also use the methods in the public interface. These methods are often somewhat implementation dependent. They allow these subclasses to have special access to details of the class's representation. Not every language provides this interface, but it is a very useful tool in those that do.

Standard Interfaces

In designing a hierarchy of classes, the class that is the root of the structure provides a model or standard interface that is the representative for those found in the subclasses. The root class should be abstract and does not necessarily implement each of the methods in the interface, but it should provide the standard signature for the method that will be implemented by each of the subclasses. There are three purposes for providing this *standard interface*:

- Our disciplined use of inheritance working with this standard interface will result in a set of classes the instances of which are acceptable parameters to routines that expect instances of the parent classes.
- The standard interface will provide a means of communicating information about the set of classes in the hierarchy to others.
- Users of the class hierarchy will find the standard interface a useful first step in learning the classes in the hierarchy.

In some languages the standard interface will provide the set of operations that can be assumed for all elements in a heterogeneous list. Figure 6.11 illustrates this with a list that is written to accept instances of class A but may have instances of subclasses of A as well. Once the instances are added to the list, as in Figure 6.11(c), each individual item will be viewed as an instance of A. The only messages that may be sent to the instances on the list are those that are valid messages to instances of A. It becomes quite important that the interface of A be as complete as possible.

It certainly does not make sense to have a method that returns the "center" of every shape just because we would like to have a method that returns the center of a circle. We might well have a method that returns the reference point for each shape; for the circle, it would be reasonable that this be the center of the circle. We might also have a method in circle that returns the center and is used only when we know that we have a circle instance; that is, when the instance is not being treated as part of an aggregation of many shape instances. Both of these methods would return the same value but only one of them would be in the standard interface for the hierarchy.

Internal Structures

Two types of data are defined within a class representation: members of the data model and support information. The members of the data model provide the representation of the concept. Support information exists only to facilitate implementation of the concept. For example, we may wish to support both cartesian and polar coordinates in a Point class. However, for the sake of efficiency, we may want to use only one representation at a time in the implementation—either x and y or rho and theta, but not both. We determine which pair of attributes to use based on the most recent operation on an instance. In this case we might use a flag, usingPolar, which is "true" if we are using rho and theta and "false" if we are using x and y. The sole purpose of the attribute usingPolar is to support the implementation. It eliminates the need to keep all four attributes, which are part of the data model, in sync with each other. The data model objects are identified and specified during the analysis and high-level design phases. The supporting data objects are not identified until the class design and implementation levels.

DESIGN GUIDELINES

A number of guidelines have been developed for the design of modules. Those given here take guidelines for modules and make them specific to classes. They provide a basis for measuring the quality of a class design. Some of these guidelines are based on those presented by Johnson and Foote[53].

Information Hiding

Modern software design relies on information hiding to enforce abstraction. The representation of an ADT should be protected from direct access by users of instances

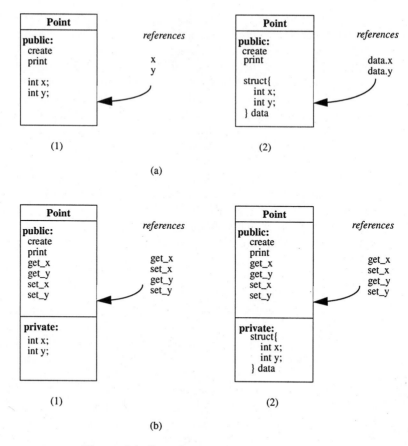

Figure 6.4: Specification for the Point class.

of the ADT. The interface should be the only avenue of access to the representation. The same is true for classes.

> *Design Guideline #1:* **The only members of the public inter-**
> **face of a class should be the methods of the class.**

Figure 6.4 shows the design of a Point class. Even a simple set of data such as two integers should be protected from direct access. When no such protection is used, as in Figure 6.4(a), changes in representation can force all references to a data value to become invalid. This requires system-wide maintenance to change all references. Figure 6.4(b) shows an alternative design of Point. If methods provide access to the data, the change in representation can be masked from users of the class. This can introduce inefficiency into the system through excessive function calls. Some languages provide techniques, such as the inline function declaration in C++, for removing these inefficiencies during compilation while permitting a better design at the programming level.

Limitations on Messages

A corollary to the previous design guideline considers the use of instances of other classes as part of the representation.

Design Guideline #2: **A class should not expose its implementation details, even through public accessor operations.**

The only operations provided by a class should be those suitable to the abstraction that the class is modeling. If the instance of class A is to send a message to a component of class B that is part of the implementation of B, then class A must know the implementation of that component and must incorporate that knowledge into its implementation. When, as inevitably happens, the implementation of class B changes, the implementation of class A must change as well.

Consider the development of a dictionary class. One simple design would use an array as the main data storage for the items entered into the dictionary. Operators of the dictionary class would determine where in the instance of the array class to place an incoming item. If an outside instance of another class, such as an inventory class, addresses the array directly, the inventory class must contain much information about the implementation of the dictionary in order to calculate the appropriate location for the new item.

If the owner of the dictionary class decides to modify that class to use a hash table instance instead of the array instance, the impact on the inventory class is serious. Much of the inventory class must be modified. The designer of the inventory class should have either used the appropriate operations from the interface of the dictionary class or should have used an instance of the array class directly in its own implementation instead of using the dictionary instance. More serious effects can be seen if we consider that when the inventory class accesses the array directly, it might modify the value in an entry that is the basis of the ordering! The dictionary may no longer be in order.

The designer of a class should provide an explicit interface to its operators. The users of instances of that class then have the responsibility to use only what is provided in the interface. Most object-oriented languages provide implementation-level restrictions that ensure that a user can only access the methods contained in the interface.

Narrow Interfaces

The previous guidelines restricted data attributes to be hidden from use by outside instances. Those guidelines indicated that methods of the class would be used to provide access to these data attributes. However, not all methods will need to be public.

Design Guideline #3: **An operator should be a member of the public class interface if and only if it is to be available to users of instances of the class.**

For the hash table class mentioned above, the interface should include methods for inserting and retrieving items from the table. The interface should not include the operator that calculates the hash value for the key of an item. The hash function is not intended for access by users of instances of the class. It should be a separate operator to make tuning the function easier, but it should be part of the hidden implementation.

Strong Cohesion

The internal structures of the module should be strongly related. That is, it should not be possible to identify separate, unrelated groups of data variables or of methods within a single class definition. A particular problem in object-oriented systems is the decision on where to place a function that could belong to any one of several related classes.

Design Guideline #4: **Each operator that belongs to a class either accesses or modifies some of the data of a class.**

Some of the methods of a class are simple accessor functions—that is, they simply return the value of some attribute. These are important to maintain the information-hiding characteristic of the class. They hide the actual representation of the attribute. Every class should provide one or more printing methods. The printed representation might not include a printed representation of every instance variable, but rather should include only those values relevant to the entity being modeled. For example, a string represented by an array and a length might be printed as a sequence of characters. A second method might be available to print the length and each character in the array. Printing methods are simple accessor functions. If, by convention, every class has a **describe**, then attributes of an object can be printed by sending a **describe** message to the value returned by an accessor function.

Other methods will modify the data of the instance. The simplest example is a **set** function, which allows the attribute to be set to a specified value. Again this allows access to the attribute but hides its representation. Modifying methods are many and varied, including what might be called "view" methods.

Consider the **Point** class mentioned earlier. Typically we think of the representation of a point as a pair of rectangular coordinates giving a position relative to two perpendicular axes. It is also possible to represent a point in "polar coordinates" as a distance from the intersection of the axes and an angle from the x axis. A completely developed point class would provide methods that allow us to access a point using the rectangular convention:

get_x

get_y

or the polar convention:

get_rho

get_theta

The class would also have methods to set the value of a point using either convention:

setRectangular(x, y)

setPolar(rho, theta)

We can know that these methods would all be available without knowing whether the internal representation is rectangular or polar! One set of these methods is behaving as a filter. If the internal representation is rectangular, then the polar-accessing functions act as filters because they present what appears to be polar information when the stored information is actually rectangular.

Suppose that the value of π is used in the processing required to produce polar coordinates from rectangular coordinates. We could place a function in the interface of class Point to produce the value of π. Is this appropriate? No. That function would not access or modify the data of the Point instance. The point class needs access to the value of π—perhaps from a component—but it should not produce the value itself.

Weak Coupling

An individual module should depend upon as few other modules as possible. A class A "depends" upon class B if instances of class A create local instances of class B, if an operator of class A takes an instance of class B as a parameter, or if A is a subclass of B.

Design Guideline #5: **A class should be dependent on as few other classes as possible.**

The amount of coupling is partially dependent upon the decomposition that is used. Class A becomes dependent upon class B because A needs the service that B can provide. This dependency can be eliminated by duplicating the functionality of class B in class A. While this lessens the degree of coupling, obviously the duplication of code reduces the flexibility of the system and increases the maintenance difficulties.

The designer must balance the competing objectives of modularity and coupling. The goal is to arrive at a decomposition that does not proliferate many small modules but that does provide discrete concepts. Object-oriented techniques produce more and smaller modules than the procedural paradigm. Designers using object-oriented techniques have found an increased need for tools to support the design and development process by managing the large number of classes.

The use of polymorphism complicates the dependency picture. In a strongly typed object-oriented language environment, polymorphism allows instances of several classes to be substituted for instances of the class used in the formal definition of a method. This means that a class often is dependent on an entire family of classes.

Inheritance can be viewed as violating the concept of weak coupling. Inheritance sets up a dependency as part of the definition of the more specialized class. Changes meant to improve efficiency that are made to classes higher in the hierarchy are propagated to those classes below. Someone making changes that improves the performance of an object for their application could adversely affect the users of classes defined lower in the hierarchy. This can be handled in one of several ways. First, policy can be made that any changes to an existing class except bug fixes are to be made as new subclasses. Second, an approval process can be established that requires notification and comment by users of that class or its subclasses prior to any modification. For simpler hierarchies or for small projects, a single developer may be in charge of all the classes in a hierarchy and can decide these issues for those classes. Finally, the changes may be handled as versions. Developers can explicitly decide which version to use or whether to switch from one version to another.

Explicit Information Passing

In addition to being dependent on a minimum number of classes, the information flow between those classes should be explicit. The sharing of global variables between classes represents implicit information passing and is a form of dependency.

> *Design Guideline #6:* **The interaction between two classes should involve only explicit information passing.**

Explicit information passing is accomplished through parameter lists. By explicitly listing the values being passed into an operator through the parameter list, errors can be traced by following these specific paths. Many object-oriented languages include an implicit first parameter, variously called "self," "this," and so on, in each message that is a pointer to the instance that originated the message. Although not necessarily to be encouraged, at least it is known that this implicit exchange occurs with each message.

Even explicit information passing should be minimized. The need to pass large amounts of data between instances is often an indication that the decomposition of two closely related classes is incorrect. The designer should always evaluate any case of excessive information passing to see if a change in the decomposition will decrease the flow between instances.

Subclassing as Subtyping

The use of inheritance is one of the characterizing features of the object-oriented paradigm. The inheritance relation allows an existing class definition to be used as the basis for the definition of a new class. There are at least two ways in which a class can be used to assist in the development of a subclass: the existing class provides service to the implementation of the subclass or provides its public interface to become part of the subclass's interface.

> *Design Guideline #7:* **Each subclass should be developed as a specialization of the superclass with the public interface of the superclass becoming a subset of the public interface of the subclass.**

C++ allows the designer to choose whether a class's parent classes are public or private. Several other languages provide a similar facility. If a parent class is public, its public interface becomes part of the public interface of the new subclass. This implies that the behavior of the parent class becomes part of the behavior of the subclass. This is similar to the relationship between a type and a subtype.

When the parent class is private, its behavior does not become part of the public behavior of the inheriting class. Rather, it becomes part of the implementation. It is present to provide its services to the implementation of the new class. The use of inheritance for implementation leads to an inheritance structure that blends the subtyping relation mentioned in the previous paragraph with the implementation structure described here. This makes the interchange of classes via polymorphism and the reuse of classes very difficult.

Consider the dictionary class discussed earlier. A designer might decide to implement the dictionary using an array. If the array class is a public parent class, then its behavior becomes part of the behavior of the dictionary class. The array class probably has a member of its interface that places an item in the nth slot. This operator becomes part of the public interface of the dictionary class. That is not an appropriate operator for a dictionary class to have. This design also implies that a dictionary is a special type of array which is not the case. If the array is a private parent class, its operations and storage are available to the dictionary; however, the array is not a separate object. Changing to another implementation later or using browsers on the inheritance structure gives unexpected results.

Inheritance should be reserved for the subtyping relationship in those languages in which the typing and inheritance mechanisms are mingled. The services of a class can be made available by declaring an instance of that class in the implementation of the new class. In the dictionary example, an instance of the array class should be declared in the implementation. This would provide storage for the items in the dictionary but not add inappropriate methods to the interface of the dictionary class.

Abstract Classes

Some languages provide a single class that serves as the starting point for the inheritance structure. All classes that the user defines must have this as a parent class either directly or indirectly. Smalltalk provides a class Object that is the root of the inheritance tree of all classes. Other languages, such as C++, support multiple inheritance structures. Each of these structures contains a set of classes that are (or should be) specializations of some concept. The concept should be abstractly expressed by the root class of the structure.

Uniform Random Variable
create
create(a, b)
describe
value
get_a
get_b

Figure 6.5: A uniformly distributed random number generator class.

Design Guideline #8: **The root class of each inheritance structure should be an abstract model of the target concept.**

This abstract model results in a class that is not used to produce instances. It defines the minimal common public interface to which each subclass adds in order to provide its special view of the concept. For example, consider a group of classes derived concerning the concept of a list. The root class in such a group should provide a set of methods as an interface that does not assume that the list is ordered or unordered. The abstract class can provide implementations of those methods that behave the same no matter what special case is being handled; but, many of the class methods will be given an implementation only in the more specific subclasses.

This guideline can be followed even in those languages that have a single root class for the inheritance structure. When a new concept that does not currently appear in the hierarchy is identified, the first class added to the inheritance structure should be an abstract description of the concept. Classes should then be added that provide specific specializations of the general concept. The documentation of the abstract classes and even the language itself should warn the users about not making instances of that abstract class.

A SMALL EXAMPLE

Consider the design of a class for exponentially distributed random variables. An exponential distribution with parameter λ ($\lambda > 0$) has the probability density function:

$$f(x) = \begin{cases} \lambda e^{-\lambda x} & \text{if } x \geq 0 \\ 0 & \text{if } x < 0 \end{cases}$$

The parameter λ is sometimes referred to as the "rate" of the distribution.

For this example, assume the existence of a class that models uniformly distributed random variables, as shown in Figure 6.5. This random variable is uniformly distributed over the interval $[a, b]$ with the interval $[0, 1]$ being the default. Method value

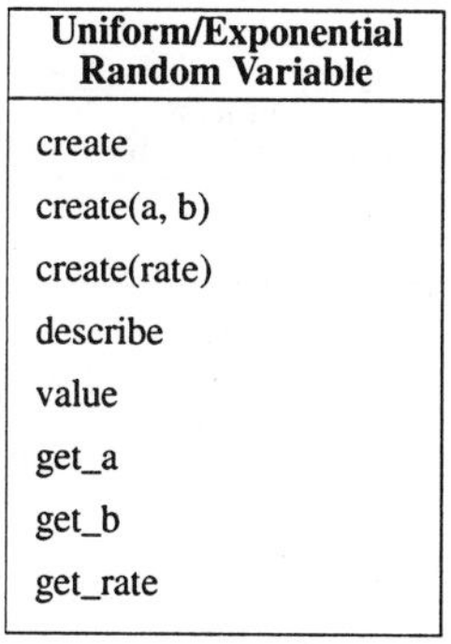

Uniform/Exponential Random Variable
create
create(a, b)
create(rate)
describe
value
get_a
get_b
get_rate

Figure 6.6: The expanded interface for the random number generator class.

returns a different result each time it is invoked, and the sequence of values returned has a uniform distribution on the designated interval. Note that once an instance of this class is created, the interval cannot be changed.

To provide an exponentially distributed random variable, we need to be able to generate random numbers with an exponential distribution. One technique for producing exponentially distributed random numbers is to do a calculation on a series of uniformly distributed numbers that changes the underlying distribution and the value. The purpose of this example is to consider the design choices for developing the exponentially distributed random variable class. In addition to choosing the most appropriate design for this example, generalizations will be drawn from the exercise.

Design Choices

There are at least three possible designs that can model the concept of an exponentially distributed random variable:

- *Design Choice #1.* The interface of the existing uniformly distributed random variable class could be modified to provide the additional capability. The interface would then look like Figure 6.6. The new operator would cause the values returned by an instance of the class to be exponentially distributed.
- *Design Choice #2.* The new class could be designed as a subclass of the existing class. This would allow the new class to inherit most of the existing class. The algorithm for generating the new value would be changed to generate exponentially distributed random numbers from a set of uniformly distributed random numbers. Figure 6.7 illustrates that in this choice the value operator of the superclass will be redefined in the subclass.
- *Design Choice #3.* A complete new structure could be developed in which both the existing class and our proposed class would be subclasses of a new class that models a more general concept, random number. This new structure is illustrated in Figure 6.8.

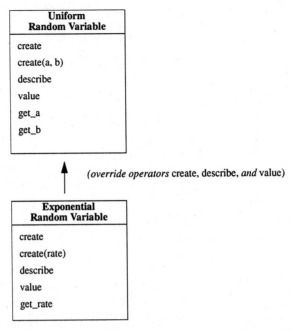

Figure 6.7: A subclass that redefined the value method.

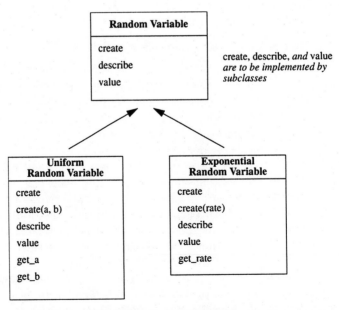

Figure 6.8: The new inheritance structure

Evaluating the Choices

Design is seldom an exact science. The discussions below attempt to illustrate the reasoning that should accompany the decision of which choice to use. Each of the choices will work in that it can be the basis of an implementation that produces the desired numbers. Our job is to determine the *best* choice and along the way to understand the reasons for that choice.

Design Choice #1. This design choice attempts to provide the desired result by expanding the interface of the existing class. This seems reasonable since the algorithm for generating one type of random number uses the other type of random number. It is equivalent to developing a random number generator function that takes a parameter to tell which type of distribution to use:

```
random(selectDistribution:  integer; var value float);
```

An important rule in module design is that a module should do one thing. This choice would bind together two concepts, uniformly and exponentially distributed random variables, into one class. Thus this module would attempt to do two "things." This is not an appropriate choice. Furthermore, we are faced with the problem of what to do with the interval $[a, b]$. If a rate is supplied, then the instance variables that record the interval are meaningless since an exponential distribution is defined over all real numbers. Similarly, for a uniformly distributed random variable, the rate is meaningless. This situation indicates that two separate concepts are being placed into the same class.

Design Choice #2. This is an attractive choice to the practical designer who wants to take the quickest route to solve the problem closest at hand. The new class would inherit most of its functionality from the existing class. This supplies the needed functionality but presents a conceptual problem.

By using the subclass relation, the design implies that the exponentially distributed variable *is a* special type of uniformly distributed random variable. The obvious difficulty is that this is not a true statement! Even though it appears to be useful and expeditious, this is not an appropriate choice.

Inheritance should only be used where there is a subtyping relation. It should not be used when the functionality of one class is needed for the *implementation* of another, as is the case here. While subclassing for implementation will work, it develops a dependency between two classes that implies a relationship that does not exist. This leads to a weak design.

Design Choice #3. This design choice is expensive. It requires that the entire class structure be modified. Some of the methods defined in the existing class would be moved up to the new parent class. The modified uniformly distributed random variable class would still have the same functionality. Some of its interface would be inherited and some locally defined instead of all of it being local. The important aspect is that *users* of this class would not have to rewrite any of their code. The new upper-level class would be abstract, one that we would never use to create instances but that does define the standard interface for a set of random variable classes. If we had identified this class originally as a result of domain analysis over continuous random variables, much effort could have been saved.

The new class for exponentially distributed random variables would use a locally declared instance of the uniformly distributed random variable class to obtain the values it needs to calculate its own value. Each of the subclasses would provide its own implementation of the generator function, but the abstract class would provide all of the other functionality needed. The inheritance structure eliminates the need for duplicate implementation of most of the needed interface functionality for both subclasses. The component instance used by the exponentially distributed random variable is an appropriate way to provide a part of its implementation. This looks like a winner!

Consider another benefit of this design choice. Many other distributions are candidates for the basis of random variables. The design represented here provides a logical structure for future extensions. It makes sense that there will be additional subclasses that differ only by the underlying distribution. The implementation of these additional classes has also been facilitated. The only new function that must be written for the new class is the specific generator algorithm. The remaining functionality is inherited.

What has been developed is a set of plug-compatible components. One type of random variable can be quickly replaced with another by simply creating an instance of a different class of random variable.

A Final Note

The classes developed in this example are continuous random variables. An instance of one of these classes is sent a message and it returns a real value that has been created using the generation process. An alternative to the type of class developed here is a random *value* class. When an instance of a random variable is created, a message is still required to produce a random value. The random *value* class would produce instances that *are* the random values. The design of this class should be very different than that described in the section above. The class **Random Value** would be developed as a subclass of the **Real Number** class. It would inherit the arithmetic and relational operators of the reals. We could, in fact, write statements such as x + y, where y is an instance of **Random Value** and x is an instance of **Real Number**. The value of y would be generated at instance creation time and not change during its lifetime. How would the value be generated? By an instance of a **Random Variable** class, what else?

REFINEMENT

The example in the previous section illustrates the usefulness of refining designs and how the impact of those changes can be mitigated by the information-hiding capabilities of objects. Programming with abstractions is difficult because finding abstractions is difficult and is certainly not a top-down process. Abstractions are usually found through experience. Existing classes can often be generalized, as was seen with uniformly distributed random number generators. Our models of application and class development must be able to accommodate the process of refining inheritance structures, and they do.

The generalization process can be hidden from users of existing classes by keeping the name of a class the same. The functionality that is removed from the class definition to the higher level class is inherited back into the lower level class. This allows messages to objects of that class to continue to behave as they always have while allowing the sharing of that method with other classes.

IMPLEMENTATION ISSUES

Several elements of design have been discussed in this chapter. Design is impacted by implementation restrictions imposed by the language to be used. Some object-oriented languages restrict the number of parent classes in the inheritance relation to one. This forces the designer to provide some services by replicating code or by declaring instances of the other classes as components in the class definition.

The design may not have the information-hiding qualities the designer would like if the implementation language does not provide a semantics of protection. One particular implementation currently on the market provides only a public area in a class definition. None of the representation definition can be protected from outside access. The designer can still provide the set of accessor functions that manipulate the data but has no way of enforcing them as the only access to the data.

The design of a class is also impacted by the resources that are available to the designer. The decision to evolve a class from an existing one assumes that the parent class does exist and that the designer knows that it exists. This implies the need for "software bases" of class definitions accompanied by sufficient tools to access the classes.

MORE GRAPHICS: CLASS DESIGN

As we saw in the previous example, class design usually occurs with a set of classes rather than just one. This can be seen in the graphics example as well. The user of the graphics system wants to draw a picture of something. To do this, the system user will draw individual shapes in the correct positions to result in the desired picture. To the user, each of these "shapes" are the same except for their "shape." This sameness can be abstracted as the general concept of a geometric figure.

Our design for the graphics classes is sketched in Figure 6.9. We have identified attributes and methods for each of the classes we identified in analysis as shown in the figure. We have omitted instance creation operations and some access operations from the figure. We have also made some decisions with respect to representations and conventions.

With respect to the reference point for each displayable shape, we have decided that it will represent the location of a displayable shape in terms of screen coordinates for the display. The other points in a shape class—for example the two endpoints of a line—are relative to the reference point. We designed it this way to facilitate the moving of figures. A **move** operation amounts to changing a reference point.

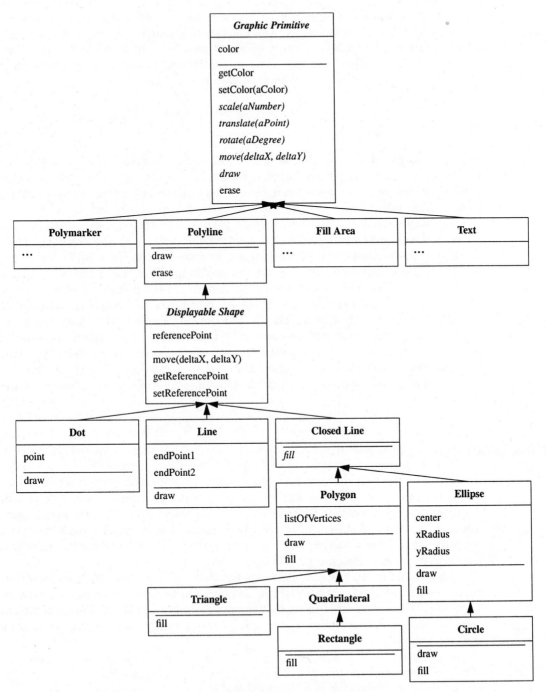

Figure 6.9: Hierarchy for the graphics classes.

We are aware, however, that this decision could lead to performance problems if our application ends up doing much redisplaying of figures. At that point we are prepared to change this decision and store all points in absolute screen coordinates. Our current design allows us to get the application running faster because we do not have to implement a move method for each shape. We are comfortable with the decision because except for the shape classes, no other classes in the system will need to be aware of this change.

We have chosen to represent a polygon as a list of points that define its vertices relative to the reference point. This representation is extended to the Triangle and Quadrilateral classes as well even though there may be more efficient representations for them. The primary advantage we see in this approach is again speed of development. The use of the relative values will be hidden from the user. Polygons will be defined in terms of screen coordinates by the user and converted to a relative representation by the methods of Polygon.

We can use the same draw method for Polygon and all its subclasses. We do implement a fill in class Triangle and in Rectangle because we think these can be considerably more efficient than a generalized polygon fill method. The class Quadrilateral exists only as an abstract class because there are so many kinds of quadrilaterals in plane geometry—trapezoid, parallelogram, rhombus, and so on.[3]

We have generalized the concept of a circle—a shape required for the draw application—to an ellipse. An ellipse is defined by a center point and two radii. A circle is an ellipse whose radii are equal. The second radius in an instance of Circle is redundant, but we are willing to use the extra space in order to model the relationship between circles and ellipses.

The ability to display a shape on a computer graphics device is a separate concept from that of the shape itself. The two concepts can be brought together using multiple inheritance to form the class illustrated in Figure 6.10. A shape exists in a coordinate system and thus can have an attribute that locates it within that system. Elements are displayed on a graphics device with color. These two attributes come together in the class Displayable Shape. It is not possible to know what other coordinate data will be needed to specify a particular shape so the definition of this information is deferred to the subclasses. The methods that manipulate the position and color information can be completely specified and implemented, but much of the functionality for these two general concepts cannot be defined at this level. Geometric shapes may, in general, be considered to have a perimeter and an area, so they are included in the interface for Geometric Shape even though at this abstract level we cannot provide an algorithm for either of the methods. Displayable Object can be drawn, moved, and erased. It is not possible, at this level, to know how to draw this general notion of a Displayable Object so this must be deferred to lower levels. However, it is possible to completely specify and implement an operation such as move for Displayable Shape. move can be defined as the sequence:

---

[3] We are omitting some of these concepts from this example in order to keep the number of classes relatively small.

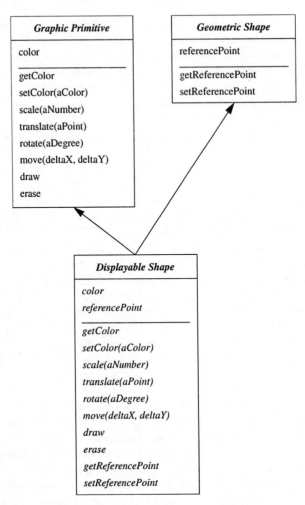

Figure 6.10: Using multiple inheritance.

Erase the shape
Change the value of the reference point for the shape
Draw the shape

So move can be defined in terms of an operation, draw, that has not yet been defined and will not be defined in this class!

The design of more specific shapes such as lines, polygons, and circles will be based on the design of these abstract ideas. Consider the design of the Line class. A line is a more specific notion of a shape so it should be designed as a specialization of class Displayable Shape. A line can be represented by two points and a color. One of these attributes—the color—will come from the Displayable Shape class when we make Line a subclass of Displayable Shape. Our decision will not be based on that consideration, however. The Line class is made a subclass of the Displayable Shape class because a line is a specific type of shape. We want the methods in the Displayable Shape class interface to become methods in the interface of the line class.

At this level we must also provide definitions for those methods that were marked as virtual in the definition in class Displayable Shape. The draw method might well send a call to the display terminal to draw the line rather than calculate each point on the line. Important to us, at the design level, is the fact that this routine does not need any data from outside the line instance in order to totally determine the line. If you look at the interface of the shape class, you will see that only the move method needs any information passed to it in order to complete its function.

Now let's consider the design of the Rectangle class. The implementation of this class might use four lines for the four sides. Inheritance is not the appropriate technique for providing the four lines because we do not want the behavior of a line to become part of the public behavior of a rectangle. For example, what would the draw method refer to in such a class? Would it draw a line or a rectangle? Four instances of line should be declared as the representation of the class. The draw method of Rectangle is intended to draw a rectangle. Its implementation would in turn send the draw message to the four instances of Line.

This is a good place to consider the value of information hiding. Declaring the four instances of line in the *private* representation area makes it easy to change the implementation—for example, to use four points (the corners) instead of the four lines or even use two points (lower left and upper right). A method to return the location of the southeast corner could be written using any of these implementations. The user of an instance of Rectangle would not see any difference in the result of the method.

Many object-oriented languages support the concept of polymorphism. The inheritance structure shown in Figure 6.11 establishes a relationship that can be used to develop a polymorphic approach to the graphics system. In a strongly typed language, only items of one type are allowed on a given list. Polymorphism allows instances declared to be of a particular class to be replaced by instances of any class that is a specialization of the declared class. This allows us to design a list class that can contain instances of any of the shape classes. This is accomplished by declaring the list to be a list of shapes. Instances of rectangles, circles, lines, and so on could all be placed in the list. Later we will see the usefulness of this concept.

SUMMARY

Class design is an important part of developing an object-oriented application. These building blocks must be developed to encapsulate an idea, hide its implementation, and provide a complete, correct model of the concept being represented. The interface of a class will model the behavior of a concept. Collections of these building blocks are developed to have a standard interface so that members of a collection may be interchanged to modify and improve the performance of an application. The data attributes of a class will provide the data model of the concept being represented by the class. These attributes will be provided by defining instances of other classes within the representation of the current class. The definition of a new class will also receive data attributes through inheritance from another class. This will not be our

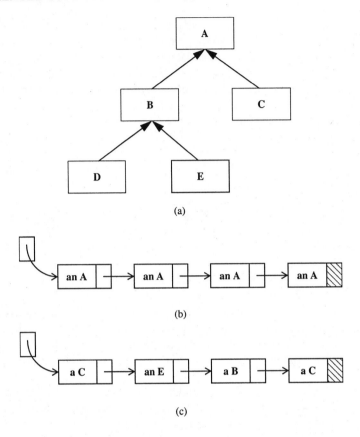

Figure 6.11: The polymorphic substitution in a list

reason to use inheritance, however. Inheritance will be used to develop classes that are specializations of existing classes.

FURTHER READING

Most of the texts on object-oriented design have sections on class design. Wirfs-Brock et al [101] consider standard approaches to class design, including the relationship of a class to the hierarchies to which it belongs. Johnson and Foote[53] provide a list of guidelines and examples for designing reusable classes. Lieberherr and Holland[64] provide the Law of Demeter which discusses style issues in design of classes. The Law has several instantiations, including one for C++.

7

Object-Oriented Languages

In this chapter we digress from the outline of the object-oriented software development process to present an overview of object-oriented programming languages. We provide a classification of the languages and look at specific features. The design and implementation of object-oriented systems are supported by and limited by the features provided by the language chosen for the implementation phase. We present examples to illustrate the impact of various language features on design.

What is an object-oriented language? This takes us back to the definition given in Chapter 1. An object-oriented language is one that supports *objects*, *classes*, and *inheritance*. There are a number of languages that fit this definition. There are also a number of ways by which each of these features may be provided by a language. The rich variety of implementations of these features will be the driving force in this chapter.

Support for dynamic binding and polymorphism adds a dimension of flexible system design. Some languages use dynamic binding of messages to methods exclusively. Others provide a combination of static and dynamic binding in order to eliminate some of the runtime inefficiencies of dynamic binding. This elimination may be under programmer control or only at the discretion of the compiler that analyzes the code and determines when dynamic binding is required.

There are several forms of polymorphism. The use of *inclusion* polymorphism, most closely associated with the object-oriented paradigm, requires the support of dynamic binding for its implementation.

LANGUAGES

Before beginning the tour of features and their implementations, we will provide a survey of several object-oriented languages. Brief capsules will provide references to further information about each language, a brief history, a characterization of how the language is used, and future directions for the language. For each language we will present a class specification and definitions of some methods for a Point class as an example of the language syntax and features. These languages will be used as the basis for examples in the discussion of features below.

C++

The basic C++ language definition has been developed at AT&T under the guidance of Bjarne Stroustrup[88]. The original versions of AT&T's C++ were implemented as translators that produced standard C code which was then compiled. This provided quick and easy porting of the new language to any system that supported a C compiler. C++ has also provided a natural progression for the large base of designers who already use C but who are interested in object-oriented techniques. These factors have resulted in widespread use of the language.

A number of implementations that remain somewhat faithful to the AT&T definition of the language are now available from several vendors. These implementations include compilers and interpreters in addition to the original translator. Many of the "new" features of C++ were provided to update AT&T's existing C to the ANSI C standard. Many designers have moved to C++ to take advantage of a "better C" and are not using the full power of the object-oriented paradigm.

Beginning with Version 2.0, C++ supports:

- *Strong type checking.* A function prototype specifies each method in the class definition. Actual parameters are checked to be certain they conform to the formal specification.
- *Abstract classes.* C++ will not allow an abstract class to be instantiated. The role of the abstract class is to form the root of an inheritance structure in which a number of more specific classes make use of the logic and/or interface defined in this root class. The abstract class provides the standard interface for classes in a hierarchy.
- *Polymorphism.* The subtyping conventions that accompany the inheritance structure allow the substitution of a subclass anywhere the use of the superclass has been specified. This provides a major addition to the architectural repertoire.
- *Multiple inheritance.* More than one class may be used as the basis for incrementally developing a new class. This provides support for multiple classification of objects. It also provides additional complications for the language and for the design of systems.

C++ combines the efficiency of C with support for the object-oriented paradigm. While many of the data elements present in a C++ program are class instances, C++ does represent certain primitive data types—for example, integers and floats—in a traditional format to improve the performance of the generated code. C++ has a more strict type-checking facility than that available in C. This includes combining the class inheritance structure with the typing system. The implication of this mechanism is that developers should restrict the manner in which the inheritance mechanism is

```
class Point<class T>{
  private:
    T x;
    T y;
    static const float pi = 3.14159;
  public:
    Point(T,T);
    Point();

    Point& operator+(Point);
    Point& operator-(Point);

    float distanceFrom(Point);

    inline void set_X(T);
    inline void set_Y(T);
    inline T get_x();
    inline T get_y();

    void print(ostream*);
}

Point::Point(T abcissa, T ordinate) {
    setX(abcissa);
    setY(ordinate);
}

void print(ostream* strm) {
    strm << "(" << get_x() << "," << get_y() << ")";
}
```

Figure 7.1: C++ realization of class Point.

used. Inheritance should be used for defining subtype relationships, but not also for opportunistic code sharing.

Most versions of the language restrict the user to the edit–compile–link–execute cycle. These are the characteristics of a language that produces an efficient, reliable executable but that are very inefficient from a design/development perspective. At least one vendor now provides an environment that supports the interactive, interpretive style of development for C++[50]. This type of integrated development environment can alleviate some of the inefficiencies in the development cycle but it does not eliminate them.

A C++ realization of a Point class is shown in Figure 7.1. Different uses of points may require either integer or real values for the coordinates. This definition uses the template mechanism described by Ellis and Stroustrup[27] to provide an implementation that allows the user of the class to determine the "type" of the coordinates at instance definition time.

We provide a more in-depth view of C++ in the next chapter.

Smalltalk

Smalltalk originated at Xerox's Palo Alto Research Center[36]. The language was designed to expand upon features in the Simula language that gave increased attention to data objects. Smalltalk was originally intended as an educational language. The language supports a design philosophy and a development environment for which modeling is the natural paradigm.

Smalltalk is implemented by an interpreter that is fully integrated into a programming environment that is written in the language itself. The environment supports interactive development, including a wide variety of tools including debuggers, inspectors, and browsers. Versions of the environment are available for high-performance workstations as well as personal computers. The compilation of methods eliminates some of the run-time inefficiencies of the interpreted implementation.

Smalltalk is easy to learn because of its simple syntax and because *every* data item in the system is an object. Referencing one "data object" in the system is the same as any other. The system supports a single inheritance structure with one root class. This allows much general functionality about being an object to be provided in the root class and inherited by all of the other classes in the system. This makes system-wide modification a convenient process.

The single root of the inheritance structure, called class Object, provides a basis for designing very general data structures with generic-like features. A Set class would be able to hold instances of any class as a result of the polymorphic behavior of the inheritance relation: Because every class in the system is directly or indirectly a subclass of Object, instances of any class may take the place of any other. However, not every message can be understood by every instance. This combination leads to the development of systems for which extensive testing is required because no compilation phase checks the validity of messages between instances.

Smalltalk provides a layer of abstraction beyond that of a class. Every class in the Smalltalk language is itself an instance of a class—Metaclass. This provides a very uniform means of reference because *every* reference—even to classes—addresses an object. This also provides a very flexible system because classes as well as instances may be manipulated at run-time.

The Smalltalk realization of the class Point is shown in Figure 7.2. The syntax for class definitions varies from implementation to implementation. (A subclass is defined by sending a message to its parent class; the spelling of that message can vary.) The syntax used in the figure to distinguish class methods from instance methods follows no particular implementation. Methods that contain parameters must use names that end with a colon—for example, the method to set the x-coordinate is named "x:" and the method to create a new instance, requiring two parameters, is named "x:y:". Operator symbols such as '+' are a special case. The caret (^) indicates the value to be returned by the method. Method attributes and data attributes can have the same name, allowing the value of the x-coordinate, x, to be accessed by the method named x.

---

class name: #Point
superclass: Object
instance variable names: x y
class variable names: pi

"class messages and methods"

"instance creation"
  x: xInteger y: yInteger
    "Answer a new instance of a Point."
        ^super new setX: xInteger setY: yInteger

"instance messages and methods"
"accessing"
  x
     "Answer the x-coordinate."
     ^x

  x: anInteger
     "Set the x-coordinate."
     x := anInteger

  printString
     "Answer a string of the form '(x,y)'."
     ^'(', (x printString), ',', (y printString), ')'

  setX: xPoint setY: yPoint
     "PRIVATE METHOD:
      Initialize the instance variables."
     x := xPoint.
     y := yPoint

"arithmetic"
 + aPoint
     "Answer the sum of my coordinates and aPoint."
     ^Point x: (x + aPoint x) y: (y + aPoint y)

Figure 7.2: Smalltalk realization of class Point.

Eiffel

The Eiffel language was developed by Bertrand Meyer and is marketed commercially through his company, Interactive Software Engineering. Eiffel is not an extension of any existing language, but rather was designed from the ground up to support the goals of software engineering. A number of pieces[73] have been written relating the features of the language to the goals of software development.

Eiffel supports a number of useful features.

- *Generics.* Classes may be written in a generic or parameterized form. For example, the definition of a stack class does not depend upon the type of the elements that will be placed on the stack. The declaration of an instance of the stack class that is intended to hold real values could look like:

STACK[REAL]

- *Assertions.* Eiffel also provides an integrated facility for incorporating statements specifying invariants directly in method definitions. This provides an automated technique for testing the interfaces between classes.
- *Exceptions.* Eiffel provides an Ada-like exception mechanism with which the class designer can signal the sender of a message that some unusual event has occurred.
- *Compiler-controlled dynamic binding.* The use of dynamic binding is determined by the compiler in Eiffel rather than the designer. The compiler considers the context of the use of a method call and determines whether it can be statically bound. This provides an efficiency increase at the cost of a loss of control for the designer.
- *Strongly typed.* Eiffel is a strongly typed language. This feature is combined with dynamic binding and polymorphism to provide very general and flexible designs.
- *Inheritance model.* Eiffel provides a very simple inheritance mapping. All attributes of a class are inherited by its subclasses. The subclass can then decide what should and should not be public.

The original Eiffel compilers were written in C, but the syntax of the language is not C-oriented. By implementing in C, the compiler can be and has been easily ported to a variety of computers. A program development environment, several libraries, and a number of tools are available.

The definition of class Point is shown in Figure 7.3. The export statement in the class header determines the public interface of the class.

Common LISP Object System

The Common LISP Object System (CLOS) is an extension of the Common LISP dialect of LISP. The specification for this facility can be found in Bobrow et al [8]. LISP was originally a purely functional language although many modifications have been made in the Common LISP dialect. For example, Common LISP includes a

```
class Point[T] export
     Create, print, get_x, put_x, ...

feature
     x : T;
     y : T;
     Create(new_x, new_y : T) is
     do
          x := new_x;
          y := new_y;
     end; - - Create
     print is
          - - io is an instance of STD_FILES and provides
          - - access to the standard output for every class
     do
          io.putchar('(');
          x.print(io);
          io.putchar(',');
          y.print(io);
          io.putchar(')');
     end; - - print

     get_x : T is
     do
          return x;
     end; - - get_x

     put_x(new_x : T is
     do
          x := new_x;
     end; - - put_x
end; - - Point
```

Figure 7.3: Eiffel realization of class Point.

```
(defclass Point ()
    ((x :initarg :x :accessor x :initform 0 :type integer)
     (y :initarg :y :accessor y :initform 0 :type integer)
     (pi :allocation :class :initform 3.14159)
     )
)

(defmethod printPoint ((instance Point))
    (format t "( a, b)" (x instance) ( y instance)))

(defmethod add ((instance Point)(instance2 Point))
    (make-instance 'point
        :x (+ (x instance) (x instance2))
        :y (+ (y instance) (y instance2)))
)
```

Figure 7.4: CLOS realization of the class Point.

number of "types" and provides some type checking. CLOS provides a blend of the functional style and the object-oriented style for applications that have traditionally used a purely functional approach. This facility is useful in knowledge-based systems that need to provide independence between reasoning algorithms and the pieces of information about which they reason.

- *Interpreted/compiled.* The basic "eval" loop is an interpreted environment, but definitions are partially compiled into a more efficient representation that facilitates interpretation and execution.
- *Weakly typed.* The LISP environment does not support strong type checking but does support a few basic types that are used to streamline the representation of an element.
- *Inheritance model.* CLOS provides a rich inheritance model that supports a number of method combination techniques. The designer of a subclass may develop code that is executed before, after, or before *and* after the method of the same name in the parent class. The attributes— or slots—of a class may be manipulated in several ways as well.

CLOS provides the designer with a powerful prototyping environment that makes system development an incremental process. A wide range of features, which will be discussed below, are provided to support the interactive development of systems. In particular, classes are represented in the system so that changes may be made to class definitions as the system executes.

Being a dynamic system, CLOS places heavy demands on the platforms that support it. Typical implementations require a large amount of memory to support the representations used, and the processor must be sufficiently powerful to support the garbage collection process. Due to the required resources and to the differences of this dialect from many other dialects of LISP, the system has not had widespread use other than in certain research communities.

The definition of the Point class is shown in Figure 7.4. Rather than having a method in the class that constructs instances, CLOS has a system-level macro make_instance that would be used, for example, to construct a point as (make_instance 'Point :x :y).

Other Languages

A number of other language implementations are available that support object-oriented techniques. Objective C[23] was one of the original object-oriented languages. It has been used to provide an extensible programming environment for the NeXT computer. Variants of APL[34], Pascal[51], and other languages have been developed that support the paradigm. Trellis[56] is a new language that supports many of the same features as C++, but uses a less cryptic syntax.

LANGUAGE FEATURES

In this section we provide a classification of object-oriented languages and a discussion of several distinguishing features of the categories of languages. This will include a look at general characteristics of the inheritance relation that are combined to provide different inheritance mappings of individual languages.

Paradigm Support

One dimension of classification is the number of paradigms supported by the language.

Pure languages support the object-oriented paradigm exclusively. Every entity in the language is a member of some class. A typing system may be associated with the inheritance structure defined on the classes. Any function that is defined must be a method of a class. The advantage of a pure object-oriented language is uniformity of reference. Every manipulable entity in an application is an object. The disadvantage is that no one paradigm is the best paradigm for every problem. The designer either must make the problem fit the object-oriented paradigm or change languages with each problem.

Smalltalk and Eiffel are examples of pure object-oriented languages that have gained widespread acceptance. Smalltalk requires that every manipulable entity in the application be an instance of a class. In fact, each class is an instance of a class! Eiffel is largely a pure language, but it has four simple types: integer, boolean, character, and real. All methods in an Eiffel application are associated with a class.

Hybrid languages are existing languages that have been extended to support the object-oriented paradigm while maintaining support for the language's original paradigm as well. There are several benefits to this approach. The first is that the language fits more than one paradigm. This provides the designer with flexibility to solve a problem with more than one approach yet use only one language. It is also possible to solve a wider range of problems with the same language. The second benefit is the ability to interface easily with existing code. An example we have run across often and will discuss in a following section is the interfacing of existing C code and new

C++ code. The dual nature of the C++ language makes this easy. Other languages support interfaces to other languages, but the mechanism is not as straightforward as a subprogram call.

C++ is an extension of the procedural language C designed to support object-orientation. The Common LISP Object System, an extension of the functional language Common LISP, supports the object-oriented paradigm as well as the functional paradigm. There are also extensions for implementations of other existing languages such as Prolog and Forth. This approach is economical because the extra syntax needed to support the object-oriented paradigm is a very small addition to most languages. It also takes advantage of the available audience already knowledgeable about the original language. These persons can begin to code applications faster because of their prior knowledge. There is the disadvantage that the prior experience and the familiar environment may inhibit the experienced person's ability to fully benefit from the new mode of thinking.

Multiparadigm languages are designed expressly to support a number of paradigms. Combining the approaches of several paradigms is attractive for the construction of large, complex systems since no one paradigm is appropriate for all pieces of the system. One approach to multiparadigm development is to combine the features of several languages, each of which supports a different paradigm, into one new language. Nial [5, 52] is a language that has been developed to support a number of paradigms. Common LISP is another language in which it is possible to support the features of several paradigms.

Zave[106] points out that often this approach results in the loss of some features of a language—sometimes the very ones that made the paradigm useful. She proposes an alternative in which individual components are each developed in a different paradigm and implemented in a different language. These pieces are then combined via synchronization primitives and are executed in parallel.

Characteristics of the Inheritance Relation

Inheritance is one of the most important concepts associated with the object-oriented paradigm. Four facets[96] to this concept result in a combinatorial number of possible different implementations: multiplicity, modifiability, flexibility, and quality.

Multiplicity

Many object-oriented languages began by supporting single inheritance. That is, new classes could only inherit the definition of one existing class as part of their own definition. More recently, languages have been extended to support the use of multiple existing classes in the definition of a new class. A number of issues are raised by the more complex structures resulting from multiple inheritance. Figure 7.5 illustrates the problem of repeated inheritance. The variable x in class A will be inherited by both classes B and C. The class D would inherit two copies of x if some mechanism did not prevent it. This is discussed in more detail later. For now we will consider implementations that utilize multiple inheritance, but we will ignore several practical issues.

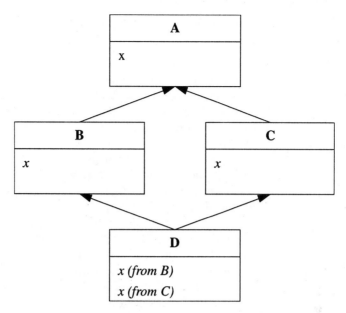

Figure 7.5: Example of repeated inheritance.

Modifiability

A number of schemes exist for modifying the characteristics of the superclass inherited by the subclass. A straightforward example of this is the modification of the visibility of C++ class members as they are inherited from the superclass to a subclass. Figure 7.6, which presents the inheritance mapping for C++, illustrates that public members coming from a public superclass become public members of the subclass. Public members coming from a private superclass become private members of the subclass. The visibility of these members is being modified by the inheritance relation. Chapter 8 will explain visibility in more detail.

If class C is to be a *public* subclass of class A:

public members of A	$\longrightarrow$	**public** members of C
protected members of A	$\longrightarrow$	**protected** members of C
private members of A	$\longrightarrow$	**private** members of C

If class C is to be a *private* subclass of class A:

public members of A	$\longrightarrow$	**private** members of C
protected members of A	$\longrightarrow$	**private** members of C
private members of A	$\longrightarrow$	**private** members of C

Figure 7.6: Inheritance mapping for C++.

The inheritance relation may provide multiple ways that a method may be modified as it is inherited:

- *Behavior compatible.* The most common case is for a method to be inherited unmodified. The method behaves the same in the subclass as it did in the superclass. As described above, the visibility of the function may be altered, but its behavior is compatible with its original behavior.
- *Signature compatible.* In an effort to provide a polymorphically compatible interface, the designer may wish the signatures—function name and types and numbers of parameters of all methods—to be inherited without modification. Certainly in the behavior compatible case this condition is met. The signature compatible case allows the actual behavior of the method to be changed as long as the signature remains the same. The interface of the Displayable Shape class is inherited in a signature compatible mode to allow subclasses, such as Dot and Line, to be able to draw but to behave differently—that is, draw a different shape—while taking the same parameters. This is the desired mapping when instances of a set of subclasses are to be used interchangeably. C++ uses virtual functions and dynamic binding to implement this feature.
- *Name compatible.* In the name compatible case, only the name of the function is inherited. Both the behavior and number and types of parameters may vary. This retains the modeling of the problem domain, but it is not often used in a type-safe language. Languages that permit a variable number of parameters can make use of this level. This feature is used by subclasses that will be used in different systems and not within a single common container because of either an incompatible interface or the system is without type checking.
- *Cancellation.* A few systems support the ability to cancel parts of the superclass—that is, to designate the pieces of the superclass not to be inherited. Cancelling members of the public interface destroys the ability of the subclass to be treated as a subtype. It is possible to cancel members of the class's representation. This does not affect the use of the subclass as a substitute but does allow for a more efficient implementation. If members of the interface are cancelled the *is a* relationship becomes an *is kind of* relationship. It provides the power to model exceptions but prevents the homogeneous treatment of the various subclasses. Cancellation is not to be confused with inheriting the signature of a function and then giving it a null implementation. The function with the null implementation is still a valid operation on instances; they simply do not perform any actions. When cancelled, a method name is no longer a valid message and an error would result if the corresponding operation is attempted.

CLOS provides another type of modifiability using inheritance. The inheritance of an operator may be modified by one of several combination types: :before, :after, and :around. A :before method provides code that is to be run before the method of the same name that is inherited from the superclass. When the method in the subclass is invoked, the :before code is executed and then the method of the same name in the superclass is invoked. This allows the designer to modify the inherited function and add code to the beginning of an inherited method. The :after and :around combinations work in a similar method. Each of these modifiers is sometimes referred to as a *wrapper*.

Flexibility

In a compiled language like C++, the inheritance patterns are fixed once the code is compiled. The designer can certainly change the pattern and recompile, but this is not a very flexible arrangement during the development process. A largely interpreted language such as CLOS allows the system user to alter the inheritance structure on the fly. When a superclass of a class is modified, its structure is changed and so are the structures of its instances. Some data attributes are destroyed and others are added, although without values.

A second dimension of flexibility is the possibility of an inheritance relation between *instances* rather than between classes. This possibility is being investigated in some research languages[2, 48]. This provides a very flexible system because each instance is a possible source of new instances, not just the classes. This allows for specialization to solve very specific problems.

Quality

The inheritance relation may act differently on the specification of a class than it does on its implementation. The inheritance mechanism might map the specification unmodified but cancel the implementation.

Classes and Types

A third issue is the relationship between the inheritance structure and the type structure. In most type-safe object-oriented languages such as C++ and Eiffel, a class is used in the same ways as a user-defined type. In addition, classes have the same status as the primitive types defined by the language.

Subclasses are not necessarily subtypes. The usual definition of a subtype assumes that membership in the type has been restricted, but that the operators defined on the data elements behave in exactly the same way as in the original type. In many cases, however, the behavior of an operator in the subclass is changed from its behavior in its superclass. The usual use of a subtype is to more specifically identify the values that are valid in some context—such as a parametric value. The declaration of subtypes is often supported by compile-time checking to assure that the actual values being used match the formal definitions. This technique supports a classification approach to representing the domain of interest.

Even if we take a more lenient definition of subtype, designers can still use inheritance for implementation. When one class inherits the data variables and operators from a class for its implementation, the interface of the new class does not contain the interface of the inherited class. These classes will compile and can be used, but the polymorphic thread back to the inherited class is broken. That is, instances of the subclass cannot be substituted where instances of the superclass are called for.

Classes as Objects

Instances of classes are always implemented as objects. The classes themselves are treated in two distinctly different ways. Smalltalk and CLOS represent classes in the runtime system as objects. This allows an application to be very flexible and self-modifying. New classes can be created and new relationships can be established "on the fly." Classes have methods that their instances do not have—usually methods for creating instances. The implication of this feature will be illustrated below. One of the results of this runtime availability of classes is the possibility of modifying inheritance patterns at runtime.

C++ and similar compiled languages treat classes as they do types. During compilation, the class information is used to bind method calls, to set up dynamic binding structures, and for type checking of expressions used in program statements. Other than information needed for dynamic binding, type—and class—information is missing from the runtime system. Classes may not be created, nor can messages be sent to a class at runtime.

The differences discussed here have an impact on design and the development process. The distinction between these two approaches can be viewed as a difference between compiled and interpreted language implementations. However, there are techniques for providing some of the features of the active class model in a compiled environment. Keith Gorlen implemented a portion of this approach in his NIH Class Library[38]. He provided a facility in which an instance could be queried about characteristics of its class, including the identity of the class's parents. An environment that provides for the runtime modification of classes supports an interactive prototyping approach to design. The developer can define, redefine, and test in a much more efficient manner than in the compiled environment.

Storage Management

Object-oriented languages make heavy use of dynamic memory allocation and support dynamic binding through some form of pointer manipulation. Allocation implies deallocation as well. Languages such as Eiffel and Smalltalk provide garbage collection as part of the runtime environment. CLOS, as with most LISP implementations, makes heavy use of dynamic allocation and garbage collection. While this does impact the performance of the application, there is an offsetting increase in ease of use since the implementer is freed from responsibility for memory management.

Other languages, such as C++, leave the specification of how to handle deallocation of dynamically allocated memory to the implementer. This provides for improved scheduling of deallocation. The designer can take advantage of knowing exactly which memory is to be recovered as well. The obvious drawback is that the designer may neglect to recover memory and may run out at a crucial time, or may accidentally deallocate an object before all program elements are finished using it.

The object-oriented paradigm reduces the resources required for automatic garbage collection. The well defined specification and the tight encapsulation of the objects clearly identifies the memory associated with a specific object. Automatic garbage collection searches all of memory for unreferenced blocks. Providing specific deallocation operators—for example, destructors in C++—is a much more efficient approach to deallocation. It eliminates the overhead of examining memory that has nothing to do with the objects being deleted and that is still active.

Single or Multiple Inheritance Structures

The number of disjoint inheritance structures is an important feature of a language. Smalltalk supports a single, unified inheritance structure. Every class in the system must be a descendent, directly or indirectly, of class Object. Much of the behavior of a class is inherited from this root class. This approach is used by several languages to provide behavior to classes that will also be objects in the runtime environment.

C++ supports a forest of inheritance structures that are all disjoint. This provides a natural grouping of classes. All the classes in one structure are concerned with one concept and specializations of that concept. This family of classes makes a reasonable size unit for assignment to a maintenance engineer. It also makes it easier to locate specific classes because each structure is smaller. Many of the languages using this approach are compiled languages. They provide the same functionality found in the root class of another language by means of the compilation process.

The single structure approach provides a central location for all the functionality needed to be a class. It can also be modified without changing the compiler. The single inheritance structure simplifies the kind of tool needed to traverse the inheritance relations between classes as well as the polymorphic relation across all objects—that is, everything is a subclass of Object. The multiple structures approach produces smaller, more easily understood groupings.

IMPACT OF LANGUAGE ON DESIGN

We have presented a short characterization of several object-oriented languages and have considered permutations of features offered by languages. The question for consideration now concerns the impact of these differences on the design of systems. The languages that qualify as object-oriented represent a diverse set of capabilities. Ideally, any object-oriented design could be implemented with any language, but the great diversity of techniques influences at least the low-level application design.

Influence of the Multiplicity of Inheritance

One of the benefits provided through the object-oriented paradigm is a factored design. Information is encapsulated in one place but provided to many places. Multiple inheritance improves the designer's ability to isolate the implementation of a feature. Consider the example of developing an interactive shape to meet the requirements for the draw application with respect to moving figures. Figure 7.7 shows two possible arrangements under single inheritance and one under multiple inheritance. An

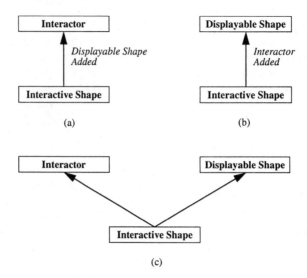

Figure 7.7: Single versus multiple inheritance.

interactor is an object that tracks mouse actions, recognizing certain combinations of button presses and cursor motions.

With single inheritance, the designer has the choice of starting with information about interactors, Figure 7.7(a), and adding information about being a shape, or vice versa, Figure 7.7(b). It is likely that information about interactors and shapes will be needed at other places in this or other systems. The information that is added at the lower level is mixed with the inherited information. Given the design in Figure 7.7(a), it is not possible to provide shape information to another class without including the inherited interactor information as well. Single inheritance reduces the amount of repeated code, but does not eliminate the need to repeat such code as the interactor or shape information. The multiple inheritance structure, shown in Figure 7.7(c), results in a design in which the interactor and shape information are each available for use in other classes without the excess baggage of the other.

Influence of Typing

Some languages require that a class be associated with every variable and return value. Two advantages of these strongly typed languages are that a compiler can use the class information to check and verify that an object can respond to every message it is sent, and that a compiler might be able to use static binding to a method. The requirement that all variables and return values be typed affects design to the extent that it can affect how inheritance and subtype polymorphism are used.

Consider the two inheritance structures shown in Figure 7.8, in which the design uses two abstract classes, A and XA. The design is such that XB and B work together and XC and C work together. When an instance of XB is created, an instance of B is created and associated with the attribute anA inherited from class XA. A similar

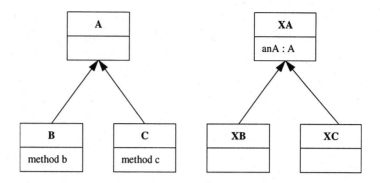

Figure 7.8: Two inheritance structures affected by "typing."

relationship exists between XC and C.

This design is easy to implement in an untyped language. However, in a typed language a problem arises if the implementation of some method m in class XB wants to send message b to anA. Since anA is declared to be of class A and since A has no method b in its interface, then a compiler will not permit the message b to be sent to anA. The only way to send b is to somehow denote that anA is actually of class B within class XB.

Different mechanisms exist within strongly typed object-oriented programming languages to help implement this design. One approach allows a method to determine the class of anA using a special kind of case statement. Within the B case a message b is permitted. Another approach allows pointers to be converted from one type to another—for example, from a pointer to class A to a pointer to class B. The latter approach requires a good understanding of how the compiler represents objects. Certain pointer conversions might be allowed by the language, but their use could result in disaster at run time. The former approach is more appealing syntactically, but any addition of new classes to our design—say, XD and D—requires changes to the code to add the new case.

One approach to the problem is to address the restriction as part of low-level design. In this example we could avoid declaring anA in class XA and declare more suitably typed attributes in its subclasses—aB in XB and aC in XC. Similarly, methods common to XB and XC that might more suitably be specified in XA might be defined for each of XB and XC if the typing restrictions demand.

Influence of Classes as Objects

A design can be affected if classes can be treated as objects. For example, a class might be used to store information useful to all its instances. We have already mentioned that class variables can implement a "bulletin board" through which its various instances can communicate with one another. A class might also be designed to keep track of all its instances to facilitate the implementation of operations—class operations—that act on all instances.

Some languages permit a class definition to be changed at run time or permit new classes to be defined at run time. The design for some applications—particularly those that involve artificial the intelligence—can be simplified if implementation allows such changes. These changes might result from the execution of the program itself or from inputs from a user.

Influence of Storage Management

If the implementation language places storage management under application program responsibility, then the problem of storage management must be considered during design. Retrofitting an existing design with storage management behaviors is very difficult.

The most obvious impact of storage management on design is the need to specify destructors. Less obvious is a need to document who is responsible for the destruction of objects—that is, which objects in an application are responsible for the destruction of other objects. An object should destroy its components, but can safely do so only if no other objects can access these components. The strict controls on access that we proposed in Chapter 5 with respect to objects in an *is part of* relationship with a given object are intended to facilitate this type of destruction as well as to reduce coupling. Responsibilities for destruction must be spelled out clearly in the design documentation for a class. This is critical for the reusability of a class.

One situation in which garbage can be generated unintentionally is within expressions. Consider, for example, a Point class that supports an addition operator. An expression of the form p1 + p2 + p3, where p1, p2, and p3 are instances of Point, results in the generation of two more points. One is the result of p1 + p2, and one comes from sending the first result the message "+ p3." However, since in this expression no name is associated with the first result, there is no way to name it in a destructor. This result becomes garbage. Senders of "+" to a Point instance must be aware of their responsibility to destroy the result at an appropriate time. This responsibility is normally communicated only through the documentation for a class.

By designing the deallocation routines as part of the original class design, memory recovery routines can be made very specific, but will the designer and implementer remember to use them? A scheme such as that for destructors in C++ can assist. The destructor is automatically called when an object is to be destroyed. This provides support in the implementation process by assuring that unused memory is recovered.

ANY LANGUAGE WILL DO

We have listed several object-oriented languages and described some of their features. It is not necessary to use one of these languages to get some of the benefits of the object-oriented approach. There are two possible levels at which benefits can be derived.

The first possibility is that of high-level design. A high-level design developed using the guidelines presented in the early chapters of this text can be implemented using a procedural low-level design and procedural language. The modeling approach of the high-level design, which is data centered, has already provided the designer with the benefits of working in the problem domain. This approach does not provide reusability or extendibility, but it does retain the model-driven orientation.

The second possibility is that of low-level design. It is possible to imitate the objects, classes, and inheritance techniques in a procedural language. This should be evident from the fact that AT&T's implementation of C++ is a preprocessor to the C compiler. The classes, objects, and even inheritance relations of C++ are represented in standard C. It is not the intent of this section to provide information about how C++ translates into C; rather, we will consider how to provide object-oriented benefits in another paradigm.

Our definition of object-oriented is admittedly an implementation-oriented one that lists the techniques of objects, classes, and inheritance. The benefits of these techniques are information hiding, abstraction, and polymorphism. Many of these benefits can be realized in a procedural language without the name mangling associated with translation.

The Ada language already provides many of the needed features. Encapsulation of objects can be implemented using generic packages or task types. The polymorphism that allows substitution of an object of one type for an object of another type can be approximated by a variant record that has all the fields needed for all of the subtypes. It is possible to hide the necessary case statements inside the implementation of a package. The disadvantage here is that the case statements must still be written and maintained. This complicates the maintenance of the system and the addition of new features.

The encapsulation and state of local variables can be provided by declaring variables that are sufficiently qualified through a naming process. The protection is possible but relies on the designer's control rather than on the automatic checking of an object-oriented language. A file-oriented language like C can use the discrete structure of a file to conceptually separate values into class-like groupings.

Inheritance can be handled through "editor inheritance." An existing package specification and implementation are copied to new files. These new files are then edited to add the new declarations and definitions for the subclass. The disadvantage of this technique is that improvements to the original files are not automatically propagated to the subclass definition.

The exact behavior of C++ code cannot be achieved in a straight procedural language without very complex structures such as those produced by AT&T's C++ translator. Designers who must remain with a procedural language can attain some of the goals of the object-oriented paradigm. They lose much of the support provided automatically via the constructs of the object-oriented paradigm.

MORE GRAPHICS: LANGUAGE IMPACT

Object-oriented analysis and design techniques provide a sound basis upon which to develop a robust implementation. The variety of object-oriented languages presents a variety of interpretations of the object model. Many developers are captives of one language—the standard for their company—but a wider understanding of the scope of object-oriented languages can lead to a better understanding of design principles as well.

A major factor in graphics systems is performance. C has been heavily used in graphics systems because it provides the performance of assembly language with many of the benefits of a higher level language. Interactive, user-oriented systems such as the draw program require a language that can support the complex, interchangeable structures created in an object-oriented design. This makes C++ the natural choice for implementing the draw program, since it blends the efficiency of C with the flexibility of an object-oriented design. The following sections will discuss the usefulness of several features of C++ in the development of the draw program, and we will consider a few features that C++ does not have.

Paradigm Support

The graphics system itself can be written in a pure object-oriented language just as it can be written in a pure procedural language. But which approach gives us the best system for the least resources? As we have seen in several examples so far, the object-oriented approach provides significant advantages over the procedural approach. Occasionally, a system will need the services of some pieces of the graphics system we have developed. In this context, a hybrid or multiparadigm language is useful if the application that needs the service was developed using a different paradigm.

A graphics system is often used in a supporting role for other types of processing. Thus, choosing a hybrid or multiparadigm language for this type of system facilitates the process of interfacing two systems developed in two separate paradigms. Figure 7.9 illustrates the combining of two systems where one is designed procedurally and the other is designed using object-oriented techniques. So, for reuse, we would like to develop these classes, but we would still retain the ability to interface this system with other non-object-oriented systems.

In this figure the two systems communicate through interfaces. Each has its own interface designed in its own paradigm. The two systems then are combined by having the two interfaces interact. This interaction is facilitated by having a language that can be used to implement both interfaces. In this case, the language should be able to support both freestanding procedures, as does a procedural language, and objects. Figure 7.9 illustrates the location of each type of support.

Perhaps the most important product of the object-oriented paradigm approach is the inventory of classes produced for this system. Three rich inheritance structures, Figure 4.12, Figure 5.16, and Figure 7.10, have been produced that represent three separate concepts. These classes can be easily incorporated into other object-oriented applications. The conceptual encapsulation at the design level and the implementation-level information hiding support the integration with other subsystems.

Inheritance

The graphics system can be designed with either single or multiple inheritance. Multiple inheritance provides a finer grain of decomposition into classes but does so at the

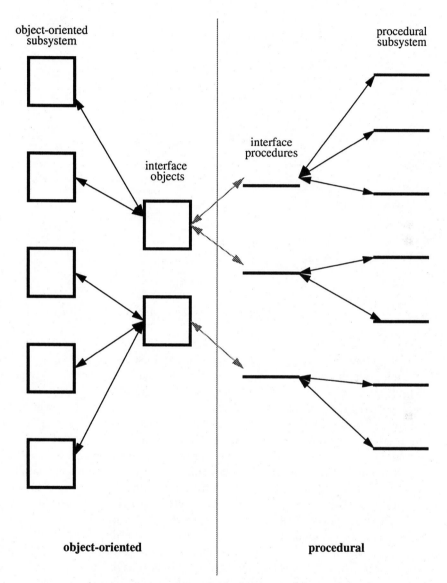

Figure 7.9: Interfacing procedures and objects.

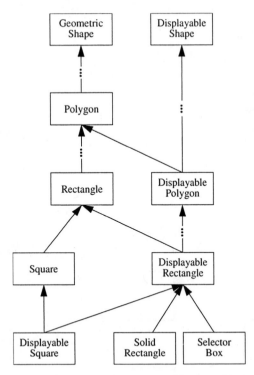

Figure 7.10: Shape classes using multiple inheritance.

cost of increased complexity. If we were in the business of writing graphical systems the fine-grained classes would pay off for us in terms of reuse, and the complexity of multiple inheritance would be acceptable. As our simple draw system is designed, single inheritance provides a sufficient classification scheme for our immediate needs. Figure 5.15 provides a simple hierarchy of shape classes. These shapes contain both the methods to be geometric shapes—having length, width, and so on—and to be graphic objects on the display device—draw, set line color, and so on.

A richer blend of characteristics leads to the use of multiple classifications and to a need for a language that supports multiple inheritance. Figure 7.10 shows that the information in Figure 5.15 can be factored into two separate hierarchies.[1] One hierarchy classifies shapes based on geometric properties and is headed by Geometric Shape. The second mixes in the capability to be a graphic primitive on a color graphics display. This is headed by Displayable Shape (we will ignore the levels above Displayable Shape for now). The benefit of this structure over that in Figure 5.15 is the availability of purely geometric classes with none of the overhead of the graphics concept. These might be used in circuit layout programs to represent regions but not to draw them on a device. There are many other uses for this set of classes.

Figure 7.10 illustrates one problem with multiple inheritance: There is a need to inherit from classes at each level down through the structure. Some information will

---

[1]Several classes are omitted from Figure 7.10 due to space concerns.

```
method draw
begin
    comment: listOfShapes is defined in the class definition.
    for each i in listOfShapes begin
        i.draw;
    end
end
```

Figure 7.11: Algorithm for a system draw method.

be redefined at each of these levels; thus, we do not get the level of code reuse we would desire. However, code reuse is only one benefit of inheritance. The common interface defined by inheritance, and used to establish a set of plug-compatible classes, is an important result as well. Consider the class Displayable Square in the figure. To create this class, we also created a class Square because a square *is a* rectangle and we want to model that in addition to making a square object that is displayable. The problem, then, is that creation of a new subclass—Displayable Square—results in the creation of additional classes—Square.

Classes and Types

Strong type checking is a language attribute that contributes to building applications in which we can have confidence. For the draw program, the typing system will provide a flexible but rigorous checking to be certain that instances being passed as parameters can respond to the necessary messages. The blending of the inheritance mechanism and the typing system in C++ does impose the restriction that the inheritance mechanism should only be used to represent specializations or subtypes. The polymorphic substitution and dynamic binding capabilities of C++ allow the development of code that can remain unchanged even though new shapes, new input devices, and new output devices are added to the application. The code for a system-level function to refresh the picture in the draw program is shown in Figure 7.11. The function will work no matter what shapes are used to create instances and no matter what output device is used. That information is "distributed" in other parts of the system.

Using Classes as Objects

C++ does not provide classes as objects. Would our graphics system be improved if that capability were available? Probably not. There are two situations in which having classes "in the system" is beneficial: (1) there are operations that naturally belong to the class rather than individual instances, and (2) there is a need to dynamically create new subclasses. The first of these was discussed in above and the second is discussed next.

There may be a need to dynamically create new subclasses in a system that allows the user to create new and unique groupings of existing classes. For example, an engineer using a CAD system may wish to define a special kind of valve assembly that will occur many times in the current design. This can be handled very naturally if classes are manipulable objects in the system. A subclass can be developed that is then used to create instances in the design. In a system developed in C++, special data structures would have to be developed to support the run-time development of subclasses. An incremental linker to add these definitions to the object code would also be required. Other types of systems, such as forms management systems, have been developed in which class-like data has been handled by one very general class. In this case, subclasses were not required because the data was handled in this general way. While this is a viable approach, new "forms" are limited to combinations of existing forms.

Garbage Collection

Many of the objects used in the graphics system are created dynamically. This requires that some attention be paid to memory management. C++ provides operations **new** and **delete** to allocate and deallocate memory, respectively, and constructors and destructors to assist in the creation of garbage. The designer is responsible for deleting any memory that is no longer needed.

The dynamic objects created in the graphics system fall into two categories: graphic objects and system entities. The system entities are instances of various menu classes and the pieces of the graphical interface. These items are created in a very regular pattern each time a menu is created. This means that it is easy for the designer to be certain that memory is cleaned up properly when, for example, a menu is destroyed. In situations where the allocation is of limited and regular circumstance, garbage collection is unnecessary overhead.

The graphics objects being developed in the system are also created dynamically. These are created in a random order depending upon the needs of the system user. In this case, there is an increased need for garbage collection. However, these dynamically created objects are all held in a constrained list of shapes. This means that the items are easy to locate. The only reason for destroying a shape object is because the system user has indicated a need to remove it from the drawing. This happens only occasionally and only as a single delete. Again this is easy to anticipate and clean up after.

Automatic garbage collection is of most use in a system in which the system user can specify the creation of a wide range of types of objects and can do so randomly. Automatic garbage collection is also of value in a pure object-oriented language where even the intermediate calculations of the expression

$$3 + (4 * 5)$$

are objects. In this expression, the final result of 23 is represented as an instance of class Integer, but an intermediate object that is an instance of Integer with value 20 is also created and should be removed either explicitly by the programmer or implicitly by a garbage collection routine. If basic computations are represented as classes in a compiled language such as C++, similar garbage is created and must be either managed by the developer or by an automatic collection system. C++ is a good choice for our draw application because the basic language does not incorporate garbage collection into each program written and in the draw program there is no need for that overhead. A garbage collection routine can be included in any application where it is desirable but does not impose overhead on those applications where it is not required.

Single or Multiple Inheritance Structures

The most important benefit from having all classes derived from a single root class is the ability to provide general functionality about being a class in the system. For example, languages or databases that provide persistence of objects as an integral part of the language often provide this capability through the single root class. This overhead becomes part of each object created in an application. Other similar facilities are often added to all objects via the root class.

The difficulty with adding this overhead is that not all objects need it. In the graphics system, it is necessary to provide persistence for the graphic objects that are part of the drawing. It is not necessary to provide persistence for the pieces of the graphical interface. It should be possible to select whether a class inherits this overhead or not. Languages that support *multiple inheritance structures* give us an option since they do not necessarily include this overhead.

SUMMARY

A number of approaches are being tried to provide implementation support for the object-oriented design paradigm. Some of these languages have been built on top of existing languages, resulting in flexible implementations that support more than one paradigm. Others have been developed as totally new languages that support only the single paradigm.

The wide range of implementations has led to a variety of features in the various languages. A number of characteristics of the inheritance relation can be varied to provide many different actual relations. Some languages support the use of multiple superclasses to develop new classes while other languages only allow a single superclass.

In addition to the object-oriented features of these languages, they provide a varying array of modern language features, including exception handling and generics. The variety of languages provides the designer with a number of choices.

FURTHER READING

A number of texts are available on the various languages. Lippman's book on C++ provides both an overview of the syntax as well as insights into the implementation of the language[67]. Bobrow et al[8] provides the specification of the Common LISP Object System. Wilensky[99] provides a readable introduction to CLOS and Lawless and Miller[63] provides good coverage of CLOS.

The idea of multiparadigm languages was explored in a special issue of **IEEE Software**[40]. This issue looks at several specific languages and includes an overview of nine research projects in the area.

8

An Introduction to C++

In this chapter we present a brief introduction to C++. Our goal is to provide a reading knowledge of C++ sufficient for understanding the examples we present in this book and for illustrating basic object-oriented concepts. We could have used any object-oriented programming language, but we have chosen C++ because it is widely used and available, and because as a superset of C it uses a syntax that is familiar to a large number of software developers. If you are not familiar with C, but you are familiar with Pascal, Modula-2, or Ada, you will probably pick up C syntax and semantics quite easily and be able to follow the examples in this book.

We first present a brief description of the structure of C programs and introduce a number of C++ features that were needed to add object-oriented constructs to C. Then we present the C++ features that support the concepts of classes, objects, and inheritance that were discussed in Chapter 2. Then we discuss some C++ mechanisms that support the techniques we are describing in this book. We end this chapter with an example that illustrates the features of C++ we have described.

FROM "OLD C" TO C++

A number of syntactic changes have been made to "old C" in addition to the support of object-oriented programming. Theses features include changes to function prototypes and dynamic memory allocation as well as support for operator overloading and inline functions. The idea of streams have been formally added to the language also.

Function Signatures

Figure 8.1 shows the typical structure of an "old style" C program, which is a variation of a "Hello, world." program. This program comprises three files:

```
/* File:  hello.h */

char *hello();
```

```
/* File:  hello.c */

# include <stdio.h>    /* has the prototype for sprintf() */
# include <stdlib.h>   /* has the prototype for malloc() */
# include <string.h>   /* has the prototype for strlen() */
# include "hello.h"    /* has the prototype for hello() */

char *hello(name)
char *name;
{
    char *value;
    /* Return the string "Hello, name.".  */

    value := (char *)(malloc(9 + strlen(name)));
    sprintf(value, "Hello, %s.", name);
    return value;
}
```

```
/* File:  main.c */

# include <stdio.h>    /* has the prototype for printf() */
# include "hello.h"    /* has the prototype for hello() */

main(argc, argv)
int argc;
char *argv[];
{
    printf("%s", hello("world"));
}
```

Figure 8.1: A typical structure for "old C" programs. By convention, header files names end with .h and program file names end with .c.

`hello.h`. A prototype for function `hello`. The prototype is needed so the compiler knows that `hello` returns a value of type character string (denoted in C as `char *`). The main program (function `main`) gets visibility to the prototype by the `#include` directive in its definition file.

`hello.c`. The definition of function `hello`, which has one formal parameter, a string, and a return value of a string. The return type must match the one in the prototype that is `included`. The include—or header—file `stdlib.h` contains the prototype for function `malloc` and the include file `string.h` contains the prototype for function `strlen`.

`main.c`. The main program that prints "Hello, world." by invoking function `hello` to construct and return a string containing the greeting, which is in turn printed via function `printf`.

Real applications written in C normally have many more files, but all have these types of files. Placing function and data definitions in separate code files (the ".c" files) supports modularity; this use of an include file (".h" files) for each code file·defines the interface to each module. In this example, the include file contains a *prototype* for function `hello`. This prototype specifies that the return type of `hello` is a pointer to a character `char *`, but note that it says nothing about the formal parameter to `hello`. There is no way to specify parameter types and numbers in a prototype in "old C," and thus there is no way a compiler can detect any error in calls to `hello` such as

> `hello()` —*missing parameter*

or

> `hello(10)` —*wrong parameter type*

or

> `hello("big", "world")` —*too many parameters*

or

> `if (hello("world") < 0)` —*wrong use of return type*

In fact, many bugs have arisen during the development of many C programs from mismatches between actual and formal parameter lists and between function return types and uses. C++ incorporates the idea of a *signature* of a function. A signature is a description of the argument list for a function. The information in the signature is sufficient for a more rigorous type checking than is present in standard C, allowing a compiler to verify that the number of actual parameters is correct, that the types of the corresponding actual and formal parameters are compatible, and that the function return type is compatible with the context in which the function call appears. Figure 8.2 shows the program of Figure 8.1 written in C++. The C++ program uses a signature in the include file for `hello`. Note that the name of the formal parameter is not needed in the signature for the prototype of `hello`. The number and type of each parameter—and the return type—completely define the interface for the function. Note, too, that C++ allows a slightly different syntax for a function's definition in that the types of the formal parameters may be declared between the parentheses in a manner similar to most modern strongly typed languages (see the definitions of `hello` and `main` in the figure.).

```
/* File:  hello.h */

char *hello(char *);
```

```
/* File:  hello.c */

# include <stdio.h>     // has the prototype for sprintf()
# include <string.h>    // has the prototype for strlen()
# include "hello.h"     // has the prototype for hello()

char *hello(char *name)
{
    char *value = new char[9 + strlen(name)];
    /* Return the string "Hello, name.".  */

    sprintf(value, "Hello, %s.", name);
    return value;
}
```

```
/* File:  main.c */

# include <iostream.h>  // declares stream cout
# include "hello.h"     // has the prototype for hello()

main(int argc, char *argv[])
{
    cout << hello("world");
}
```

Figure 8.2: A typical structure for C++ programs. In addition to the standard comment delimiters (/* ... */), C++ accepts comments starting with // and continuing to the end of the line.

Operator Overloading

C++ provides a designer with the ability to define more than one function with the same name. This capability is termed *overloading*. For example, we can name a function to zero an integer, say `clear(* int)`, and another function to clear an array of integers, say `clear(int[])`. In "old C" we would have had to use names such as `clearIntArray()` and `clearInt()` to distinguish between the two. In C++, the compiler can identify which version of `clear` to use in a particular call by comparing the number of actual parameters and the type of each to the signatures of functions having the same name. Overloading allows the use of very descriptive function names without the need for qualification.

In support of object-oriented programming, C++ provides the ability to overload binary operators such as '+' and '<'. This facility lets us extend the syntax of the language to make programs both more readable and more natural to write. For example, we might define arithmetic on points—for example, the addition of two points (x_1, y_1) and (x_2, y_2) as the point $(x_1 + x2, y_1 + y_2)$. We might define a "less than" relation for two points p_1 and p_2 as $p_1 < p_2$ if p_1 is closer to the origin (point $(0,0)$) than point p_2 and we might define the division of a point $p = (x, y)$ by an integer i as $(x/i, y/i)$. It would be nice to be able to write expressions in a programming language such as $(p_1 + p_2)$, $(p_1 < p_2)$, and (p_1/i). This is possible with C++ by using operator overloading:

```
Point operator+(Point p)

Point operator/(int i)

int operator<(Point p);
```

Some expressions using these new operators are:

```
        Point midPoint = (point1 + point2) / 2;
and
        if ( midPoint < referencePoint ) ...
```

Note that there is only one operand to each of these operators because each is defined for a point object—for example, the application of (`point1 + point2`) is actually a message—that is, a member function call—to the point object `point1`, which has attributes (or *state*) that determine the value of the first operand.

This capability to overload operators allows user-defined types to be used in expressions in the same manner as built-in types such as `int` and `float`. In essence, the language itself is being extended. This allows improved readability over the same statements in a language that does not allow overloading of operators. It is important, however, that any overloading of an operator maintain a close relationship between the usual meaning of the operator and its meaning in the new context so that programs don't become misleading. For example, it would be very confusing if we decided to overload the operator for multiplication ('*') as the operator for the addition of two points.

Dynamic Memory Allocation

In the program in Figure 8.1 we used a function `malloc` to allocate space that `hello` needed to build the string that it returns as its value. Function `hello` has to rely on its callers to free up this space once they are finished using the function's return value. (Our program does not free this space. If we called `hello` enough times, we would eventually run out of memory.) This type of storage management is common in C programs.

C++ provides two new operators for dynamic memory allocation: `new` and `delete`. They manipulate the memory that is part of the free store and replace the library functions `malloc` and `free` in "old" C. There is no garbage collection in C++ so memory allocated using `new` must be explicitly deallocated using `delete`. Operator `new` takes as an argument the type of object to be created and returns a pointer to the newly allocated space. (Function `malloc`, on the other hand, required a caller to provide the *number* of storage locations needed, and hence the computation in the program in Figure 8.1.) C++ allows variable declarations at any point in a function so we may write:

$$int* \; ip = new \; int;$$

or

$$Point* \; p = new \; Point;$$

to allocate an integer and a point. Each of these combines the declaration of a pointer variable (*type * name*) and the dynamic allocation of memory (**new** *type*).

`delete` must be able to know how much memory `new` has allocated. Therefore, when deleting data structures such as dynamically created arrays, `delete` must be given the number of elements contained in the array. For example, if we create the following array of 100 points:

$$Point* \; p = new \; Point[100];$$

then freeing that memory is carried out by:

$$delete \; [100]p;$$

Had we left off the "`[100]`," then only the initial element of p would be freed and we would have "lost" the reuse of the space occupied by the other 99 points. Had we used some expression having a value other than 100 in the brackets, then the program would be incorrect and the results unpredictable. Care must be taken to properly manage memory with `new` and `delete`.

Inline Functions

There is often a conflict between the design principle of small but meaningful pieces of functionality and the need for efficiency. The `inline` prefix to a function definition is a hint to the compiler to place the function's statements directly in the generated code, thereby eliminating the overhead associated with a function call. This capability has aided C++ in overcoming the execution speed difficulties encountered by some object-oriented languages. Of course, the space needed to expand the code in-line is sometimes greater than the space needed for an out-of-line call, depending on the size of the called function's definition.

The definition of an inline function is identical to any other function definition except for the `inline` keyword:

```
inline Point operator+(Point p);
```

Streams

C++ includes the notion of a *stream* to address file input and output. A stream is simply a sequence of characters. Two predefined classes, istream and ostream, define input streams and output streams, respectively. The standard input, output, and error files of C—stdin, `stdout`, and `stderr`, respectively—are defined in C++ as streams cin, cout, and cerr. The operator "<<" is used to write to an object of class ostream, and the operator ">>" is used to read from an object of class istream. Function `main` in Figure 8.2 uses the stream cout ">>" to print "Hello, world."

CLASSES IN C++

The centerpiece of C++'s support for object-oriented programming is the class declaration. A class is very similar to a `struct` in C. Like a struct, a class has data members. Unlike a struct, the class may have functions as members, and not every member of a class is directly accessible to users of a class.

Three levels of access are available for members of a class definition. Consider the class declaration for a point in Figure 8.3. The keywords `public` and `private` indicate levels of access. The functions declared in the public area constitute the public interface of this C++ class. Instances of other classes may request that an instance of the Point class perform these public operations. For example, Point and get_x, as well as the operator + to add another point, are among the functions available to users of class Point. Members declared in the private area may only be accessed through the functions declared in the public area or those declared as "friends." (A *friend* is a function that has access to the private data and functions of an object.) In the Point class, the representation of a point consists of two integer instance variables, x and y. Users of the class do not directly access these two integers because they are declared in the private section. However, the member functions for Point and the member functions for friends—including the stream input and output operators—do have access to them.

Two member functions, get_x and get_y, are provided to access the x and y components of a point. Why protect the representation with the `private` keyword and then provide access functions? In "real world" use of points, we often use the individual parts of a point so the ability to access these pieces is an important part of the class functionality. The access functions allow the use of these pieces of the point but prevent the users of the class from writing code that uses the internal representation.

```
class Point
{
    public:
        Point(int, int);
        Point(Point&);

        int get_x();
        int get_y();

        Point operator+(Point);
        Point operator+(int);
        Point operator*(int);
        int operator>(Point);
        int operator<(Point);
        int operator=(Point& );

    private:
        int x;
        int y;

        friend istream& operator>>(istream&, Point&);
        friend ostream& operator<<(ostream&, Point&);
};
```

Figure 8.3: A C++ definition for class Point.

Thus the abstract quality of the class is maintained. For example, should we decide to represent a point in polar coordinates—that is, as an angle *theta* and a distance from the origin *r*—then we can change the class implementation without any effect on users of the class as long as we can still provide the rectangular coordinates of the point through get_x and get_y. (We wouldn't want to alter the existing interface because other objects might rely on rectangular coordinates. However, we might want to add methods get_r and get_theta if we implement points using polar coordinates—or even if we continue to use rectangular coordinates.)

The preferred method for system development is to place the class declaration, such as the one above, in a header file. The implementations of the member functions are located in a separate code file. The implementation of a function in the code file is attributed to the appropriate class by the scope resolution operator, ":::." The implementation of the output function for the Point class would be given in the code file as:

```
ostream& Point::operator<<(ostream& strm, Point p)
{
    return strm << "(" << p.get_x() << ","
    p.get_y() << ")";
};
```

This function puts the value of a point p in the format "(x,y)" to the output stream designated by strm.

The development of classes is a large part of object-oriented design. The member functions of the classes constitute a large portion of the functionality of an object-oriented application. Instances of the classes are the bricks from which an application is built.

INSTANCES AND OBJECTS IN C++

An instance of a class is created in the same ways that data variables are created in C: automatically, statically, and via dynamic allocation. Examples of statements to create an instance of a point are:

Point a(6,3);	*automatically*
Point b;	*automatically*
static Point c(3,4);	*statically*
Point *d = new Point(1,1);	*via dynamic allocation*

Objects a, b, and c are all instances of the Point class. When each of the above statements is encountered, a function termed a *constructor* is implicitly called. A constructor function has the same name as the class to which it belongs. Two constructor functions are declared in the Point class of Figure 8.3. The arguments to the constructor function are used to initialize values in the representation. In the declaration

```
Point a(6, 3);
```

the constructor

```
Point(int, int)
```

is called when the instance a is created. As the instance is created, its x component
is set to 6 and its y component is set to 3 by the following definition:

```
Point::Point(int a, int b) {
    x = a;
    y = b;
};
```

Any number of other activities can be carried out within the constructor—for example,
a constructor might allocate instances of other classes.

When objects are about to be destroyed, another function is implicitly called.
This is called a *destructor* and is named the same as the class, but is preceded by a
tilde ('~')—for example, ~Point.

Although several constructors may be defined for a class, only one destructor may
be defined. The destructor is called when control is about to move out of the scope
of an automatic variable or when a dynamically allocated variable is deleted (via the
delete operator). Statically declared variables are destructed when function main
terminates. We have not defined a destructor for class Point because there is not
much for a point object to do when it "dies." A destructor is used to clean up as an
instance of a class is destroyed. In the case of class Point there is nothing to clean up. If
some memory had been allocated within the instance, the destructor could be certain
that memory is deallocated. The destructor may also perform related operations—for
example, shutting down the display operation when an X-Windows-based application
is terminating.

INHERITANCE IN C++

Inheritance is the technique for incrementally modifying an existing class definition
to produce a new class. The class declarations given in Figure 8.4. are the C++
declarations for the classes presented in Chapter 2.   Class Polygon, declared in
Figure 8.4(a), is the base class for class Quadrilateral, declared in Figure 8.4(b). The
phrase :public Polygon in the header of the class Quadrilateral indicates that class
Quadrilateral is a subclass of class Polygon. It also indicates that public members of
Polygon should be made public members of class Quadrilateral. The notation "= 0" in
the declaration of member function Polygon::draw indicates that a definition for this
method should be provided by a subclass. The "= 0" notation also makes Polygon
an *abstract class* (see below). This means that no instances of the Polygon class can
be created because not all the operators have been implemented. Its declaration here
puts draw in the interface for all public subclasses of Polygon.

Figure 8.4(c) shows the complete definition of Quadrilateral that results from the
composition of classes Polygon and Quadrilateral. Note that the private member referencePoint of Polygon does not become a private member of Quadrilateral and can only

```
class Polygon
{
    public:
        Polygon(Point);
        void move(Point);
        void isInside(Point);
        Point referencePoint();
        virtual void draw() = 0;
    private:
        Point referencePoint;
}
```

(a) A definition for class Polygon.

```
class Quadrilateral:public Polygon
{
    public:
        Quadrilateral(Point, Point);
        void isInside(Point);
        void draw();
    private:
        Point vertex2;
}
```

(b) A definition for Quadrilateral, a subclass of Polygon.

```
class Quadrilateral
{
    public:
        Quadrilateral(Point, Point);
        Point referencePoint();
        void isInside(Point);
        void move(Point);
        void draw();
    private:
        Point vertex2;
};
```

(c) The effective definition of class Quadrilateral. Inherited attributes are italicized.

Figure 8.4: Polygon class declarations.

```
class Quadrilateral
{
    public:
        Quadrilateral(Point, Point);
        Point reference();
        void isInside(Point);
        void move(Point);
        void draw();
    protected:
        Point referencePoint;
        Point vertex2;
};
```

Figure 8.5: The effect of **protected** members in a superclass. Inherited attributes are italicized.

be accessed using the reference() member function defined in class Polygon. Thus, the first vertex of Quadrilateral, called referencePoint, cannot be directly accessed in member functions declared in class Quadrilateral.

An alternative declaration for class Polygon can make the members of a class available to its subclasses. Figure 8.5 changes how class Quadrilateral inherits from class Polygon. If the **protected** keyword replaces the **private** keyword in Figure 8.4(a), subclasses of Polygon inherit those members declared as protected. The member functions of class Quadrilateral can now directly access the reference point as illustrated in Figure 8.5.

ABSTRACT CLASSES IN C++

Our development methodology stresses abstraction and the flexibility that it introduces to the design process. There are three ways in which abstraction is supported in C++. The first is through the use of abstract classes and the second uses of templates. A third approach is through the use of the **void** * construct. This technique is illustrated in [88] and will not be described here. It will be made largely obsolete by the provision of templates in a forthcoming version of C++[27].

The purpose of having an abstract class at the root of each inheritance hierarchy is to provide an interface that describes the functionality of the subclasses but describes it at such a high level that complete implementations of all the operators in the interface is impossible. Instances of such a class should not be created. C++ has a provision that prevents the accidental creation of such instances.

The official use of "abstract class" in C++ is reserved for a class that has one or more of its virtual functions set to zero. In Figure 8.4(a), the draw operator is set equal to zero to indicate that no implementation of draw will be given in the class definition. This notation "= 0" signals the C++ compiler to disallow the creation of any instances of the Polygon class. Subclasses of the Polygon class will either provide an implementation of the draw operator or be abstract classes themselves. This feature

```
template<class T> class Point {
private:
    T x;
    T y;

public:
    Point(T,T);
    Point(Point p);
    T get_x();
    T get_y();
    ⋮

    Other operators the same
}
```

Figure 8.6: A C++ template for a Point class.

allows a class to provide a very general definition and to defer implementation specifics to a subclass.

The concept of a *template* is being added to C++ to provide a "generic" facility similar to that found in Ada and Eiffel. The purpose of this facility is to be able to abstract out the logical functioning of a component that is not dependent on the type of data being acted upon. For example, a queue provides a first-in, first-out input/output policy regardless of the type of items being placed into the queue. A generic **Queue** class would describe this logical functioning in terms of some generic item without considering the size or the format of the items. This approach can be useful in a variety of classes. Consider the **Point** class defined in Figure 8.3. The designer must make a decision about the type of the x and y values in the definition. Integer values are required for screen coordinates in a graphics system, but floating-point values are required for the world coordinate system. The definition in Figure 8.3 could be rewritten using the template mechanism shown in Figure 8.6. This provides a very general class that can be used to instantiate objects that have either integer or real coordinate values. The statement:

`Point<int> a;`

creates an instance of the template class **Point**. This instance will use the integer type int for x and y.

VIRTUAL FUNCTIONS

One of the powerful implementation techniques that have been incorporated into object-oriented languages is the concept of dynamic binding of function calls. This is the standard practice in interpreted languages, but it has not been used widely in compiled languages. Dynamic binding is used in compiled object-oriented languages to support inclusion polymorphism. In this section we will illustrate how of virtual functions invoke dynamic binding, and we will illustrate how it is helpful in design.

Figure 8.4(a) illustrates that the syntax for a *virtual function* includes the keyword "virtual" in front of the function signature—in this case the draw member function—in the class specification. This notifies the compiler to build a special structure that is interpreted by the runtime environment to resolve calls to this function. The implementation of a function declared as "virtual" is handled in one of two ways:

1. A default implementation for the draw operator could have been provided in the code file for the Polygon class. Any subclass that did not provide its own specific draw operator would have inherited this default.
2. No implementation for the draw could have been provided as illustrated in Figure 8.4(a). In this case, the draw operator is set equal to zero. This prevents instances of the class Polygon from being created because the class contains an operator with no implementation.

The notation "virtual" in the declaration of draw indicates that the actual member function called will be determined dynamically at run time rather than at compile time. To see how this works, consider an example in which we have some function display that draws its argument among its activities:

```
void display(Polygon& p)
{
    .
    .
    .
    p.draw();
    .
    .
    .
}
```

and consider the code segment:

```
Quadrilateral q(Point p1(1,1), Point p2(2,2));
    .
    .
    .
display(q);
    .
    .
    .
```

Function display knows only that it is receiving a polygon object as its argument. However, the draw is not implemented by class Polygon, but only by its subclasses. It would be an error for the compiler to generate a call to the member function Polygon::draw. Instead, the desired behavior is to use the draw that is associated with the actual argument to display, in this case q. This cannot be determined until run time and requires the dynamic binding of the function call to the code to be executed. This is exactly what happens with **virtual**. In this example, the member function Quadrilateral::draw will be invoked since q is of class Quadrilateral. If we were to pass another object of some subclass of Polygon to display, then its draw would be invoked. The binding of member function calls to member functions is depicted in Figure 8.7.

Virtual functions implement inclusion polymorphism, a very powerful design feature.

WRAPPERS IN C++

Several object-oriented languages provide the ability to encapsulate an inherited operator within a *wrapper* (see the discussion in Section 7.) that is defined in the new class currently being defined. The inherited operator and the wrapper have the same name and therefore the same intent. The term *wrapper* is used to denote that the inherited operator is enclosed in the new operator with the new code coming either before the existing operator, after the existing operator, or both.

Wrappers can be implemented in C++ in a straightforward way. Consider the draw operator in the Polygon hierarchy. If every draw operator was going to be different (as they undoubtedly would be), but some start-up code was needed in each subclass's draw operator—say to set the drawing line width—this could be given as the implementation of draw in Polygon instead of setting it's draw operator to zero. The draw operator in each subclass would then be written as:

```
SomeClass::draw() {
    Polygon::draw();
        ⋮
}
```

Even though the draw operator is being overridden in the subclass, we can still access its original implementation in the parent class or even higher in the hierarchy. "::" is referred to as the *scope resolution operator*. It allows us to specify the class to which the definition belongs:

```
SomeClass::draw
```

as well as to resolve references:

```
Polygon::draw
```

The wrapper concept allows the development of functions to be hierarchical just as the development of classes is hierarchical.

EXAMPLE: CONSTRAINT NETWORKS

We will now work through an example to demonstrate the use of C++. In this example we consider an implementation of constraint networks. We will not look at all of the implementation details, but rather the building of an application using some classes that have already been defined. The focus of this exercise is the demonstration of the use of C++ and the reuse of existing classes.

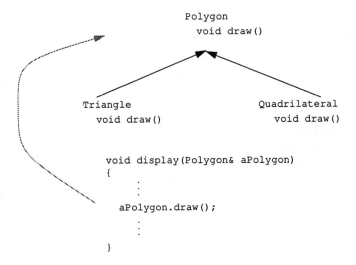

(a) Static binding of member function draw.

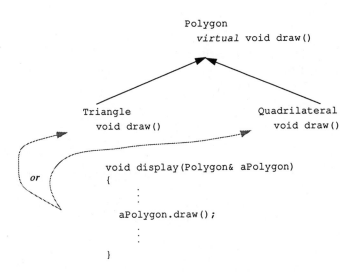

(b) Dynamic binding of virtual member function draw.

Figure 8.7: Static versus dynamic binding in class **Polygon**.

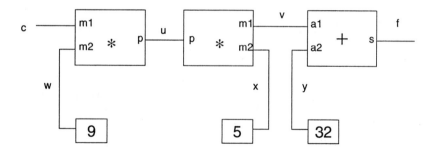

Figure 8.8: A constraint network for conversion between degrees Celsius and degrees Fahrenheit.

The Problem

Abelson and Sussman[1] present an implementation of *constraint networks*, the principle behind the spreadsheet concept. They give an application using constraint networks to develop a converter that represents the relationship between degrees Celsius and degrees Fahrenheit. The formula is:

$$C = \frac{5}{9}(F - 32)$$

where C represents degrees Celsius and F represents degrees Fahrenheit. It can be rewritten as:

$$9 * C = 5 * (F - 32)$$

A constraint network for conversion between degrees Fahrenheit and degrees Celsius is shown in Figure 8.8. Changing the value of C causes the network to propagate the change throughout and ultimately results in a new value being calculated for F. Similarly, changing the value of F causes the network to calculate a new value for C. This network behaves as follows:

> When one of the input connectors, labeled either f or c, receives a new value, the constraint associated with that connector recomputes its value and adjusts the value(s) of its other connectors as necessary. This adjustment of the value(s) causes connected constraints to adjust their values, which causes changes to ripple through the network. For example, if the value 100 is input to the c connector, then the multiplication constraint to which it is connected is forced to adjust its other connectors. Since the new value is arriving at the port labeled $m1$ and the value at the port labeled $m2$ is constant, the only possible adjustment is to

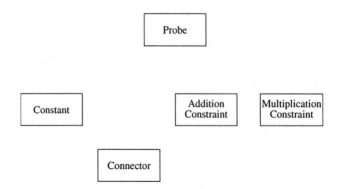

Figure 8.9: Classes of objects in a constraint network.

set the connector at p such that $p = 9 * 100 = 900$. The
change to p changes the value on u, which in turn causes
the other multiplication constraint to adjust its values such
that $m1 * m2 = p = 900$. Since $m2$ is connected to constant 5, the constraint must set $m1 = 900 \div 5 = 180$. This
change to $m1$ is propagated over connector v to the addition constraint, resulting in an adjustment to the sum
at s to $180 + 32 = 212$. We see at connector f that
$212°F = 100°C$.

The problem is to develop a program in C++ to convert between degrees Celsius and
degrees Fahrenheit using a constraint network.

A Solution

The components of the constraint network shown in Figure 8.8 can be classified into a
number of categories shown in Figure 8.9. The pieces include an addition constraint,
two multiplication constraints, three constants, and seven connectors between constraints. The connectors are actually the storage locations for values between the
constraints, so they represent significant objects. Each of these objects will be represented in the final application. The objects will be created by declaring instances of
classes.

Abelson and Sussman's implementation of constraint networks uses a two-phase
approach to calculating a new value for each connection in the network. When a value
is modified by an outside agent, the network first sends a message to each connector
to forget its current value to every node in the network. As soon as this message has
propagated throughout the network, a second message is sent requesting that each
constraint calculate a new value based on the value it receives as a parameter to the
message.

Besides the Addition Constraint and Multiplication Constraint classes, we can identify classes named Constraint, Binary Constraint, and Mono Constraint. These classes

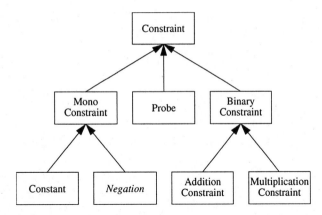

Figure 8.10: Inheritance structure for the constraint network classes.

are designed to allow constraints to be *generalized*—that is, a number of the operators that would be defined in the Addition Constraint and Multiplication Constraint classes would be exact duplicates of each other. By use of inheritance, new classes Mono Constraint and Binary Constraint can be created to generalize certain of the operators from the more specific classes. The first phase operator, processForgetValue, would be identical for both addition and multiplication constraints. Thus it can be defined at a higher level—once—and then added to both of the lower-level classes through inheritance. Figure 8.10 shows the inheritance structure for the constraint classes. The inheritance relation is stated in each class documentation page by the phrase:

```
superclass:  binaryConstraint
```

Two other classes—Connector and Probe—are also needed. The Connector class provides the connectors between constraints in the system. The connectors are the data stores for the system. The Probe class is used for debugging or—in our case—for providing a simple user interface. A probe is attached to a connector in the same way that a constraint is. When the connector announces that it has a new value, the probe prints this value so that the "outside world" can see the current value of the connector. Since the probe will be attached to a connector in a slot reserved for an object of class Constraint, it is convenient to view a probe as a kind of constraint that prints instead of calculating. This relationship is shown in Figure 8.10.

The Application

To actually solve the given problem, we now need to use these classes to provide the functionality. We will declare instances of the appropriate classes to model the entities shown in Figure 8.8. The instances must be able to send messages to each other so parameters in the constructors are used to provide pointers to other system components. This results in a set of declarations seen in Figure 8.11. Compare these declarations with the network shown in Figure 8.8 and satisfy yourself that the declarations are a faithful model of the needed network. Two statements we can use to test the system are:

```
connector c;
connector f;
connector u;
connector v;
connector w;
connector x;
connector y;

additionConstraint adder1(&v, &y, &f);
multiplicationConstraint mult1(&c, &w, &u);
multiplicationConstraint mult2(&v, &x, &u);

constant constant1(9.0, &w);
constant constant2(5.0, &x);
constant constant3(32.0, &y);

probe probe1("c", &c);
probe probe2("f", &f);
```

Figure 8.11: C^{++} declarations for the constraint network

```
              f.setValue(32.0, 0);
and
              c.setValue(25.0, 0);
```

These statements modify values of the *c* and *f* connectors to have the system convert between them.

Final Notes on the Application

The reaction of many people to this example is that it is a lot of trouble just to convert between Celsius and Fahrenheit temperatures. But the purpose of this example was to provide an implementation of a set of classes that represent constraint networks, not just a temperature converter. This would not be a good example at all if we never intended to use the network components for any other calculations. We have built a set of reusable components that can be easily extended to include additional types of constraints. We can use these components to build *any* constraint network, although we might have to add new subclasses to represent additional mathematical functions. For example, we could use these classes to build a spreadsheet application. We could take the classes from our existing set and add some others—for example, a constraint to compute loan amortizations.

The definition of class Binary Constraint has a number of operators defined for it, while its Addition Constraint subclass has only one additional operation besides a new constructor. This is a good example of the power of inheritance. The operators defined in Binary Constraint would have been defined in both Addition Constraint and

```
class negationConstraint:  public monoConstraint {
    public:
        void processNewValue()                              (a)
}
```

```
void negationConstraint::processNewValue() {
    result->setValue(-1 * input1->getValue());             (b)
}
```

Figure 8.12: The class definition and implementation of a negation constraint.

Multiplication Constraint were it not for inheritance.

Also consider the work needed to add another specific constraint, such as *negation*, to the system. Most of the operators and data elements it would need are already defined in class Mono Constraint, a class that addresses constraints involving operations on a single value. Adding the negation constraint would only require that one new function, processNewValue, be defined. Figure 8.12 shows that the implementation of a Negation Constraint class has two important features. The class header in Figure 8.12(a) indicates that it will inherit from Mono Constraint. The second important feature is that the implementation of the Negation Constraint class only requires a constructor for the class — which simply calls the Mono Constraint constructor, and the implementation of the processNewValue function.

The polymorphic nature of many object-oriented languages means that instances of the Negation Constraint class can be used any place that instances of other constraint classes are used. There is no need to modify any other pieces of the system to accommodate this new structure. This ability to extend an existing system facilitates the writing of open systems that will evolve over time.

MORE GRAPHICS: C++ IMPLEMENTATION

In this section we present C++ representative implementations of some of the classes in our design of the draw application. The remaining figures show declarations for the classes Color, Graphics Primitive, Polyline, Displayable Shape, and Line. We also provide an implementation for the member functions of Line. Our purpose is to illustrate what C++ "looks like." Attributes are omitted from many of the classes to keep the examples short. For simplicity, we use the class hierarchy based on single inheritance.

Following what we consider to be good programming practice, each class is coded in two files. A header file provides a class definition, and an implementation file provides an implementation for each member function. We assume the existence of an object terminal, an instance of class Display Device, which has operations to draw points, lines, and text.

```
/* color.h */
# ifndef COLORH
# define COLORH

class Color {
  public:
    Color(int r, int g, int b);

  private:
    short int red;
    short int green;
    short int blue;
};

# endif
```

Figure 8.13: A C++ specification for class Color.

```
/* gprimitive.h */
# ifndef GPRIMITIVEH
# define GPRIMITIVEH

# include "point.h"
# include "color.h"

class GraphicPrimitive {
public:
    GraphicPrimitive();
    GraphicPrimitive(Color&);

virtual void scale(float) = 0; // scale factor > 0;
virtual void translate(Point&) = 0;
virtual void rotate(int) = 0; // in degrees
virtual void move(int, int);
virtual void draw() = 0;
virtual void erase();

inline Color *getColor();
inline void setColor(Color&);

private:
    Color color;
};

# endif
```

Figure 8.14: A C++ specification for class Graphics Primitive.

```
/* polyline.h */
# ifndef POLYLINH
# define POLYLINH

# include "point.h"
# include "gprimitive.h"

class Polyline:  public GraphicPrimitive {
  public:
    Polyline();

virtual void scale(float) = 0;
virtual void translate(Point&) = 0;
virtual void rotate(int) = 0;
virtual void draw() = 0;


};


# endif
```

Figure 8.15: A C++ specification for class Polyline.

```
/* dispshp.h */
# ifndef DISPSHPH
# define DISPSHPH

# include "point.h"
# include "color.h"
# include "polyline.h"

class DisplayableShape:  public Polyline {
  public:
    DisplayableShape(Color&, Point&);
    DisplayableShape(Point&);

inline Point *getReferencePoint();
inline void setReferencePoint(Point&);

virtual void translate(Point&);
virtual void scale(float) = 0;
virtual void rotate(int) = 0;
virtual void draw() = 0;

  private:
    Point referencePoint;
};
# endif
```

Figure 8.16: A C++ specification for class Displayable Shape.

```
/* line.h */
# ifndef LINEH
# define LINEH

# include "point.h"
# include "dispshp.h"

class Line:public DisplayableShape
{
  public:
    Line(Point& point1, Point& point2);
    Line(Color& lineColor, Point& point1, Point& point2);
    Line(Point& refPoint, Point& point1, Point& point2);
    Line(Color& lineColor, Point& refPoint, Point& point1, Point& point2);

    void scale(float);
    void rotate(int);
    void draw();

    Point *point1();
    Point *point2();


  private:
    Point endPoint1;
    Point endPoint2;
};

# endif
```

Figure 8.17: A C++ specification for class Line.

```
/* line.C */
# include "globals.h" // provides access to terminal
# include "line.h"
Line::Line(Point& point1, Point& point2):  (point1)
{   // Use point1 as the reference point
    endPoint1 = Point(0, 0);
    endPoint2 = (point2 - *getReferencePoint());
}


Line::Line(Color& c, Point& point1, Point& point2):  (c, point1)
{   // Use point1 as the reference point
    endPoint1 = Point(0, 0);
    endPoint2 = (point2 - *getReferencePoint());
}


Line::Line(Point& refPoint, Point& point1, Point& point2):
               (refPoint)
{
    endPoint1 = (point1 - refPoint);
    endPoint2 = (point2 - refPoint);
}


Line::Line(Color& c, Point& refPoint, Point& point1, Point& point2):
    (c, refPoint)
{
    endPoint1 = (point1 - refPoint);
    endPoint2 = (point2 - refPoint);
}



void Line::draw()
{
    terminal.line(
        endPoint1 + *getReferencePoint(),
        endPoint2 + *getReferencePoint());
}

Point *Line::point1() { return &endPoint1; }
Point *Line::point2() {     return &endPoint2; }
```

Figure 8.18: A C++ implementation for class Line.

SUMMARY

This has been a very quick introduction to C++. It is intended only to give you a basic reading knowledge of the object-oriented features of C++. The code used in this book will not be written in the terse style of C but will be sufficiently verbose that most readers should have no trouble understanding the intent of the code. C++ code will only be used to discuss actual implementation issues.

The example used in this chapter is intended to illustrate the use of existing classes. The code for the application itself is very small and easy to relate to the original problem. As the application is being developed, the focus is on the services provided by the various classes rather than on their internal implementation.

FURTHER READING

Many C++ books are available and new ones are coming out all the time. We recommend two that, as of this writing, are very useful. Stan Lippman's *C++ Primer*[67] is now in its second edition and provides comprehensive but understandable coverage of C++ in a format suitable for a novice. Ellis and Stroustroup[27] have provided a language reference model that is useful for answering questions about the language, but this book is not intended as a learning device.

9

Implementation and Testing

In this chapter we will return to considering the life cycle by looking at implementation and testing issues. We will try to be as generic as possible, but we will use C++ examples to illustrate some of the concepts.

The implementation of classes is a central focus in the development process. In a system written purely in the object-oriented style, all data is encapsulated within instances of classes. In most systems, these instances are encapsulated within instances of other classes and the entire application is encapsulated within one very high-level class. As an aside, this encapsulation and the narrow interface provided by a class make it much easier to incorporate the behavior represented by the class into an application.

The implementation of the application can take much less time and effort in the object-oriented paradigm due to the use of existing components. Much of the needed functionality will have been designed into classes prior to the development of a particular application. Unlike adding procedural components, adding an object to an application brings along a large amount of potentially complex behaviors. Implementation at the application level should be reduced to creating instances of many classes, developing a few new classes, and manipulating pointers to these objects so that they may communicate with each other.

Our emphasis on reuse makes the testing of object-oriented applications and components a high priority. We need to have a very high level of confidence in components that will be used in most of a company's applications. The testing of object-oriented components is still a relatively new idea and techniques have not been refined; we will present existing information and propose some techniques and algorithms.

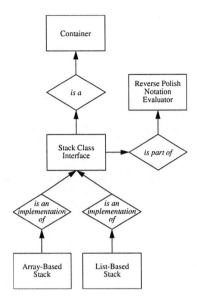

Figure 9.1: Software base captures many relationships.

CLASS IMPLEMENTATION

Class implementation moves along several dimensions. One alternative is that implementation moves from simple to complex with the smaller, simpler classes implemented first, serving as the basis for the development of larger, more complex classes.

As an alternative, classes can be viewed as developing in layers, wherein a new class is often built upon existing classes. In turn, these are built on top of other existing classes. Through such relations as *is a* and *is part of*, new classes begin with much existing code. This is an asset if the existing code is well written and thoroughly tested, but it is a disaster if the code propagates bugs into the new components.

The Software Base

The *software base* is the term used by Tsichritzis et al[92] to refer to the pool of existing software components. Many companies have recognized the value of a centralized store of code developed within the company or purchased from other sources[82]. The value of this software base is directly tied to the reliability of the code stored in it. Some type of certification process is necessary to ensure the integrity of the components being added to the software base. It is beyond our scope to specify this process here. What is important for us is that we have confidence in the code we are reusing to form the basis for our new class.

The software base is more than just a repository of pieces of code. The classes stored in the base are related in a number of ways, and the base must keep track of these relationships (see Figure 9.1). The tools associated with the software base use these relations to provide a variety of capabilities to the developer.

Reuse

As with class design, class implementation should begin with reuse. The design may use a variety of abstract classes. During implementation, we must develop "concrete" objects in those classes.

Our goal should be to write as little original code as possible; however, reuse does not happen by accident. It must be planned for. We will consider the tools needed to support reuse in Chapter 11, on supporting technologies. Classes must be accessible to be reused. This implies not only tools but techniques for organizing large numbers of classes as well. Chapter 10 will discuss design issues affecting the reusability of classes.

Once a data object is identified as being required for an application, a class must be made available that provides the needed model. The needed functionality should be produced according to the following priorities:

1. Locate an existing class that can be used "as is" to provide the needed behavior.
2. Locate an existing class or classes that can be used as a basis for developing the new class.
3. Develop a new class without any reuse.

Each of these is explained below.

- *"As is" Reuse.* The needed class may already exist, and an instance of it is created to provide the needed behavior. This instance may be used directly by the application or it may be used as part of the implementation of another class. By reusing an existing class we get tested code that should work without further modification. This type of reuse is more likely to be successful because of two characteristics of most object-oriented languages: separation of interface and implementation (information hiding) and encapsulation.

  The separation of the interface—class specification—from the implementation of the class allows the use of the class's functionality without understanding how that functionality is implemented. This requires much faith in the quality of that existing code. It also requires more information than just the specification of the class. Libraries of classes need to provide sufficient information so that developers of time-critical or space-critical applications can judge the suitability of the class, can select from available implementations, or can tune the class to their specifications.

  The encapsulation of information within the class definition prevents the presence of an instance of one class from interfering with the operation of an instance of another class. The data names declared in one instance are local to that instance. Data values with the same name do not conflict with those defined within other instances of the same class

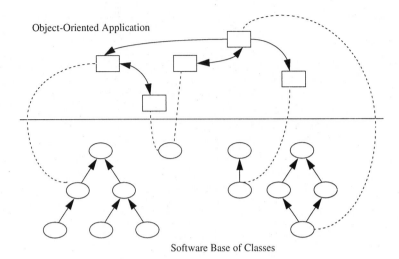

Figure 9.2: "Off-the shelf" reuse.

or within instances of other classes. Whether the data is declared in the public area of a class or in its private section, references to a data value must be qualified by the name of the instance that contains the specific data value desired. Thus, it is possible for multiple instances of a class to peacefully coexist when they have data values with identical names. Each access to a data value, even if it is publicly declared in the class, is still a message to a particular instance first and to one of its data values second.

These two characteristics support the as-is reuse of classes. New instances can be declared with assurances the they will not interfere with existing code. This supports a form of incremental application development in which the application is developed quickly to the point where it provides some limited functionality correctly. Additional functionality can be added to the application as additional classes are either located or developed. Adding instances of these new classes will seldom require that existing parts of the system be reworked to correctly interface with the new instances (see Figure 9.2).

- *Evolutionary reuse.* A class may not exist that provides the exact behavior required. However, if existing classes provides similar kinds of functionality, the new class can be designed incrementally by inheriting from them. The new class should inherit all the behavior of an existing class if it is to be a subclass of the existing class. The new class can then define locally the additional data and functions necessary (see Figure 9.3). The new class may also be developed by mixing together the behavior of several existing classes. Each of the existing classes is a model of some concept. The blend results in a class that provides a multifaceted concept in an application-specific way.

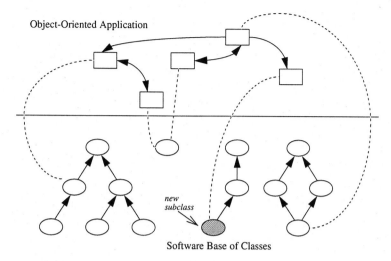

Figure 9.3: Creating a new subclass.

The needed class may point out a requirement for an additional abstraction in the software base. An existing class may provide some needed behavior plus some behaviors not needed in our new class. One new, more abstract class is created and becomes the parent class to the class we are attempting to design and to the existing class that is then modified to inherit from the new parent class. In Figure 9.4 some of the behavior of existing class A becomes a portion of new class B and is inherited by class C as well as class A'. Some of class A's behavior remains in class A' and is not inherited by class C.

Evolutionary reuse is unique to the object-oriented paradigm. Many of us have used a form of "editor inheritance" in which we reused an existing component by copying the file that contained its definition. We then edited the copy to provide the exact functionality needed in the new application. The difficulty with this approach is that the copying process does not produce a dependency between the original code and our new version. If an error is found and repaired in the original code, no formal means exists for that modification to be propagated to the new file. Inheritance does establish a dependency between the existing definition and the new one. Changes made to a superclass are passed on to all subclasses the next time they are compiled.

A second feature of evolutionary reuse is that it is nonintrusive. The existing class is not modified in any way when it is used as the parent of a new class. A class can be used as a parent many times without complicating the implementation of that class or any of its subclasses. The relationship between the two classes is recorded in the definition of the new class, not in the existing one. Even if a restructuring such as that of Figure 9.4 is required, the result of these modifications is that

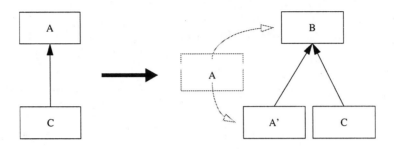

Figure 9.4: Restructuring to add a more abstract parent class.

class A' is still the equivalent of class A.

- *"From scratch" development.* We have covered this issue already, but we would like to say a little more. Even if there is no class that can be used to evolve a new one, there may still be reuse possibilities. The implementation of a class can still be speeded along by declaring instances of existing classes in the implementation portion of the new class. A list, a hardware interface, or some other capability can provide a portion of the new class.

Assertions

A positive way of implementing classes is to include information from the class design directly in the code. In particular, it is useful to incorporate the constraints on parameters, loop execution, and so on in the code. This is accomplished by some language mechanism for representing assertions. An *assertion* is a statement of a requirement for a procedure, a value, or even a piece of code. In the typical description of a stack abstract data type, assertions can be made that control the operation of the push and pop functions:

> **procedure** push(**var** S: Stack_Type; New_Item: Item_Type);
> {**assert**: *The stack S is not full*}
> $\quad$ *vdots*
> {**assert**: *The top of stack S contains New_Item*}
> **end**;
> **procedure** pop(**var** S: Stack_Type) **return** Item_Type;
> {**assert**: *The stack S is not empty*}
> $\quad$ *vdots*
> {**assert**: *The stack S has one fewer items that it did on entry*}
> **end**;

This type of assertion is termed a *precondition* because it states a condition that must be true before the operation can be performed. A *postcondition* states a condition that must be true after the operation has been performed. For example, with the pop operator, after its execution the number of elements in the stack should be one less than the number before the operation.

Both C and C⁺⁺ have a header file, assert.h, that provides a form of support for assertion. This file contains macros that allow the implementer to insert conditions in methods. The macro expands the condition to provide a checking facility. The facility provides both a runtime checking facility with a reporting facility. The implementer might state an assertion for pop as

$$\text{assert}(\text{TOP} > 0);$$

The macro would check to be certain that the stack was not empty before attempting to remove an item. If the condition fails, a message is printed that identifies the source file and line number in that file where the failure occurred.

This is a simplistic approach, but one that allows the implementer to quickly provide checking at critical points in the code. The code remains simple with no conditional structures cluttering the implementer's source code. There is no choice other than aborting the application with this system.

Eiffel provides assertions as an integral part of the language. Meyer, the designer of Eiffel, refers to the use of assertions as contracting for reliable software. He states the contract as[73]:

If you promise to call *r* with *pre* satisfied then I, in return,
promise to deliver a final state in which *post* is satisfied.

This statement places more responsibility on the designer of the calling routine.

Meyer believes this approach leads to a simple, clean design that does not force the implementer to deal with issues that are not possible to handle. For example, if the push operator discovers that the stack is full, there is no way for the implementer of that operator to know whether aborting the application is appropriate or not. The concept of an *exception* will be considered later as a way to handle this.

We believe in redundant checking, unlike Meyer. By implementing code that checks preconditions before performing the intended operation, the implementer has the opportunity to report the exact error before program termination. This is an approach that gives safety plus supports development of the class by providing error messages as the class is implemented. The exceptions talked about below will also support this approach.

Debugging

Debugging a class is a constrained process. In a properly designed class the data are in the region of the object, protected from outside access. Thus the methods of the class represent the only functions that can modify the data values. This limits the number of ways in which a data value can be modified, and limits the functions that must be examined to find the reason for an erroneous data value.

Some object-oriented programming environments support debugging with interactive facilities. These environments are usually built around interpreted language systems such as Smalltalk and the Common LISP Object System. Facilities include the setting of breakpoints, accessing source code, inspecting objects—including an ability to modify data values and evaluate expressions—and editing source code. For compiled languages, debugging tools are generally those available for procedural languages, perhaps with some modifications to support classes. For example, the standard Unix debugger, `dbx`, has been extended for use in debugging C++ programs. We will have more to say on this subject in Chapter 13.

Error Handling

The expectation that a class be self-contained implies a responsibility for handling errors. Depending on the severity of the error and how it must be handled, it may not be possible for an instance of a class to have complete and final responsibility for fixing or reporting an error.

C programmers have used a status code approach to error handling. A function is designed to return an integer value that serves as a status code and that can be checked by the routine that called the function. Status codes of different values indicate either success in carrying out the task or else varying degrees of failure. Typical is the status code returned by `fopen` function in C, which attempts to open a file. The value zero is returned if the attempt fails, and the handle to the file is returned if it succeeds.

The difficulty with this approach is that each level of code must know about the status codes of the functions that are called at that level and must check those codes and take action. The problem is handled at a level higher than it occurs. This creates a higher degree of coupling than is desirable. Fi possible, the error should be handled at the level at which it occurs. For example, with a failure in `fopen`, an application might request that the user enter another filename if the current name does not exist.

Built-In Error Handling

Ada programmers have the exception mechanism to aid in error handling (see Figure 9.5). An exception covers a wider scope than the traditional term *error*. An *exception* may be nothing more than a special case that must be treated differently than the vast majority of occurrences. An *exception handler* is a piece of code that is invoked when a specific exception is raised—that is, when it occurs. This code may abort the application, it may signal a higher level exception handler, or it may fix the problem.

Exception handling is becoming part of an increasing number of languages, including object-oriented languages. Eiffel has an exception-handling mechanism. The GNU C++ Version 1.37.1 also has a preliminary implementation. Stroustrup[89] has indicated this as a future direction for C++.

The complex nature of objects has made the cleanup associated with handling exceptions a difficult task. This has slowed the development of built-in exception handling. An exception-handling scheme has been developed to work on top of C++ with no modifications to the language[74, 75].

User-Defined Error Handling

Two relatively simple techniques have been used to provide simple error-handling facilities. These techniques provide for printing error messages and aborting the ap-

```
package SIMPLE is
    EQUAL : exception;
    function max(a : in INTEGER; b : in INTEGER) return INTEGER;
        - - Returns the maximum of a and b,
        - - but raises the exception EQUAL if a = b.
end SIMPLE;
package body SIMPLE is
    function max(a : in INTEGER; b: in INTEGER) return INTEGER is
    begin
            if a = b then        raise EQUAL;
            elsif a < b then     return b;
            else                 return a;
    end max;
end SIMPLE;

with SIMPLE;
procedure MAIN is
    x : INTEGER;
begin
    begin
        x := SIMPLE.max(7, 7);    - - should raise the exception
    exception
        when SIMPLE.EQUAL => x := 7;    - - handle the exception!
    end;
    - - The exception was handled and x has value 7.
end MAIN;
```

Figure 9.5: An example of exceptions in Ada.

plication. They do not allow for nested handling of errors. The techniques are no substitutes for the exception mechanism mentioned earlier, but they are quick, easy, and can be used in any language. They provide localized error handling that is quickly tailored to new classes.

The first possibility uses a global error object. The user adopts a style of design in which every class developed assumes that it will have access to this global object. When an error is detected in one of the user's objects, a message is sent to this global object. The message carries a string that is the error message to be printed and an integer that indicates the severity of the error. The message:

```
ERROR_HANDLER.handle("Message to be printed", 1);
```

would have the ERROR_HANDLER print the message and abort the application.

The benefit of this approach is that the ERROR_HANDLER is responsible for formatting and displaying the message. At the time the object ERROR_HANDLER is created, the output can be directed anywhere the system user chooses. The designer can also easily modify the actions taken for the various levels of error severity.

The second approach to user-defined error handling requires that each class define—or redefine—a method named error. This should not be part of the public interface of the class. Rather, it should be a hidden part of the implementation that is called by the public methods when an error is detected.

This error method can print messages, ask for additional input if appropriate, or abort the application if necessary. What this application cannot do is clean up the stack and back out of a routine in a special error state as an exception handler could. Using this approach, the error method often invokes the error method of the parent classes and component classes.

Neither of the approaches described here provides the comprehensive and system-integral facility that an exception handler does. Either can be used for a simple facility in a language that does not provide any more complete solution.

Multiple Implementations

The concepts of a software base presented in this section and the concept of a relation presented in Chapter 5 form a basis for handling multiple implementations of the same class specification. The software base must be capable of maintaining sufficient information about each piece in the base so that a specification can be related to more than one implementation at a time. Attempts to do this in the Ada Programming Support Environment (APSE) have been uneven in their success. The use of relationships (made more explicit by the object-oriented paradigm) to associate elements in the software base provides a great deal of flexibility in modeling relationships between software components.

Figure 9.6 illustrates the relationship used to associate a specification to several implementations. A designer should be able not only to indicate the class of which an instance is needed but also to specify the particular implementation that is desired. Choosing between static and dynamic memory management or between tree-based and hash table-based implementations can be represented so that subclasses are not needed for each different implementation.

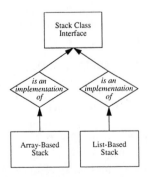

Figure 9.6: Multiple implementations.

APPLICATION IMPLEMENTATION

The implementation of the application seems almost an afterthought once all the classes have been implemented. In fact, the actual implementation of the application is a much simpler, shorter process than in the procedural approach. A college senior once became quite concerned because her main procedure in a C++ program was so small. The project worked—and the first time, too!

Actually we have been implementing the application all along as we developed the classes. Each class provides some piece of the functionality needed for the complete application. The process, of completing the application requires that instances of these classes be created. Some of the needed instances will be created as part of the initialization process for other classes. Others will have to be declared explicitly in some type of main procedure or as a part of the representation of the highest level class in the system.

In C++ there is a `main()` function, as there is in C. This procedure can be used to declare instances of classes that comprise the major objects of the application. In the graphics example, a single instance of the User Interface is created. Once created, one message is sent that starts the command loop of the draw program. This object is then responsible for coordinating the messaging and object creation for the remainder of the life of the system.

The constraint network example in Chapter 8 contains a mainline that creates a number of instances of both connectors and constraints. These instances must communicate with each other so, as the instances are created, addresses of some are provided as parameters to the constructors of others. The two principal duties of the main procedure in a C++ system are creating instances and establishing communications between objects through pointers.

For pure object-oriented languages, every "thing" in the system is an object. There is no "main procedure" in these languages, which are often interactive. The user creates an instance of a class in that environment, which then takes control and executes a method either as a result of instance creation or upon receipt of some message sent by the user. The sequence of messages that result from that original message is the application.

TESTING AN OBJECT-ORIENTED APPLICATION

Testing in the object-oriented paradigm has not received a lot of attention.[1] The literature consists mainly of attempts to adapt procedural testing approaches to the object-oriented paradigm[17]. Perry and Kaiser attempted to show some of the difficulties in testing object-oriented systems by applying Weyuker's adequacy criteria[97]. Unfortunately, their analysis did not adequately accommodate the differences between procedural systems and object-oriented systems. Weyuker's criteria[97, 98] provide a sound basis for determining the adequacy of a test set for a procedurally-developed system that can be viewed as having a single-entry, single-exit structure. Classes

---

[1]The authors would like to thank Dr. Mary Jean Harrold for her leadership in the research program that was a major contributor to the development of this section.

cannot be viewed as having this kind of structure and so Weyuker's criteria cannot be directly applied to the testing of object-oriented systems. However, Harrold, McGregor, and Fitzpatrick[43] provide a restatement of two of the critical axioms in object-oriented terms. Frankl and Doong[30] discuss the testing of object-oriented systems but limit themselves to the behavior of data abstractions. Thus, their work contributes to a testing methodology but is not sufficient because it does not consider the implications that inheritance and polymorphism have for the testing of software. We will present some new ideas on the testing of object-oriented systems based on the techniques reviewed here.

The testing phase in object-oriented application development has the same goal as in the procedural paradigm—to ensure that the software solves the target problem correctly and consistently. To achieve this goal, the testing methodology should detect faults in the software as well as determine whether the software performs the function for which it is being developed. The testing procedure includes the development of a suite of test cases, each of which is intended to exercise a particular element of the application. The results of executing the software with each test case is analyzed to collect information about the software.

Applications undergo many types of testing during the development and delivery process. The testing conducted during the active development of a software system is usually divided into unit testing and integration testing. Unit testing is concerned with testing individual modules. It examines the correctness of the algorithms implemented in the units and the conformity of the return values to the specified results. Integration testing is concerned with how well the individual units work together. The use of appropriate data types as parameters, and so on are of concern. In the object-oriented paradigm, we test at different levels. We test the individual methods within a class, but we are concerned primarily with *class* testing, which combines some aspects of unit testing and some of integration testing.

As before, we will assume that testing an application is the same as testing a class. Even those multiparadigm implementation languages that do not require that every function be associated with an object will require only minimal procedural testing. The testing we will discuss in this section will focus on testing classes and their individual methods, and will not consider acceptance testing or other system-testing issues. As in procedural-testing methodologies, we will assume the existence of an "oracle" that can determine the outcome of a test by reviewing the results of executing a method with a set of test cases. This oracle will most often be the developer of a particular class.

The test suite for a class will consist of cases chosen to satisfy the testing requirements that we will discuss in the following sections. Figure 9.7 gives the skeleton for such a test suite. Each test case is a sequence of values that serves as inputs to the system to carry it through the manipulations required to satisfy the testing requirements. Each test case should include the arguments to a constructor function to place the object in a known state before beginning to test methods. We will also assume a layered approach to the testing. There is some primitive level of classes that we will consider as having been tested. We will consider the interaction of our classes with these primitive classes, but we will assume that any message sent to an instance of one of these primitive classes will behave properly given appropriate inputs.

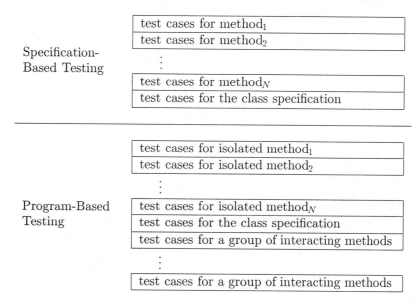

Specification-
Based Testing

| test cases for method$_1$ |
| test cases for method$_2$ |
| $\vdots$ |
| test cases for method$_N$ |
| test cases for the class specification |

Program-Based
Testing

| test cases for isolated method$_1$ |
| test cases for isolated method$_2$ |
| $\vdots$ |
| test cases for isolated method$_N$ |
| test cases for the class specification |
| test cases for a group of interacting methods |
| $\vdots$ |
| test cases for a group of interacting methods |

Figure 9.7: Test suite for a class.

Class Testing

Class testing is the initial testing phase in the class life cycle. These individual components, the classes, may be used in a number of different applications over time. The users of those components must be able to assume that each class is reliable and can be reused without having to explore the implementation details. The class will be tested in isolation as much as possible so that our confidence is based on the unit and not on the context in which it is tested.

The test suite for a class can be defined by first testing each of the methods in it. The suite is then further expanded to provide a form of interaction testing in which methods that call other methods in the class and those that access the same class data are tested together. If both pre- and postconditions have been developed for the methods in a class, they will provide guidance in the development of the test cases for the individual methods. Doong and Frankl use an algebraic specification technique as the basis for generating test cases. This can be adapted to the object-oriented technique by using a formal specification technique such as Object-Z, an object-oriented extension of the Z specification formalism.

Class testing includes two major forms: *specification-based* and *program-based*. Specification-based testing treats the class as a black box. This is intended to determine whether the class is performing according to its specification. For example, if the class is a Stack, testing should ensure that the LIFO policy is being enforced. Program-based testing considers the implementation of the class. The testing is intended to determine whether the code has been written correctly. For example, in the Stack class, we want to be certain that all code has been exercised at least once and that it performed the appropriate actions.

Specification-Based Testing

The specification-based testing includes two levels: class specification and method specification.

- *Class specification.* The specification of a class is a combination of the specifications of each individual method and a broader statement of the concept that the class is intended to represent. For example, a Stack class would include specifications for the methods push and pop, but these specifications would not convey how these two operations behave when working together in a class. The specification for push would state that the parametric value is added to the "top" of a stack but would not say anything about deletions, and the specification for pop would similarly not describe how the removed item had been placed on a stack. Only in the class-level specification is the LIFO idea represented. The formalisms for expressing and reasoning about types can be used to provide some support for specifying the class, but a class is more than a type so these methods lack support for the full semantics of a class. In particular, inheritance is most often not represented in those formal techniques.

  The specification of a C^{++} class is multitiered. For most other classes, the specification of the class are those methods contained in the public area of the class definition. Subclasses will see an expanded interface that includes both the *public* and *protected* areas. The methods defined within the class will see an interface that includes all three access levels: public:, protected:, and private:. While these could be considered separately, a class should have all of its specified behavior tested.

- *Method specification.* The specification for an individual method is defined by the preconditions and postconditions for the method as well as by its signature. Based on the preconditions, test cases are selected to produce outputs that permit the oracle to judge whether the postconditions are being met. The testing of the individual method specifications will not differ significantly from the testing of the specifications for individual procedures.

Program-Based Testing

The program-based testing of a class will test the individual pieces—the methods—of a class, and it will test the class as a unit. On the first level, the testing plan will consider the code in the individual methods that belong to the class. The second level of testing will consider the interactions between methods. Figure 9.8 presents a *class graph* that illustrates the cases in which two methods access the same data within the class representation or that interact by one method calling the other. Each method can be tested over its full domain of inputs, but this is still insufficient to claim that the testing is adequate until the interactions of these methods are also tested. The testing of the complete unit should ensure that the class be exercised over a representative set

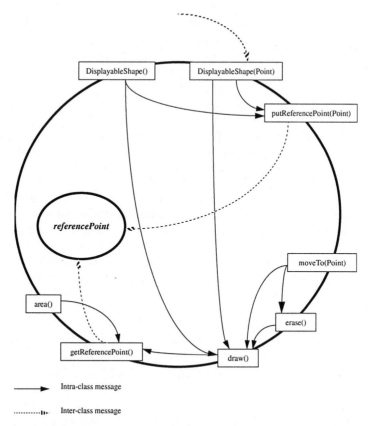

Figure 9.8: Interaction between Displayable Shape and Point classes via messages.

of its states. The selection of parametric values for the constructors and the sequences of messages should be chosen to meet this criterion.

- *Methods in isolation.* The first level of program-based testing considers each individual method. These can be tested in much the same way as any procedure. The most significant difference between testing a method and a procedure is that the method may change the state of the instance to which it belongs. The oracle will need access to this hidden state information to evaluate the result of a test. Any messages that are sent to other objects are ignored and replaced by stubs that return appropriate values. Test data is selected using conventional testing techniques to assure adequate coverage of the code in the class.

- *Methods in integration.* This second level of testing considers the interaction of one method calling another within the same class (*intra*class) and messages from one class to another (*inter*class). Testing either of the two methods in isolation examines the quality of their implementation but may not uncover subtle problems of sequencing. Test cases that invoke these interactions will be added to the test suite and the oracle must determine whether the interaction is handled appropriately. The intraclass testing involves little or no flow of data since both methods have access to the representation of the class. Exercising all major states of the class is an important adequacy criterion for this type of testing.

Integration Testing

In the object-oriented paradigm, integration testing occurs at two levels. Testing a new class also tests the integration of those classes that participate in its definition. The *is a*, *is part of*, and *refers to* relations establish dependencies between classes that require testing and that imply an ordering to the testing of the several classes. Once primitive classes first are tested, classes that use them can then be tested, and so on in layers. Each layer uses as the building blocks for its representation those classes that have been previously defined and tested. When a message is sent from the class being tested to an instance of another class, the current testing can be limited to *domain* testing (in which the message is examined to be certain that the actual parameters come from the appropriate domains if the receiving class has already been tested.)

The special challenge for integration testing in the object-oriented domain is that elements are being brought together that were not specifically written for use in the current application. Since the focus of integration testing is the coordination between modules, it is important to test the coordination between classes that have never worked together. Termed *interclass* in the previous section, this testing will assume that each class has been tested separately in isolation. It includes messages to an instance of a class used as part of the representation of that class. It also includes a message sent to a parameter that has been passed to a method. The challenge in this testing is the use of instances of classes as parameters to methods of classes that were developed, tested, and integrated before the classes being used as parameters were even created!

The second level of integration testing is the formal process of bringing together all the pieces that make up the completed application. In the main procedure of a C++ application, appropriate instances of a few high-level and global classes are created. Often these instances must communicate with each other. The top level of the application may, as it creates these instances, provide the address of one object to another. The test cases chosen for this testing should address the purpose of the application and should provide data for the testing oracle to use in determining whether the application accomplishes its purpose.

Testing a Subclass

Many claims and counterclaims have been made about the testability of object-oriented systems. Perry and Kaiser use Weyuker's test adequacy criteria to argue that testing object-oriented systems is not as much improved over testing procedural systems as one might believe. Their analysis, however, mistakenly compares Weyuker's notion of a program to a class. There is much that must be tested in an object-oriented application; however, the structure of the application class definitions can be used to support an approach that reuses test cases from one class to another. The outline

```
class DisplayableShape {
  private:
    Point referencePoint;
    Color shapeColor;
    Matrix transformMatrix;

  protected:
    void setReferencePoint(Point);
    Point getReferencePoint();

  public:
    DisplayableShape();
    void erase();
    virtual void draw() = 0;
    void move();
    void rotate();
    void translate(int xDistance, int yDistance);
}
```

Figure 9.9: The class specification for Displayable Shape.

above presents a methodology for testing an individual class that has no ancestors. Harrold and McGregor[42] have presented an algorithm that takes advantage of the complete testing of the base class and the inheritance relationship to reuse existing test cases from the test suites of the parent class(es) in the test suite of a subclass. This technique incrementally develops the test suite for a class based on its hierarchical relationships with its ancestors, and is thus termed *hierarchical incremental testing*. We will first lay out a test plan for an individual class and then consider the hierarchical incremental testing algorithm to show how to develop the test suite for subclasses.

Let's consider testing a class that models shapes that can be displayed on a graphic display device. Figure 9.9 shows the interface of a class Displayable Shape. Figure 9.10 shows the implementation of a selection of some methods, and Figure 9.11 shows two other classes upon which the implementation of our class depends.

Before developing the test suite for this class, we need to consider a complication that is introduced by our C++ realization of it. The class defined in Figure 9.9 is termed an *abstract class* because the draw method does not have an implementation, as indicated by the "= 0" after the signature of the draw method. No instances of this class can be created to support execution of program-based test cases. Technically, we can, and will, replace the "= 0" with a null implementation, "{}." However, we must be aware that for a class we may not be able to test the complete specification because not every method will necessarily have a complete implementation. This has wider implications. The implementation of move uses the draw method. The null implementation of draw would allow that method to execute but, if there had been a required return value from draw, we would have needed to build a stub for draw that would return an appropriate value.

```
void DisplayableShape::move(Point newLocation)
{
    erase();
    setReferencePoint(newLocation);
    draw();
}

void DisplayableShape::setReferencePoint(Point p)
{
    referencePoint = p;
}
```

Figure 9.10: Implementations of some methods for Displayable Shape.

```
class Point {
  private:
     Integer x;
     Integer y;

  public:
     Point();
     Point(int, int);

     &Point operator=(Point);
     &stream operator<<(&stream);
     :
}

class Integer {
  private:
     int value;

  public:
     Integer();
     Integer(int);

     &Integer operator=(Integer);
     &stream operator<<(&stream);
     :
}
```

Figure 9.11: Classes used in the implementation of Displayable Shape.

The setReferencePoint method in the protected area of the Point definition illustrates another problem for testing object-oriented systems. The result of the method is not outwardly obvious because the data it is setting is in the private area. So the oracle will have to introduce temporary access functions to provide a view of this private area, if they do not already exist, to be able to determine whether some of the methods correctly performed their functions.

The Test Plan

The specification of Displayable Shape will not be completely testable. Most of the methods cannot be tested as part of an instance of Displayable Shape because their explicit behavior includes drawing the shape. Since the draw method is not implemented in the shape class, it is not possible to be certain that move, erase, or rotate work properly. We can test the low-level methods like getReferencePoint and setReferencePoint. Program-based testing can be performed on each of the methods except draw. For methods that rely on draw, the dummy implementation will not draw the shape, but it will provide a means for testing the remainder of the code. The most likely stub would draw the reference point at its current location.

Let's consider testing the setReferencePoint method. Figure 9.12 shows the hier-

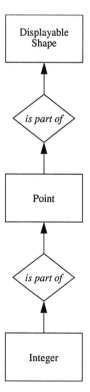

Figure 9.12: Implementation hierarchy for Displayable Shape.

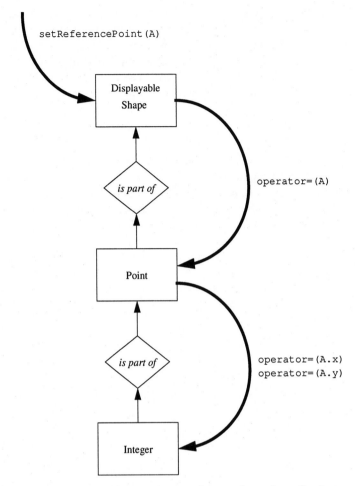

Figure 9.13: Hierarchy of messages to change the value of referencePoint.

archy of classes that support the implementation of setReferencePoint. In other words, when the setReferencePoint message is sent to an instance of Displayable Shape, a series of messages is initiated. Figure 9.13 shows the sequence of messages that occur as a result of this message. A testing plan would first test primitive classes such as the Integer. Domain-specific classes that are still very general such as Point would be tested next, and finally application-specific classes such as Displayable Shape would be tested. Obviously, classes should not have to be totally retested for each new application.

Testing the Subclasses of DisplayableShape

The hierarchical incremental testing algorithm allows the testing of a subclass to begin with the test cases of the ancestor classes, just as the inheritance relationship allows the definition of the subclass to begin with the definitions of the ancestor classes. The test suite is developed by examining the definition of the subclass and determining those parts of the class that are new. Many test cases can be eliminated from the ancestors' test suite because the pieces of the definition to which these cases correspond do not need to be retested. By treating specification, program-based, and interaction testing separately, we have three distinct sets of test cases from which to select those that require retesting. Other test cases will be added because those pieces have been newly defined, either as additions to the previous classes or as redefinitions of existing pieces.

GRAPHICS CLASSES

We will consider a number of issues that relate to the implementation of our graphics example and present a few of the C++ header files that help illustrate the concepts without too much detail. We will not give details of the implementation of any graphics classes here.

Development of Graphics Classes

The design of any computer-based system requires assumptions, and object-oriented systems are no exception. Perhaps the most fundamental assumption in the graphics system is how the image is to be displayed. In our system there is a set of classes, each representing a different type of display device. For our simple purposes here, a global instance of the Display Device class is considered to be available to each shape class. This instance might be included in a header file in the Displayable Shape header if we implement in C++, as it was in the implementation of the class line in Figure 8.18 using file `globals.h`. While global variables are not desirable, our system has very few compared to the usual draw program.

Display Device Classes

The display device classes encapsulate the mechanics of accessing each of the types of displays upon which we wish to run. A set of graphics primitives was chosen as the basic functionality that a device must provide. For this system, the graphics primitives were a point and a line. (The X-windowing system, for example, uses point, line, and arc.) Users of the display device family of classes are assured that each of these classes can provide the two specified primitives. The graphics system is based on this assurance, which is provided via the interface of the first class in the display device inheritance hierarchy. This interface is the minimum we can expect *every* class in the family to support. Subclasses may define additional behavior, but designers who want portability will only assume the functionality defined in the top-level class.

The history of the hierarchy of devices shown in Figure 9.14 illustrates the evolution of these classes. This hierarchy started some time ago when only a Tektronix 4014 terminal was being used for the graphics system. Later a Tektronix 4105 terminal was available and a class had to be created to represent that device. The initial reaction was to make the Tek 4105 class a subclass of the Tek 4014 class. The Tek 4105 terminal did almost everything that the 4014 did, with some new features. However,

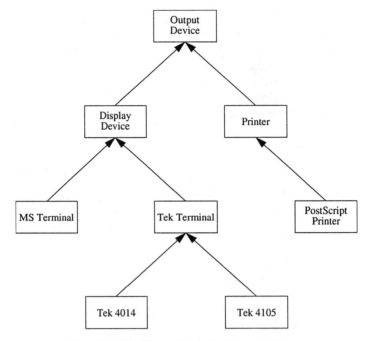

Figure 9.14: Hierarchy of output devices.

it had eliminated a small part of the functionality of the 4014. Because of this small difference, the generalization operator was used to factor out the commonalities between the 4014 and 4105 classes and place those in a higher level class, Tek Terminal. This structure is a true picture of the relationships between the types of Tektronix terminals and provides a sound base for adding other Tektronix devices later.

Figure 9.15 shows the interface of the Tek Terminal class. This interface includes the capabilities to draw a dot and a line at a given location on the terminal. Exactly how this is done is hidden from the user of the terminal instance, and will differ. With one device, the arguments to the terminal object will be used as input to a line-drawing algorithm, which will use the dot class to produce the final line. In another, the arguments will be passed directly to the terminal, which has built-in line-drawing capabilities.

The Polygon Class

The assumption about graphics primitives impacts each of the shape classes. The draw method of each shape uses the graphics primitives and the global terminal instance to display its image on the device. The interface of the Polygon class is shown in Figure 9.16. There are two elementary approaches to the basic representation of a polygon. We may think of a polygon as having N vertices or locations in space that determine the sides of the polygon. The second approach is to consider the polygon to consist of N lines, which are the sides of the polygon. The first approach has a slight advantage

```
class TekTerminal
{
  public:
    void setHorizontalScreenSize(int);
    void setVerticalScreenSize(int);
    int getHorizontalScreenSize();
    int getVerticalScreenSize();

    inline void initiateIncPlotMode();
    inline void initiateGraphicalMode();
    inline void initiateAlphaMode();
    inline void initiateGraphicsCursorMode();

    tekTerminal();

    inline void eraseScreen();
    inline void plotPoint(int, int);
    inline void moveDrawPosition(int, int);

  protected:
    char *encodeInteger(int);

  private:
    int horizontalScreenSize;
    int verticalScreenSize;
}
```

Figure 9.15: Interface for class InterfaceTek

```
class Polygon
{
  public:
    void Polygon(ListOfPoint);

    void draw();
  protected:
    ListOfPoint *listOfVertices;
};
```

Figure 9.16: Interface of class Polygon.

in that no redundant information is stored. If we use the lines as sides, then each vertex is stored twice—once in each of the instances of the lines that intersect at that location. For a rectangle shape, the storage requirements could be reduced to two points, but only if we assume that each side of the rectangle is parallel to an axis. We could save some storage in this case, but it would require the re-implementation of the draw method in class Rectangle.

The implementation of the Polygon class is made easier, faster, and safer by the use of inheritance. Many of the functions needed in the final polygon class are inherited from higher level classes. For example, the move method will work with any shape we can imagine by changing the reference point. A general fill routine can be implemented for any closed figure in class Closed Line. Each new shape has very few methods that must be written specifically for it. The draw and perhaps some methods that support the geometry domain—for example, perimeter and area—must be specialized for each new shape.

During implementation, we must take care to recognize problems that did not show up during design. One example is a problem with storage management. This arises when we design our representation of the vertices in a shape being stored relative to the reference point for the shape. Consider the C++ implementation of the draw method for the class Line in Figure 8.18. In that implementation, we used a point addition operator to convert the endpoints of a line to screen coordinates. The problem arises because point addition returns a Point instance, which we use once as a parameter to the display device in a line-drawing operation. Once that operation is completed, the returned value is "garbage" and must be reclaimed via a `delete` operator. Our implementation of the class does not do this. However, the fix is easy: Assign the result of the point addition to a local variable, say `pt`, and include the statement `delete pt;` after the terminal draw operation.

At this stage in the development process, we may wish to reassess our decision to store shapes relative to the reference point, or we may find a way to design Point to provide some other operator—for example, move—that would modify the existing instance rather than return a new instance that we will have to manage in the code.[2] If we decide to store the vertices of a polygon in absolute coordinates, we have to revise the design of the move method. In any case, we will need some form of point addition. Our final decision will be based on how the system eventually performs. The encapsulation provided by the classes in a structure allows us to change the implementation with no effect on users of those classes.

As we implement the design, we must avoid exposing component objects. In the implementation of the method referencePoint in the Displayable Shape class, we must take care not to return a pointer to the instance of referencePoint, but rather a pointer to a *copy* of the reference point. Similarly, when we set the reference point, we should set it to a copy of the point received as a parameter to setReferencePoint. By returning a copy, we can eliminate any possibility of another object's manipulating the reference point directly. This is important; if, for example, we decide later to store the vertices of a polygon in absolute coordinates, then any change to the reference point in an instance implies a change to all the vertices as well. If a reference point can

---

[2] In the latter case we must be *very* careful about how point instances are shared among objects!

```
class UserInterface
{
  public:
    void draw();
    void refresh();
    void go();
  protected:
    int numberOfChoices;
    selectorBox selectorBoxes[];
    shapeList shapes;
    Rectangle outerFrame;
    Rectangle drawingAreaFrame;
}
```

Figure 9.17: Interface for class User Interface.

be manipulated directly, then any update to the vertices will not occur. Returning a copy completely hides our implementation, but at a cost of more objects "floating around" in the application whose storage must be managed.

Interface Class

The implementation of the user interface class is the final assembly in this application. Once the user interface class has been built, it totally encapsulates the behavior of the application. The user interface object has few methods—only those needed to start up the draw program. The main routine in this object is the command loop that waits for a user action and then determines what function to invoke.

The invoked functions are class methods from the Displayable Shape classes. The implementation of the user interface is modular so that new shapes can be added without major revision to the user interface class. The design also includes a flexible design of the user interface. The pieces can be moved anywhere the user wishes because the shapes in the interface come from our shape classes. The outer frame and the box around the drawing area are instances of the Rectangle class. Figure 9.17 provides an illustration of the internals of the User Interface class.

The small boxes that form the menu of actions are Selector Box instances. They are held on a polymorphic list that accepts instances of any selector box class. Selector Box is a general class that provides methods that can determine if a mouse button press/release has occurred within its boundaries. Specialized Selector Box classes are created for each shape class. The use of specialized classes is the one piece of overhead that is imposed by this approach to the user interface design. Figure 9.18 illustrates the relationships among these classes.

The user interface is also responsible for maintaining the image, which is actually the sequence of individual shape instances that are selected and positioned by the user. This image is maintained as a list of Displayable Shape instances. This polymorphic list holds instances of any of the Displayable Shape classes and is used to refresh the

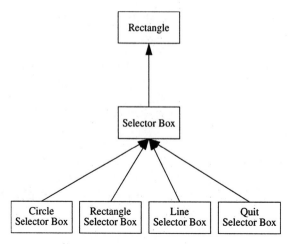

Figure 9.18: Selector classes.

display. The draw routine for the system does nothing but iterate over this list and sends the "draw" message to each shape on the list.

Testing the Line Class

We have chosen the line class to illustrate testing because it is not very large but is representative of all the shape classes. The testing plan of the class should:

1. Exercise each method in the class.
2. Use values chosen using the preconditions of each method.
3. Consider interactions of the methods.
4. Account for all states of the class.

The person developing test cases should consider the common problems with algorithms in the area of the concept being modeled. This can often be related to the domains of the inputs. By considering significant milestones such as changing from positive to zero to negative, test cases can be developed that explore the usual areas of difficulty. For a line-drawing algorithm, for example, lines with positive and negative slope as well as horizontal and vertical lines should be tested to be certain that they will be displayed properly.

The line class uses two points to model the line. Routines for allowing the user to enter the two endpoints via the mouse have already been tested. Thus we have a case of integration testing. These instances of the Point class are being integrated with other code to model the concept of a line. If the Point routines are well tested, then writing the routine to enter a line via the mouse is a quick task.

Consider the hierarchy of Displayable Shape classes. Based on the work done to test class Displayable Shape, there are test suites available for the methods of that class. There are specification-based test cases for all the methods in the class, program-based test cases for those methods that were implemented in the class, and interface test cases for those methods that interact in the Displayable Shape class. When we begin to test the more specific classes such as Line, some of these test cases will be reused. Let's consider a few of the methods in Line.

- move. The method move is completely implemented in the superclass. Therefore, the specification-based and the program-based testing will not be repeated at this level. If the move method interacts with any methods in Line, then interaction test cases will be developed and executed. These test cases will be added to the class's test suite. Much effort has been saved by not retesting the class.
- draw. The draw method was not implemented in the superclass so no program-based test cases were developed, nor could they have been executed. The specification-based test cases were developed based on the intent and signature of draw, but were not executed. To test class Line, program-based test cases are constructed and executed. The reuse of these test cases saves time.
- *New attributes.* Two new attributes are introduced at this level—the two endpoints of the line. However, since we do not provide new operations for these attributes and their only role once a line is constructed is in connection with the draw operator, no program-based test cases are required just because of these attributes. draw is a newly defined method, as is the constructor for the class. These must be tested as they would have been even if no new attributes were present. If new methods were provided for an added attribute, then new test cases would need to be constructed and executed. Reuse cannot be expected at all.

The Draw Application

The length of this discussion should indicate the effort necessary to produce the desired application from the component parts. Figure 9.17, which exhibited the internals of the user interface, shows "the application." In the C++ implementation, the main routine need have only two lines. One line creates the instance of the user interface and the second initiates the command loop via the message go.

SUMMARY

There are a number of considerations in the implementation of a class. Our first concern should be to reuse existing components whenever possible. This reuse may be direct in the sense that an instance of the class is created with no modification to it. The reuse may be evolutionary in that the new class is created from an existing class or classes. When reuse is not possible, a class that is a robust model of the needed abstraction should be created from scratch. The information-hiding and encapsulation properties available in most object-oriented languages support this task.

The testing of object-oriented systems is an evolving methodology. The procedures presented in this chapter attempt to address the class as a collection of methods and as a unit that is a model of a concept. The testing of object-oriented systems is more efficient but more complex than the testing of procedural systems. The methodology should and does take advantage of the special characteristics of the object-oriented paradigm. The inheritance relationship is exploited to reuse test cases and to incrementally build the test suite for a class.

We have not talked about coding in this chapter on implementation; that may be viewed as an unusual approach. However, there are many excellent texts on specific programming languages, and we cannot do any of them justice in such a small space. The concepts we have discussed are important implementation issues no matter what the language.

FURTHER READING

Most implementation issues are addressed in language-specific texts. The C++chapter includes references to applicable books on that language. Goldberg and Robson[37] provide a comprehensive view of Smalltalk-80. Meyer[73] provides a good overview of the Eiffel language. Many other languages are available but we will not attempt a comprehensive list here.

The testing of object-oriented systems is still an active research area. Perry and Kaiser[79] provide a good overview of some of the concerns in object-oriented testing. Harrold, McGregor[42] and Harrold, McGregor, and Fitzpatrick[43] provide details of a reuse-oriented class testing methodology.

10

Designing Reusable Classes

One important goal for software design in today's environment is to produce components that can be reused. This has certainly been one of the central themes of this text. Reuse does not happen by accident. The developer must explicitly make decisions intended to generalize and standardize the results of the design process. Decisions that affect the reusability of classes are made at both the design and implementation levels. One technique for producing reusable components is to develop general components. This is both an attribute of a class and a *kind* of class. As an attribute it refers to a continuum, ranging from seldom to often useful, that describes the applicability of the class in application development. As a kind of class, it describes a class that can be applied to a wide range of inputs without modification.

At the design level, the possibility of reuse can be enhanced by modeling concepts at a level that is as abstract as possible. The responsibilities of a class should be specified as generally as possible. For example, when a parameter is specified, the designated class should be the highest one in its inheritance structure that provides the appropriate functionality. This provides the broadest range of classes that can provide instances for actual parameters to the method.

During the implementation phase, decisions about reuse can have a profound impact on the performance and generality of class instances. A number of language features are available that facilitate building generality into classes. They provide powerful mechanisms while supporting the writing of safe and reliable code.

The term *general class* is a relative one. We are concerned with the decisions that will make a class more general than it might be if it were simply designed to perform a specific task within a specific application. Some classes will be sufficiently general to be used in almost any application, while others will be of use to a select group of domain-specific applications. The guidelines and techniques presented in this chapter will increase the generality of classes.

Why should we care about making classes more reusable? The economics of software development are forcing companies to search for ways to improve productivity. Two widely used measures of software development productivity are percent of project completed and number of lines of code completed. If many of those lines of code can be produced through the reuse of existing code, the cost of software can be reduced significantly and the time to bring a product to market will also be reduced.

A second reason for making more classes more reusable stems from the fact that we are beginning to see a market for reusable components. Chances are good that if you need a set of classes, some other developer also needs them. Many companies are willing to pay for quality software packages rather than pay for the development of the same software.

In this chapter we will distinguish between reuse and generality. We will take generality as a characteristic that supports reuse. As a consequence, this chapter is also about generality. Not all techniques that improve reuse affect the generality of a class. We will consider these other techniques in the next chapter.

CHARACTERISTICS OF REUSABLE CLASSES

What qualities characterize classes that are general and reusable?

- *Domain independence.* The class should be as independent as possible of any problem domain. It is easy to see that artifacts such as counters and timers can be defined, implemented, and used in a variety of applications, but it is more difficult to build application-specific classes that are general.
- *Complete functionality.* The class should provide the complete behavior expected of instances of the concept being modeled.
- *Multiple implementations.* The class should have multiple implementations that provide different runtime characteristics to allow designers a choice. The techniques of abstraction and information hiding support this characteristic.
- *Genericity.* A generic component specifies an algorithm without regard to a specific data type. The type is provided at the time that an instance of the component is instantiated. This is an implementation-dependent characteristic; in typeless languages this feature is available basically for "free."

TYPED VERSUS NON-TYPED IMPLEMENTATIONS

Removing the limitations imposed by typing systems would appear to make components more widely usable because there are no language restrictions on where a component may appear. The fact is that a component's appropriateness is a matter of design that is unrelated to the type name associated with the component. Declaring the types of components and parameters supports the automation of discriminating legal from illegal usage. Removing the type checking in a language does not broaden the applicability of a class, but only suppresses complaints about potentially illegal use of a component. We do not get more reuse in a non-typed environment, but we do get a system in which we have much less confidence!

Many veteran C programmers have encountered the strong type checking of C++ and have decided C++ is "too complicated." Languages range from the essentially typeless environment of LISP to the strongly typed Ada. C and C++ lie between these two extremes. C functions impose type restrictions on parameters, but C does not require that the actual parameters match the declaration of the function's formal parameters. C++ does require that formal and actual parameters match but introduces the flexibility of polymorphism to allow a range of actual parameter types to match the one formal definition.

A typed language relieves the programmer from the ultimate responsibility of compatibility because the translation process will provide the checking. The typed language environment does impose a discipline upon the developer that forces attention to conformity to typing rules. This can slow the development process by causing the programmer to cross-reference information. The typeless environment of a language such as Smalltalk can free the programmer to think more about modeling and abstractions of the application and thus may result in more general classes than in a typed environment.

Typing of parameters and checking the conformance between formal and actual parameters is important to the systematic development of reliable software components— particularly in the object-oriented paradigm. When an instance of a class is a parameter in a message, it is the recipient of messages from within the method that processes the message in which it is a parameter. Type checking ensures at compile time that the particular instance used as the parameter can legitimately be the recipient of these messages. Interpreted, typeless environments do not provide this kind of safety.

Type checking does not diminish the potential for reuse. A typed container class may not be quite as flexible as an untyped one, but it is still very reusable even though the domain of objects to which it can be applied has been narrowed. We almost always know some reasonable restriction on the objects that will be encountered. We will see later that the technique of generics will assist in developing classes that provide both type checking and generality. The flexibility introduced into a typing system by polymorphism also supports reuse and generality. The combination of these two techniques produces very powerful components.

We will, in general, have more confidence in a system implemented in a strongly typed environment, but we will also be able to prototype more quickly in a less strict environment. This has long been recognized and has resulted in a number of translators, such as LISP-to-C converters. This allows initial development in one language that supports quick and easy modifications, followed by conversion to production-quality code in another language that will provide many static checking facilities.

GENERAL CLASSES

By a *general class* we mean a class that can be used across many application domains. These are utility classes that provide a basic implementation functionality. Classes that implement basic data structures—lists, trees, and so on—or that count or that perform operations such as windowing are general purpose components.

There are several ways that classes can be made more general. The purpose for which the class is intended can contribute to its generality. The container classes, first prominently used in Smalltalk, are intended to hold instances of classes. The behavior of these classes is independent of the types of the instances being held. These classes are general in that they may be used in a variety of applications that need groups of objects held, ordered, or returned in a systematic manner.

This idea can be carried beyond the usual container classes to include a number of general data structures. These standard organizations of data apply in the object-oriented world as much as in the procedural world. The lists—linked, one-way, or circular, with headers and without—are containers of a sort, as are graphs.

The most powerful and broadly applicable approach to generality is to provide a model of an abstraction. The recognition and design of good abstractions is very difficult. In a language such as C++, the individual inheritance structures should begin with a class that is a model of an abstraction. Even in languages with a single root class, it is possible to organize groupings of classes in the structure that are derived from a model of an abstraction.

In this section, we will consider classes that illustrate each of these approaches.

Container Classes

One of the attractive features of Smalltalk is that it provides a number of very general classes—such as bags and sets—that hold and organize instances of other classes. These classes, coupled with those that represent the standard data structures such as stacks and queues, provide an environment in which an implementer has several basic resources. A number of such classes can be developed in most any language environment.

The container classes from the Smalltalk programming environment have now been replicated in and adapted to a number of object-oriented languages. These classes, described in [37] and shown in Figure 10.1, provide a variety of ordering and accessing possibilities. We will consider a few of them, their purpose, and their interface.

The Bag class is one of the most general container classes. A bag holds objects that are placed "in" it with no assumptions about order and no considerations regarding duplicates.

The Set class is very much like the bag class except that no duplicates are allowed. This is a very important consideration. How is something defined as a duplicate? Generally, duplication is determined based on the use of an equality ("=") operator defined for the classes being placed in the set. Thus, any instance placed in a set must respond to a message to check equality.

The Sequenceable Collection class makes assumptions about the order. It maintains items in the order in which they were placed in the collection. This is an important class because it can serve as the basis for a number of other classes that maintain specialized orderings. For example, the Array class extends the Sequenceable Collection class by placing the instances it is to contain in order based on a provided integer key.

In a typeless environment such as Smalltalk these classes are very general. In a

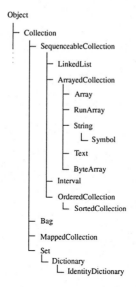

Figure 10.1: Some of the Smalltalk collection classes.

strongly typed language such as C++, it is more difficult to support this generality. Although the basic functionality can be provided, it must be duplicated and modified to provide typing information for different situations. The discussion on generics below will give some approaches to handling this.

Figure 10.2 provides a hierarchy that places the classes mentioned above in relation to each other as implemented by Gorlen in the NIH Class Library[38]. The top class in the structure provides the basic interface for the classes in the remainder of the structure. The basic operations on a collection include:

addItem
removeItem
isIn
print

Each class is free to add operations to the interface, but the most useful idea is for a class to redefine the behavior of the existing operations. This allows for plug-compatible objects that may be interchanged to modify the operation of a given system.

Standard Data Structures

There is a fine line of distinction (sometimes a nonexistent line) between the container classes above and the abstract data types encountered in "Data Structures 101." Polymorphism is still important in these structures. These general classes will not often be entities that are recognized in the analysis phase. Most often they will be used to support the modeling of some real-world entity rather than being the direct representation of the concept.

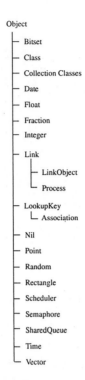

Figure 10.2: The NIH Class Library class hierarchy.

Gorlen, in the NIH Class Library, provides several general data structures. Linked lists, stacks, and queues are all recognized as useful members of the developer's tool kit. Another general class that is not often found in toolkits is a graph or network structure. In the same vein as our earlier discussion about modeling a linked list (see Chapter 7), this probably is a concept that would best be represented by more than one class. The typical decomposition would be a class for the nodes and a class for the edges. The node class would actually be one of several subclasses, depending upon what the node is to hold. As with the linked list, a traverser class would provide instances to allow algorithms to "keep their place" in the graph as they go away to process and return to continue traversing. Finally, a class to represent the graph itself would be a container of nodes and edges.

Abstractions

An abstraction is an idea formed by separating a concept from particular instantiations of that concept. We are looking for ideas that could be the basis of a number of more specific classes. One place to look for these classes is in our experience. A domain analysis of software engineering should provide many ideas. In software design we often see commonalities among the components that we design. We will present two examples.

<table>
<tr><td align="center">Counter</td></tr>
</table>

Counter
counterValue
baseValue
initialValue
limit
increment
decrement
initialize
reset
showValue
create(stepSize)

Figure 10.3: The large-class approach to the design of a counter.

Counters

Many classes behave like a simple counter. In fact, many systems need counters. Calculating summary statistics for a set of data may involve an array of simple counters that keep track of the number of occurrences of a discrete set of events.

The design of a set of counter classes can illustrate the two different approaches that can be taken in class design. First, we could design a class that incorporates all the features we can ever consider for a counter. This leads to a laundry list of methods, many of which are not needed for a given application. The resulting class might have an interface like that in Figure 10.3.

This design of the counter class has advantages and disadvantages. The class will often be larger than necessary and may introduce inefficiency into the system. The implementation of an all-purpose counter may include data values that are not often required for most uses of a counter. Users of the class may inadvertently use the incorrect method, leading to incorrect results. For example, a counter might be used to represent time in a simulation. A developer might, accidentally, reset the counter or decrement it, thereby causing time to run backwards!

The advantage of this design is that this one component has all the features of all counters. The developer need only learn one class. Larger numbers of smaller components forces the developer to spend more time comparing classes to determine the one best suited for the current application.

The design illustrated in Figure 10.4 uses a layered, incremental approach to the development of a set of counter classes. At the root of this structure is a very basic class, **Simple Counter**. A **Simple Counter** has a value, it can be initialized to a starting value, it can be incremented, and it can return its current value. This class fulfills the role of a normal elementary counter. It cannot be accidentally reset.

A second class provides more functionality and flexibility. **Unidirectional Counter** builds on the **Simple Counter** by adding the ability to set the amount by which the counter is incremented with each "bump." Since the step used in this class can be

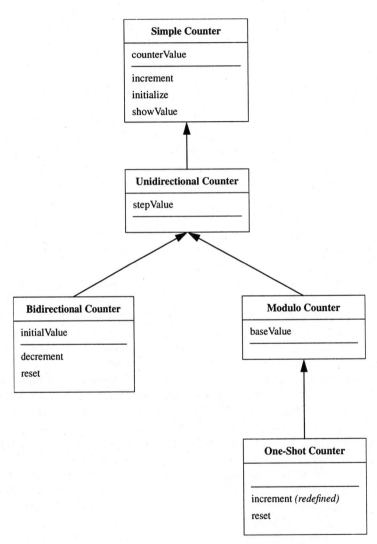

Figure 10.4: An incremental, small-class approach to the design of a counter.

either positive or negative, the Unidirectional Counter may either increase or decrease, but a given instance can only do one or the other.

At the next level, a Bidirectional Counter is defined. Similar to the Unidirectional Counter, this class defines counters that may either be incremented or decremented by the amount of the specified step. Once the ability to move in both directions is provided, the ability to reset the counter can also be added with no loss of safety—that is, a reset method provides convenience for an operation that can be performed using the other methods. Also at this level, a Modulo Counter is defined. This counter counts until it reaches a specified limit and then it "wraps around."

These specializations require additional data values to support their operation. The Bidirectional Counter requires that the original value, given to the counter during initialization, be saved so that the reset method will return to the appropriate value. The Modulo Counter requires a base value that signals the end of a cycle.

A final specialization can be seen. The Modulo Counter can be specialized to provide what we call a One-Shot Counter. This is a counter that does not reset automatically when it reaches the limit. It will count to a certain value and then stop. Specific implementations of the increment method might issue an error message when attempts are made to increase the counter beyond the limit, might raise an exception if such a facility is available, or may simply return a value indicating failure.

Access-Oriented Classes

Unlike the container-type classes, a complete hierarchy is not always necessary to provide a good abstraction. We consider here the development of an abstraction to support the access-oriented paradigm[86].

Here the concept is simple: formal, controlled side effects. The idea is to provide an encapsulated value. Whenever the value is "touched"—initialized, set, or read—an action is carried out in addition to the expected action of updating or returning the value. This additional action is provided in the form of user-defined functions. There should be one function for each of the standard methods of initialize, set, and read. These may be—and often are—the same function.

This class is an example of a small *framework*, which is an abstraction of abstractions. It is developed by considering many instances of the structures in various applications. From these instances, a parameterized section of code is developed that can be instantiated to provide a significant component in an application.

Figure 10.5 shows the class description for a realization of the access-oriented paradigm. The constructor for the class takes as its parameters pointers to user-defined functions. These will be used as the side effects when any of the three methods is activated. Figure 10.6 shows a subclass of the access-oriented class that specializes the definition to protect instances of integers.

An example of the use of this abstraction is the development of a gauge class for use in a user interface. The class we are interested in is actually a discrete-valued gauge that has been termed a *digi-meter*. The digi-meter is the visual representation of a discrete value—we will assume integer for this example. This value is what will be protected. Any attempt to reference or change the value must use one of the three interface methods: initialize, set, and read. Each of these will not only perform the

```
typedef void (* func)(void *);
    // pointer to function having one parameter,
    // a pointer to anything

class ActiveValue {
  public:
    ActiveValue();   // constructor
    ActiveValue(func, func, func);   // constructor

    void set(void *);   // set the encapsulated value
    void *get();   // return the value
    void initialize(void *);   // initialize the value
    void setFuncs(func, func, func);   // set trigger fcns

  private:
    void *value;   // encapsulated value
    func setFunction;   // function triggered by a set
    func getFunction;   // function triggered by a get
    func initFunction;   // function triggered on init
}
```

Figure 10.5: A C++ specification for class Active Value.

```
typedef void (* funcInt)(int *);
    // pointer to function having one parameter,
    // a pointer to int

class ActiveInteger:ActiveValue {
  public:
    ActiveInteger();   // constructor
    ActiveInteger(func, func, func);   // constructor

    void set(int *);   // set the value
    void *get();   // return the value
    void initialize(int *);   // initialize the value
    void setFuncs(funcInt, funcInt, funcInt);
            // set trigger fcns
```

Figure 10.6: Specification for class Active Integer.

```
class Digimeter :  public ActiveInteger
{
  public:
    Digimeter();
    void draw(int *);
}
```

Figure 10.7: Specification for class Digimeter.

appropriate action on the value, but will also redraw the gauge with the new value shown in the user interface. The user is notified visually as soon as any change to the value occurs. Figure 10.7 presents the class specification for a digi-meter.

GENERICS

Many of the classes discussed so far in this chapter realize a concept that can be stated quite generally, except for the necessity of type information. The Access Value class must be specialized for each new type of data value that is to be encapsulated. The logic of the algorithms in the class are valid regardless of the type of data being manipulated. In a strongly typed environment, however, the data types used in the class must match their use in the remainder of the application.

One approach to providing the various implementations in a variety of data types is to use subclasses. In C++, for example, an abstract base class can be developed that defines all of the logic. Subclasses are then developed that specify the type of the data and that use the logic of the parent class. While these specific classes are easy to develop from the abstract class, the development of all these classes quickly becomes tedious and cumbersome.

A second approach is to use macros, which take specific data types as parameters and expand a template definition to include the specified data type. The problems with this approach are typical of the problems with macro expansions. For one, it is difficult to have multiple expansions of a macro in the same program unless there is some support for resolving duplicate names that result from the multiple expansions. Macros comprise an error-prone technique that should be used carefully.

The third—and most acceptable—choice is to use generics. The generic language feature is an integral facility for doing much the same as the macros. The definition of a unit is written completely, but in terms of a parameter rather than a specific data type. At the time of declaration of an instance of the unit, a parameter is provided to the instantiation process. That parameter is the specific data type to be used in this instance.

Ada provides support for generics. It is possible to develop both generic subprograms and generic packages. A generic sort procedure is given in Figure 10.8. This procedure sorts an array of elements whose type—ElementType—is a parameter to the generic unit.   The user of such a generic procedure must create an instance of the procedure before actual use. The creation of the instance requires a param-

```
generic
  type ElementType is private;
  type ArrayType is array (INTEGER range <> of ElementType;
  with function "<" (Left, Right : ElementType) return BOOLEAN is <>
procedure Sort(A : in out ArrayType);

procedure Sort(A : in out ArrayType) is
  - - This implements a bubble sort.
  switched : BOOLEAN;
begin
  switched := TRUE; - - Force through the loop once.
  while switched loop
    switched := FALSE;
    for i in A'FIRST..(A'LAST-1) loop
      if A(i+1) < A(i) then
        declare
          temp : ElementType;
        begin
          temp := A(i);
          A(i) := A(i+1);
          A(i+1) := A(i);
        end;
        switched := TRUE;
      end if;
    end loop;
  end loop;
end Sort;
```

Figure 10.8: An Ada generic procedure to sort an array of any element type.

```
with Sort;
procedure Main is
  type FloatArray is array (INTEGER range <>) of FLOAT;
  X : FloatArray(1..10) :=
    ( 1.0, 4.0, 3.0, 2.0, 5.0, 8.0, 0.0, 6.0, 9.0, 7.0 );
  procedure SortFloatArray is

    new Sort(  ElementType   => FLOAT,
               ArrayType     => FloatArray,
               "<"           => STANDARD."<" );
begin
  SortFloatArray(X);
end Main;
```

Figure 10.9: A program instantiating the generic array sort procedure.

```
template<class T,int size> class vector {
  private:
    T* elements[size];
  public:
    vector();

       :

    vector& operator+(vector&);

       :

    void print();
}

vector& operator+(vector& v) {
    vector& result = new vector;
    for ( int i = 0 ; i < size ; ++i )
        result[i] = elements[i] + v[i];
    return result; }

void print() {
    for ( int i = 0 ; i < size ; ++i )
        elements[i]->print();
}
```

Figure 10.10: A C^{++} template definition of class Vector.

eter that specifies the type for which the instance will be used. Figure 10.9 shows an instantiation of the generic function for float values. This instantiation sorts the array in ascending order by specifying the use of the predefined "less than" operator for floating point, designated by STANDARD."<." By changing the comparison function in the instantiation, we can effect a different ordering—for example, using STANDARD.">" in the instantiation will effect sorting in descending order.

Some object-oriented languages, such as Eiffel, also provide a generic facility. The most common generic unit in an object-oriented language is the class. The complete supporting detail, data values, and methods are developed but written in terms of a parameter.

For example, consider a Vector class. A vector is an ordered list of elements all of the same data type. Most operators manipulate all of the elements in a vector in parallel. To add two vectors, the elements are added pairwise with corresponding elements in each vector being added together. The addition used to combine the elements is the addition defined on the type of the elements. The addition of vectors then can be totally defined without direct access to the addition operator of the element type. As long as the element type has an addition operator defined for it—and the compiler can check this at compile time—then the generic definition of vector addition can work. Each of the other arithmetic operators can be similarly defined. Figure 10.10 shows the definition of the vector class as a "template," a new feature of C++. This experimental feature should be included in the third release of AT&T's C++ translator, but the feature is detailed in [90].

A generic vector class has the logic of all the methods as well as all the necessary auxiliary data values defined. What is missing is access to the code for the operators on the vector elements, which is provided by a parameter in the class definition. When an instance of the Vector class is declared, a specific type name and a size must be provided as a parameter. In our example, we needed to create an instance of class Vector in the addition method to hold the result. Any type may be used as the parameter provided that it possesses definitions for all of the operators required by the generic definition. A vector of characters would be possible if operations such as addition have been defined for the character data type.

It is easy to see that generic classes are powerful abstractions. They allow the designer to concentrate on the essential features of the entity described by the class. At the same time, the designer can take advantage of the safety provided by a strong typing system.

POLYMORPHISM VERSUS GENERICS

A polymorphic typing system and generic units are intended to provide controlled flexibility. The polymorphic typing system provides flexibility in the set of types that may be substituted for instances of a specific type. In the object-oriented paradigm, the set of acceptable substitutes is determined by the inheritance relation.

Generic pieces provide flexibility in the definition of abstractions. The definitions only require that the parameters to that abstraction define certain operators.

These two concepts are similar but distinctly different. Generics provide a "static" flexibility in that generic routines may be instantiated for a broad range of different data types, but an instance of the generic component only accepts the one data type that was used as the parameter. Polymorphic routines provide a "dynamic" flexibility. A polymorphic routine only accepts objects from a limited—by inheritance—range of data types, but it will accept those objects in any mixture at any time. It is not necessary to provide complicated mechanisms for creating multiple routines, each of which provides functionality to one data type in the range. The polymorphic routine can handle in rapid succession instances from a wide variety of data types, but these types must all be related by inheritance to the type used as the formal parameter to the component.

An object-oriented language that provides both a generic facility and polymorphic substitution supports the development of very powerful, flexible components that are essentially parameterized by an inheritance structure. For example, Figure 10.11 shows a stack class designed using the template facility of C++. An instance is created using the syntax shown in Figure 10.12(a). The top class of the inheritance structure shown in Figure 10.12(b), class A, is used as the parameter for creating an instance of Stack. The instance of Stack, shown in Figure 10.12(c), contains instances of several of the classes in the hierarchy—all instances of subclasses of A.

```
template<class T>class Stack {
  private:
    T* top;
    T* list;

  public:
    stack();

       ⋮

    void add(T);
    T remove();

       ⋮

    int empty();
}
```

Figure 10.11: A generic stack class.

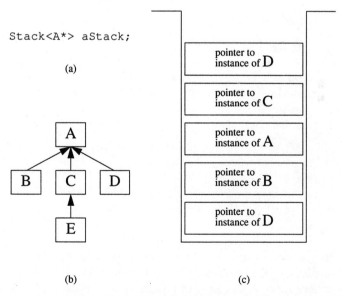

```
Stack<A*> aStack;
```

(a)

(b)   (c)

Figure 10.12: Using the generic stack.

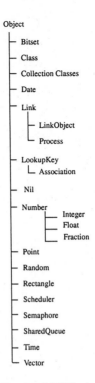

Figure 10.13: Revised NIH class hierarchy.

DESIGNING FOR REUSABILITY

Johnson and Foote[53] provided a list of 13 rules for the designer of reusable classes. Some of these have become standard fare and were the basis for some of our guidelines in Chapter 6. We will consider a couple of special rules directly related to the design of reusable components.

Design Guideline #9: **A set of reusable classes should make maximum use of inheritance to model relationships of the problem domain.**

There are several reasons for using inheritance, but the most important is subtype modeling. Building an inheritance structure that is shallow negates this benefit of inheritance. A large set of classes is hard to learn unless there is some logic to their interrelationships.

It is easy, when we are confronted with a large collection of classes, to not take the time to locate an appropriate slot for the new class. That appropriate parent class—or set of parent classes—is sufficiently high in the hierarchy to not have any

```
class DisplayableShape {
  private:
    Point referencePoint;
    Color shapeColor;

  public:
    DisplayableShape(Point, Color);
    DisplayableShape();

    void move();
    void erase();
    virtual void draw();
    virtual float area();

    void setReferencePoint(Point);
    Point getReferencePoint();
}
```

Figure 10.14: Specification for class Displayable Shape.

unnecessary methods, but sufficiently low to inherit as much as possible. Following this layering approach to design will also result in a smaller amount of source code.

The learnability of a collection of classes can be enhanced by adding structure. Figure 10.13 shows the NIH Class Library as it has been rearranged to have a Number class with subclasses Float, Fraction, and Integer. Compare this with the original structure in Figure 10.2. The new structure is more logical, with fewer classes to learn at the two levels. It is useful even though few attributes can be defined at Number because of the fundamental differences in representation. This very abstract class defines the interface for a Number and provides a meaningful grouping of classes.

Design Guideline #10: **Limit the number of methods that must understand the data representation of the class.**

We have said throughout this text that the implementation of a class should be hidden from its users. Now we go a step further and say that knowledge of the data representation should be limited even within the class. This supports the concept of having multiple implementations of each class. The critical methods that access the representation may use other "private" functions to "interpret" so that there is no need to modify the signature of any of the methods in the class specification. This can lead to inefficiencies due to a large number of function calls, but some languages provide mechanisms—for example, `inline` in C++—for optimizing this concern away. The most important concern in defining such a class in a language such as C++ is the definition of private data.

Consider the design of the Displayable Shape class. The specification of such a class is shown in Figure 10.14. Figure 10.15(a) shows one possible design of the move

```
void DisplayableShape::move(Point newLocation)
{
    erase();
    referencePoint := newLocation;
    draw();
}
```

(a)

```
void DisplayableShape::move(Point newLocation)
{
    erase();
    setReferencePoint(newLocation);
    draw();
}
```

(b)

Figure 10.15: Implementations of the move method.

method. This version directly accesses the referencePoint instance. The second version, shown in Figure 10.15(b), replaces the direct references in the previous design with calls to setReferencePoint. This reduces by one the number of methods that must directly access the data representation.

MORE GRAPHICS: GENERAL CLASSES

Several levels of generality are present in the graphics example. This results in components that are reusable and an application that is easily modifiable.

The shapes being created in the graphics system must be held for use in redrawing the screen, saving the image to disk, printing, and so on. This is accomplished by a list. This list is not a generic unit, since we are using C++ for implementation and C++ does not currently (Version 2.0) support generics. The list does, however, accept the polymorphic range of shape types. The inheritance structure shown in Figure 5.15 is the hierarchy of shape types as it is currently defined. Once a list is created for the Displayable Shape class, instances of any of its subclasses, such as Rectangle, can be placed in the list.

The design of the list class we are using is borrowed from Stroustrup[88]. Its design contributes to its generality. The concept of a "linked list" is actually divided among three classes. The linked list class itself handles the head of the list. A second class represents the links between items in the list. Instances of this class provide the actual linkage. The third class provides the ability to iterate over the list. By separating the iterator class from the list class, we gain the ability to have multiple iterators on a given list at one time.

The resulting set of classes is very general, but must be tailored to the particular data types being used. The linked list classes are so general and reusable that we now have, in our library, subclasses for a wide range of data types. For the graphics system, it is fairly quick work to specialize the links to work with Displayable Shape instances. Once that is accomplished, it is possible to declare an instance of that class that can now hold any combination of circles, rectangles, and so on.

A second level of generality is also present in the design of the graphics system. Each of the shape classes represents a particular type of figure, such as a circle, but is not limited to providing that representation to this one graphics system. For example, the Rectangle class requires only that it be displayed on a system that can draw lines given two endpoints. No assumptions are made about the type of display device or whether the rectangle is actually visible in the current viewport. These same classes could provide the basic shapes for use in a computer-aided design system or a modeling system. The classes can also be used to draw a figure such as a logo or to provide a graphic illustration as part of any computing application.

One assumption that has been made is that of single inheritance. The assumption requires that we produce a class such as Displayable Shape that combines the ideas of being displayable on a color graphics system and that of being a geometric shape. We discussed multiple inheritance for this in Chapter 6. The result of using multiple inheritance is that we have to manage more classes. However, these classes are more general than those used for single inheritance in the sense that they are more broadly applicable. Class Geometric Shape could be used in applications that do not call for the ability to display shapes.

Careful design of most of the classes in an object-oriented system results in a high degree of reusability. Perhaps the most application-specific part of any system design is the user interface. In our case, the user interface has been designed using existing or specialized objects. The major features of the user interface (see Figure 5.14) are all rectangles. The selection menu to the left consists of specialized rectangles, termed *selector boxes*. These boxes were developed specifically for this user interface as a subclass of Rectangle so that users may rearrange them to suit their taste. This is accomplished through the move method, which was derived for the Displayable Shape class, an ancestor of the Selector Box class. One new class was developed from scratch for this application: the User Interface class. This class defines the command loop that searches the list of selector boxes to find the one that was selected via a mouse button press. Control is then turned over to the routine contained in the selector box, which is a method associated with the shape represented by the selector box. A complete application has been developed with perhaps only one class that has limited reuse potential!

SUMMARY

Reuse is a reality for software development in the 1990s. Our current level of reuse is such that most companies can make great strides by paying any modicum of attention to reuse. The object-oriented style of development provides some special support for reuse. The polymorphic structures and the dynamic binding provided by most object-oriented languages can be combined with the standard interfaces and distributed responsibility design techniques to produce flexible and extensible components.

FURTHER READING

The design of reusable classes often must be considered within the context of a complete hierarchy. Gossain and Anderson[39] present considerations for designing a hierarchy of reusable classes. Perhaps our most referenced paper is Johnson and Foote[53] which presents a comprehensive set of guidelines that include designing in reusability.

11

Support for Reuse

Reuse, one of the fundamental goals of our methodology, has not been explicitly addressed—as a phase—in our life cycle models because we do not want to limit consideration of reuse to any one phase of the cycle. At each phase in the development process, we should be considering how previously completed work can be used to reduce the effort needed for the current task. Our discussion of documentation and testing techniques shows that incremental approaches support our reuse philosophy in more areas than just code sharing. Supporting these types of reuse will require retention of much information so that it will be available to support operations on later classes. These lead to requirements for automation in the software development process.

We will apply a broad definition: *Reuse is the use of any artifact that has been previously used.* This implies that our view will include the reuse of analysis information, design plans, and implementation details. We will be particularly concerned with beginning reuse at as high a level as possible; this will expedite the reuse of the products from lower levels that support the analysis-level concept and ultimately increase reuse.

Several areas will be discussed. We will present three techniques that support reuse of various products in the software development process. An approach will be adapted from the reuse of abstract data types to support the reuse of classes. We will also consider the issue of class libraries. Guidelines for the purchase of libraries will be developed by considering several existing libraries.

LEVELS OF REUSE

Reuse in the procedural paradigm means that either the component is used "as-is" or it is not used at all.[1] Reuse in the object-oriented paradigm actually may refer to one of several levels [61]:

- *Abstract-level reuse.* A set of object-oriented inheritance structures will include a number of high-level abstractions. Some reusers will only use these abstractions to give them ideas for additional classification dimensions or to simply understand the problem domain modeled by the structures.
- *Instance-level reuse.* The most usual form of reuse will be to simply create instances of existing classes. This is the easiest, quickest, and most economical form of reuse. Most widely used will be the classes that provide general structures such as the "Data Structures 101" content. The payoff for writing and reusing the more domain-specific classes may be far greater per use than for the easily developed and widely available components, but there will be fewer occasions for reuse.
- *Customization reuse.* A powerful feature of the object-oriented paradigm is the use of inheritance to support incremental development. Reuse is not an either/or proposition as it is in the procedural style. A class may be modified with far less effort than a set of procedures. A reuser can inherit information from the existing class, override certain methods, and add any new behaviors that are required.
- *Source code reuse.* A reuser may wish to modify an existing class to change its performance characteristics. This would probably be handled by the reuser creating a subclass of the existing class rather than modifying a class that others may be using.[2] Library support would make it possible to maintain multiple implementations of a specification without creating new "subtypes" for reasons of implementation.

FUNDAMENTAL TECHNIQUES

We believe that three fundamental approaches to reuse are well supported by the object-oriented paradigm.

- *Software components that are based upon problem-domain information will be more reusable and require fewer modifications than those based on solution-specific information.* Domain analysis identifies the fundamental abstractions of a problem domain. These abstractions provide a basis for developing the abstract classes that will be used as the roots of

---

[1]This is true if we assume only binary is available. If source code is available, then we can reuse existing code by copying it and then modifying the copy, a form of reuse we term *editor inheritance*.

[2]An interesting property of inheritance is that with proper class design, a subclass may be added without any knowledge of the implementation of the parent classes. In a procedural paradigm, source code must be available in general.

inheritance structures. These structures will contain classes that model the domain and will form the basis for applications that solve problems related to the domain. As advances in or changes to this domain are made, these classes will have to evolve to reflect these changes; however, this evolution will be slow compared to the changes that would be required if the classes reflected the structure of a particular solution rather than the structure of the domain.

- *Software components can be designed and implemented to anticipate reuse.* A number of the techniques discussed in this book have contributed to the reuse potential of these classes. These include:

  Abstraction. Object-oriented languages provide for the development of a specification of a class that is separate from the implementation of the class. This provides an effective means of communication with other developers on the same project and it provides for the hiding of implementation details from direct reference by anyone other than the developer of that class. This allows the class to be (re)used effectively without the user understanding or relying on a specific implementation of the class. In fact, more than one implementation can be made available.

  Standardization. The standardization of class interfaces is important to reuse. Consider a set of "container" classes such as lists, stacks, and queues that all use different names for the action of removing an element to the container. A list typically "deletes" an item from the list, while a queue "dequeues" that item and a priority queue has an operator termed "deletemin." To change from one container to another, not only must a different class be used, but the messages sent to that class must be modified as well. If queues, priority queues, and lists all were to "remove" items, then the three containers become essentially plug-compatible components that may be quickly interchanged.

  Incremental development. Incremental development is a fundamental design technique that takes advantage of the inheritance relationship. It *is* reuse in the sense that it requires the results of previous work in order to develop new products. This incremental reuse does not use existing components in an "as is" state; rather, it supports an evolutionary reuse. In fact, a class need not be fully implemented to be useful. The incremental testing and documentation techniques reuse products from previous processes to reduce the effort needed to create some new product.

  Polymorphic typing systems. Polymorphic typing systems support reuse through a flexible substitution policy. By using an appropriately abstract class as the formal parameter specification, the developer can create a broad range of classes whose instances serve as the actual parameter to that method. The method to which these classes are parameters can be reused over a wider range of possible parametric values. This increases the (re)use of the method and of the class to which it belongs.

- *Collections of software components that are organized into structures that model the relationships among the components will be more reusable than collections that have an arbitrary structure.* The inheritance mechanism provides support for the development of classification schemes that construct structures of components. These structures can model the domain from which the components are derived. Libraries can use these structures to provide an organization to their member components that is logical and that assists the developer in locating the appropriate component. These collections also become easier to remember and help the developer to learn the domain.

A REUSE METHODOLOGY

Uhl and Schmid[93] presents a Reuse Paradigm for ADTs. We have modified their approach to illustrate the reuse of classes.

- *Identify the classes required for an application.* Classes are identified at each phase of the development process by considering the basic concepts that are required for an application. In a computer-aided design (CAD) graphics system—which is somewhat more complex than our draw system—the concept of a segment is needed. A segment is a set of shapes that the user has constructed. By employing multiple segments, the user can separate the shapes that constitute the total picture into manageable pieces. This phase is an integral part of the life cycle we have presented.
- *Determine the behavior needed from this class in this application.* The behavior for a particular class is determined by modeling the concept. From the reuse perspective, however, we consider what behavior the system needs from this component. A CAD system expects that an instance of **Segment** will receive instances of various shape classes. The CAD system can determine whether a segment will be displayed as part of the current display. The segment can be edited to remove shapes or to modify them.
- *Abstract these methods from the application domain to a more general domain.* It is only at the lowest data structure level that we will find an exact match of a component with each of the methods, just as we have specified them. It is necessary to abstract the behaviors to determine the general characteristics of the behaviors that are required. In the **Segment** class, the reception of instances of shape classes can be considered to be "add"ing the instances to the segment. Part of the editing process corresponds to a "remove" behavior.
- *Select the abstract class with matching behavior.* A general characterization of the behavior of a **Segment** class corresponds to the concept of

a container class. An appropriately organized library will have an abstract class with a name such as Container or Collection. Beginning here, the designer can browse the inheritance structure to find an appropriate class.

- *Select the appropriate subclass.* It is at this level that we see the greatest deviation from Uhl's paradigm. The ADT approach does not support the evolutionary possibilities provided by the object-oriented paradigm. The ADT Reuse Paradigm would require that we select the component that *matches* our need. The object-oriented reuse paradigm allows us to select the component that is most closely associated with the needed concept. It need not be an exact match, nor will it often be so. Inheritance will allow us to efficiently evolve a subclass. For example, the segment in our CAD system might be expected to retain the instances of shapes in the order in which they are received. The abstract class, Container, provides the basic set of behaviors: add, remove, and clear. The designer now must consider the additional important specifications, such as the order of the shapes. An inheritance structure might have the classes Bag, Set, Ordered List, and Stack. If a segment is to maintain the instances of shapes in order, the class Ordered List is appropriate and the classes Bag, Set, and Stack are not.

- *During the application's lifetime, tune the performance of the component perhaps by choosing or developing different implementations.* Different applications will have different performance requirements. Some will need real-time response, others will have less stringent requirements. Some of the applications will handle large quantities of data while others will handle a small amount. A number of implementations can be provided through a series of subclasses. These will be plug-compatible components that can be used in place of the original with no modification to those instances that communicate with this instance. The Ordered List could have array and linked-list implementations as well as other implementations that have been optimized for real-time control.

Our reuse methodology is a process of iterative refinement. The class structures evolve and expand while hiding much of these modifications from the user. The steps described here concentrate on the reuse of classes, but a number of products will be reused in this methodology. Figure 11.1 shows our application life cycle with an indication of the products that can be reused at each level.

The reuse methodology relies heavily on libraries, which we will discuss next. The methodology also requires the support of management. These problems will be briefly discussed in Chapter 15.

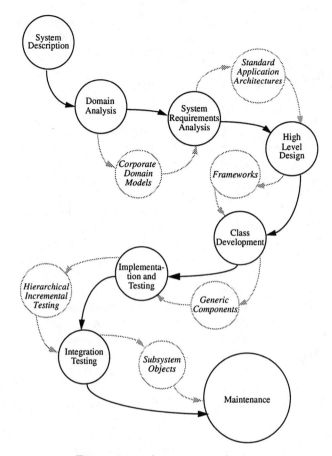

Figure 11.1: A reuse paradigm.

LIBRARIES

In this section[3] we will consider some of the existing object-oriented libraries and will use them to justify a set of guidelines for the purchase of libraries. We will also consider guidelines for the development of your own library.

Survey of Existing Libraries

New libraries appear on the market almost daily, so this is not intended as a broadly based survey nor is it sufficiently comprehensive to be a product review. We will present a few libraries and discuss their characteristics. This presentation will provide an introduction to a set of criteria for purchasing libraries in which we will further discuss the characteristics.

---

[3]The authors gratefully acknowledge the participation of Tim Korson, Clemson University, in the research that led to this section.

- *NIH class library.* The NIH (National Institutes of Health) Class Library was previously called the OOPS Library. It was developed at NIH by Keith Gorlen[38]. This was an early effort at a library to support system development in C^{++} that addressed a number of interesting issues. The library consists of the single hierarchy shown in Figure 10.2. The root class Object was used to provide a large amount of functionality to the library classes. Users of the library could create subclasses of the library classes and inherit all of the functionality provided by Gorlen in Object. The use of the single hierarchy allowed the library to implement a simple system of persistence, which we discuss in more detail in Chapter 14.

    The use of the single hierarchy for the library also supported the polymorphic substitution for the container classes provided in the library. Many of the Smalltalk collection classes were included in this library. In each case they were implemented to hold instances of Object. Since each class is a subclass of Object, instances of any of the classes in the library can be held in the collections. This can have two purposes.

    First, we could build very general, heterogeneous collections. A Stack class might have instances of Bag, Set, and even other instances of Stack pushed on it. This is very flexible and powerful, but in typed languages such as C^{++} it is also very difficult to take advantage of. An instance of Bag is pushed on the Stack, which has a formal parameter of Object. That instance of Bag will now be treated as an instance of Object and can only respond to messages that are in the interface of Object. These messages must be very general since Object is a very general abstract class. The only way to again be able to address the instance as a Bag is to cast it—that is, do a type conversion. In a heterogeneous usage where instances of Bag, Set, and Stack are all mixed together in a collection, it is impossible to know the origin of each instance in the collection, so casting is not practical.

    Second, we can build very specific, homogeneous collections quickly and easily. In a strongly typed environment like C^{++}, a collection class must be defined to hold instances of a class that is compatible with the actual instances being sent to it. If that class is a general one like Object, then every method that interacts with the collection class instance must cast any instance that has been placed in the collection class. In a homogeneous use of a collection class, every instance coming out of the collection class can be cast to the same class.

    It is very seldom that we design an application in which a container must hold instances of just any class in the system. Usually there is a constraint on the range of classes that a container must be able to hold, and usually it is limited to the classes in a single hierarchy with an abstract class at the root that establishes a standard interface for all of the classes in that one focused structure. In the draw program, there is a list of the shapes that the user has drawn. This is a heterogeneous list, but the range of classes is limited to those that are a subclass of Displayable Shape. The standard interface of Displayable Shape provides all of the

Classix Standard Interface

constructor - no parameters	Class_name::Class_name()
copy constructor	Class_name::Class_name(const Class_name&)
destructor	Class_name::~Class_name()
deep copy - 1 argument	Class_name& Class_name::deep_copy (const Class_name&)
deep copy - no arguments	Class_name& Class_name::deep_copy const Class_name&)
shallow copy - 1 argument	Class_name& Class_name::shallow_copy (const Class_name&)
shallow copy - no arguments	Class_name& Class_name::shallow_copy (const Class_name&)
returns class name as a string	inline const char* Class_name::type()
deep equal	int Class_name::equal(const Class_name&)
shallow equal	int Class_name::same(const Class_name&)
assignment	inline Class_name& Class_name::operator= (const Class_name&)
equality	inline Class_name& Class_name::operator== (const Class_name&)
inequality	inline int Class_name::operator!= (const Class_name&)
input	friend istream& operator>>(istream&, Class_name&)
output	friend ostream& operator<<(ostream&, Class_name&)

Figure 11.2: The Classix Library's common interface.

operations needed for the individual shapes. Therefore, there is no need to cast instances as they are removed from the list and manipulated.

Gathering many of the classes needed by a corporation, or even a project, into one inheritance structure can produce a complex lattice; however, it can have benefits as well. The entities in the hierarchy can all be used as parameters to high-level methods that may be able to handle a wide range of events. The entities can also all inherit some common set of attributes for purposes such as becoming persistent objects. That is, any class belonging to this structure may have the data attributes and method attributes to interact with a file system or database. Many of the object-oriented databases discussed in Chapter 14 require that any class to be stored in the database be a subclass of a database system-supplied class. The NIH library provides a simple and early example of this feature, but we will delay discussion of this topic until Chapter 14.

- *Classix.* The Classix Library is a collection of C^{++} classes divided into four groups: primitives, general data structures, mathematical classes, and the Smalltalk collection classes. The mathematical classes include the areas of vectors, matrices, and complex numbers. This library provides at least two noteworthy features.

    First, the primitive classes in the Classix library encapsulate the C^{++} primitives: integer, float, char, string, and boolean. This provides a uniform means of referencing in a C^{++} program. Integer values become objects just as do the instances of user-defined classes.

    Second, the designers of the library provided a common interface that is shared by *all* the classes in the library. The library documentation provides the user with an overview of this set of very commonly used methods that have been implemented for every class in the library. Figure 11.2 presents this interface. In addition to providing a set of functions that are needed often, this common interface makes the library easier to learn. The library user begins learning about each class knowing a lot about its functionality due to this common interface.

- *Compiler-coupled libraries.* Many of the language vendors provide a library with their product. Zortech and GNU provide libraries with their C^{++} compilers and ParcPlace Systems and Digitalk provide libraries with their Smalltalk environments. No two of these libraries are the same. In keeping with tradition for personal computer language products, Zortech provides support for graphics but unfortunately not in the form of classes. Zortech's tools include an event queue class and an event class that uses a data attribute to determine the type of the event: keyboard, mouse, or other. This would have been a natural place to use subclasses. GNU provides a library, `libg++`, that includes some unique classes and macros.

    The basic syntax of Smalltalk is sufficiently simple that if the vendors did not provide an extensive set of classes the purchaser would have very little functionality. The central strength of Smalltalk is the set of collection classes. Given the fact that inheritance is commonly used for the purpose of implementation in Smalltalk, it is not surprising that two vendors would provide libraries with significantly different structures. The open approach of Smalltalk results in a library that includes classes that implement the behavior of the Smalltalk development environment. Windows, for example, are provided in the library partially because the development environment makes extensive use of them.

Guidelines for the Purchase of a Library

Companies have always been faced with build or buy decisions. As libraries become more extensive and useful, firms will have to consider whether the cost of a library will be justified by the resources saved during the system development process. Most of the commercially available libraries are relatively small and are provided at little or no cost. Even if the purchase price is small, however, the effort needed to integrate it

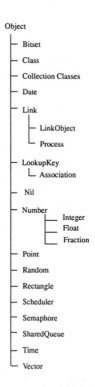

Figure 11.3: A reorganized NIH Class Library.

into the company's development environment and to learn the library can still require extensive resources. The following criteria are intended to assist in the determination of whether to purchase a particular library.

- *For those concepts it claims to provide, the library should give a complete general model.* A library becomes easier to learn if there is some rationale to its contents. The NIH Class Library, for example, provides several number-oriented classes: Integer, Float, and Fraction. We have already argued that the NIH library would make more sense if it had a more coherent organization of these numeric concepts. Figure 11.3 shows the revised version of the NIH class library in which a Number abstract class provides organization for the numeric concepts. The library does show that an area such as container classes can be represented by a sufficient number of classes to model the general domain. This does not assume that no other collection classes could be designed. It simply means that including only one class in an area does not provide a sufficient structure to facilitate the development of further classes.
- *The library should be designed around a few key abstractions.* The "more coherent organization" noted above can be provided by abstract classes. The high-level class Number is used to provide a standard interface for

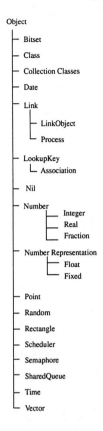

```
Object
  ├─ Bitset
  ├─ Class
  ├─ Collection Classes
  ├─ Date
  ├─ Link
  │    ├─ LinkObject
  │    └─ Process
  ├─ LookupKey
  │    └─ Association
  ├─ Nil
  ├─ Number
  │    ├─ Integer
  │    ├─ Real
  │    └─ Fraction
  ├─ Number Representation
  │    ├─ Float
  │    └─ Fixed
  ├─ Point
  ├─ Random
  ├─ Rectangle
  ├─ Scheduler
  ├─ Semaphore
  ├─ SharedQueue
  ├─ Time
  └─ Vector
```

Figure 11.4: A further reorganization of the numeric classes.

the three numeric classes in the library. A top-level Collection class also provides an entree into the layers of classes that represent varieties of containers. The abstractions serve several purposes. They provide an organization to the library that makes it easier to learn and to browse. They support extensibility by defining a standard interface that can be the nucleus for new class specifications. Finally, an abstract class at the top level of a structure makes it unlikely that the structure will have to be reorganized to accommodate a more abstract concept.

- *The design of the library should model standard knowledge in the domain.*
  There has been much said in this text and others about using inheritance to model the subtyping relationship. The classes in the library should represent the concepts in the domain of the library, and the inheritance structure should model the standard classifications within the domain. The NIH Class Library is difficult to understand in the numeric area because of poor organization and because of a mix of concepts in the names of the numeric classes. Figure 11.4 shows a further clarification in that inheritance structure. The mixture of numeric representations,

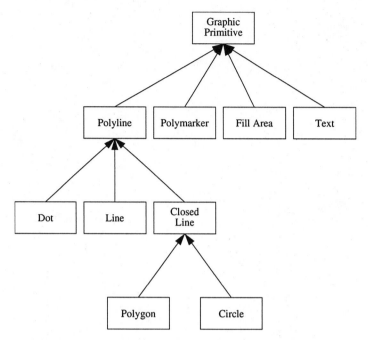

Figure 11.5: A hierarchy of GKS primitives.

Float, is separated from the conceptual mathematical entities of Integer and Fraction. A library of classes that represent the GKS graphics standard should have a structure that represents the GKS structure. Figure 11.5 provides a structure that contains the primitive graphic elements of GKS.

- *The library should use inheritance to implement the generalization/-specialization relationship.* We have already argued for this approach. The importance of this to a library is that the inheritance relationship can serve as a classification scheme that can be used to browse through the classes in the library. Multiple inheritance is used to represent multiple classification schemes.

- *The library should be designed as networks of classes without free-standing data or procedural items.* Hybrid languages, such as C++, allow the developer to use a mixture of styles. It is possible to develop procedures that are not methods of a class. If a concept requires class definitions, function definitions, and global data declarations to provide its definition, the chance for name conflicts, missing pieces, and incorrect references is much greater. When all the data and methods belong to one class, one declaration encompasses the complete definition of the class. Many names are hidden inside the unit thus reducing the possibility of name conflicts and accidental referencing. The Zortech Flashgraph graphics library is an example that declares many publicly available names.

- *The library should be designed with a low level of coupling between classes.* The relationships between classes are explicit. The use of the inheritance mechanism, the component relationship, and messaging are syntactic devices that can be automatically detected and managed. By creating discrete, well defined structures, the small amount of coupling can easily be handled. Many of the dependencies between classes are in the implementation and thus are hidden.

- *The library should provide a consistent and easily understood approach to the handling of errors and exceptions.* A number of exception-handling mechanisms have been developed for classes. Eiffel includes such a mechanism as a built-in feature of the language[71] and thus it is available for the Eiffel libraries. Other mechanisms have been developed as add-ons to existing languages such as C++[74]. The use of a single class as the parent of all other classes provides a technique for propagating an exception mechanism or for uniform techniques of reporting errors for every class in the library.

- *An "inspector function" should be available to check the preconditions of every partial function.* A partial function is one for which a precondition must be satisfied for the function to perform properly. For example, the **push** method of **Stack** should use an inspector function full? to decide whether the remainder of the **push** method can be executed.

- *It should not be possible for a library user to violate the abstraction represented by a library class.* For example, a number of ordered list classes available in commercial libraries allow the user to directly access an element of the list and modify the value of the attribute used to order it. A change to the element's key field can have the undesirable effect of "un-ordering" the list. Such classes should be designed to return copies of elements rather than the actual element.

- *Classes in the library should conform to a minimal set of standards that are enforced throughout the library.* The library should have a standard class structure around which variations are built. The Classix Library provides the standard interface shown in Figure 11.2 as a foundation for all of its classes.

- *The implementation should be the most efficient available within the stated time and space parameters.* A set of subclasses can be available that provide a wide range of implementations. Each implementation should be carefully tuned. If we are to rely on libraries for portions of our applications, we must spend time developing quality components with above-average implementations.

- *The definitions and naming of items in the library should be consistent.* Subclasses, for example, may be named by prefixing the name of the class with modifiers that describe the distinctions between subclasses. The documentation of the NIH Class Library uses the phrases "Integer Number Object," "Rational Arithmetic," and "Floating Point Number" for the classes **Integer**, **Rational**, and **Float**. It is impossible to recognize the relationship between these classes with the existing names and the existing structure. In fact, the use of "Integer" and "Float" as opposed to "Integer" and "Real," or "Fixed" and "Float," is confusing.

- *The library should provide generic classes where possible.* The container classes in a library can be specialized for every other class in the library using a set of subclasses, one for each class. This is tedious and errorprone. If the implementation language has a generic facility, the development of generic classes is easy. If that facility is not available, a macro facility should be designed. This reduces the number of classes needed in the library.

- *The user should be aware of the degree of completeness of the implementation of the classes in the library.* Every library has a number of abstract classes that cannot be used to create class instances. Each should provide classes beyond these. Some libraries have a ratio of two abstract classes for every concrete one. This is good design, but it can be misleading for the purchaser to see a list of classes without realizing how many of them are abstract. The documentation for the classes should make this obvious.

- *Documentation should be organized in a manner that reflects the structure of the library.* The documentation for a library might be grouped so that all the classes in a single inheritance hierarchy are together. Within this structure, the class information can be laid out using an array-based tree representation—that is, in layers.

- *Documentation should be provided that presents an overview of the library, including contents and structure.* An illustration that presents the tree or graph of inheritance relationships among classes can provide an overview of the library. This picture will assist the new user in learning the structure. The diagram can also include page numbers for each class definition.

- *The library should provide different documentation for different levels of users.* Some readers will only use instances from the library, others will create subclasses from the classes in the library, and finally some may wish to alter the inheritance structure. The increasing sophistication of each level of user requires an increasing amount of detailed information.

A user who will only create instances needs the complete specification for the class but no information about the implementation. The documentation for the class should include preconditions and postconditions for each method in the class interface. The class documentation should also include an overall specification for the class.

To create subclasses, the user must know those parts of the class that will be accessible in the subclass. In C++ this means that all the declarations and definitions in the public and protected areas of the parent classes should be made available.

Finally, to modify the inheritance structure, the user will need access to all details about the implementation of a class. The user will also need access to the source code because the implementation of a class must be modified to alter the inheritance structure. This is obviously a serious step that should require the approval of the library manager and should include the notification of all library users.

- *Documentation for each library should have a minimum of three access methods: alphabetic by class name, hierarchical via the inheritance structure, and a keyword facility.* It is a simple matter to maintain three separate indexes into the paper documentation of a library. Automated systems of documentation can provide even more flexibility. In particular, an affinity browsing system[92] can provide a means for automatically selecting a set of classes that have many of the properties we are seeking in a class. A built-in thesaurus to recognize similar terms such as "sorted" and "ordered" is also useful.

- *Commercial libraries should be supported.* We cannot develop commercial applications in which major portions are purchased externally unless there is some guarantee that the library is supported. We do not want to spend our time fixing problems in a purchased product, nor can we wait very long for a vendor to fix problems we encounter. Libraries and their technology will continue to evolve for some time. It will be important for the purchaser to receive upgrades.

Developing Your Own Library.

Purchased libraries will play an increasingly important role in software development, but so will the development of original libraries that capture the expertise of the company. Reports of the development of corporate libraries are just beginning to appear in the literature[21, 29, 24, 102], but they are still very small, narrowly focused libraries. Many of the criteria that were just presented for purchasing libraries can be viewed as guidelines for the development of a library as well. There are other considerations from the development perspective; we shall mention a few.

Each inheritance structure and each group of structures that claims to represent an area of knowledge should be based on domain knowledge. This implies that a library is the result of a domain analysis. Uhl and Schmid provide a catalogue of reusable abstract data types[93]. In spite of the broad implication of the title, Uhl considers a set of abstract data types that are some of the basic data structures from "Data Structures 101." Since this is an ADT approach and not an object-oriented approach, inheritance is not used to structure the catalogue. Each ADT is defined separately, but the catalogue does include an implementation hierarchy that shows simpler, lower-level ADTs being used to construct the more complex, higher-level ADTs. The specifications for these data structures provide the beginnings of a classification scheme that would be useful in structuring a library of classes. Even small libraries should—and many have for some time—provide references to the sources of their knowledge. Van Wyk[102] describes the development of a library of classes to solve simultaneous equations. In this description, much space is given to the theoretical foundations of the library. This provides the prospective user with information to use in judging the appropriateness of the library.

The classes and structures in a library should be validated by domain experts.

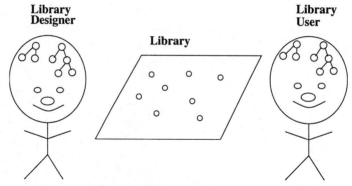

Procedural libraries have no structure so the library users
must have the same mental models as the library designer.

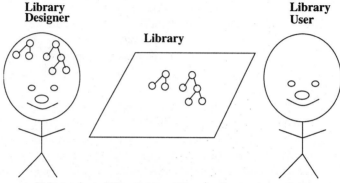

Object-oriented libraries can represent the structure of the
domain so the user does not have to have the same mental
model as the library designer.

Figure 11.6: Procedural versus object-oriented libraries.

The initial designs of class specifications can provide the experts with information to
be evaluated and modified. These same experts should have input into the test data
used to validate the conformance of the class's implementation to its specification.

The structures in an object-oriented library will provide a model of the relationships present in the problem domain. This provides an important advantage for the
use of object-oriented libraries. Figure 11.6 illustrates that a procedural library has
no internal structure. It is simply a collection of pieces that a user must assemble
in meaningful ways. The user must have a mental model of how to use these pieces
that parallels the model intended by the library designer. This is easy to do in well
understood and rigidly structured domains such as mathematics, but is not so easy in
specific application domains. The object-oriented library contains the model as well
as the pieces from the problem domain. The user of the library can actually learn
something about the domain by studying the library's structure.

The library should be developed in an organized manner rather than having classes added to the library as they are needed in the application development process. This is difficult to do in practice unless a dedicated library development group is formed. A good compromise is to use the domain analysis to identify the major high-level abstractions. As classes are developed for applications, they can be added to the library by classifying them using the structure developed from the abstract classes. This process needs to be accompanied by a refinement process. Periodically the library should be examined as a whole to identify reorganizations that will improve its structure and classes. There are many issues associated with this reorganization that we will not consider here; Casais[14] provides an extensive discussion of them.

Using Libraries

We have already discussed several levels of reuse, which correspond to types of reusers. No matter the level, the reusers all need to learn the library and must be able to browse the library during use.

- *Learning.* Learning a new library is one of the most time-consuming processes in object-oriented development. If the user only intended to create instances of classes in the library, then learning the specifications of the classes would be sufficient. However, most users will need to understand the structure of the library as well as the specifications. If the structure is arbitrary, this will be a difficult task. Numerous psychological studies over the years have shown that expert knowledge is represented in chunks. Structuring information to correspond to these chunks improves recall. Structuring the library according to the structuring of the underlying domain will facilitate a user's recall of the classes in the library.

    Our previous discussions on naming are applicable here. Not only must the structures be characteristic of the problem domain, but the names for the concepts represented in the structures must also be appropriately chosen. The combination of structuring and naming provides more than just a library that is easy to learn; it provides a library that is a sufficient model of a discipline that it can assist software developers in becoming familiar with a new domain for which they are to build systems.

- *Browsing.* If the library follows the criteria presented above, the documentation should provide multiple means of accessing the classes. If the documentation is in printed form, these multiple access paths will take the form of indexes. If the classes are arranged alphabetically, traversing the inheritance structure will require much page turning. For a fixed-size library, parent classes may actually contain references to their child classes, but this approach cannot be expanded to include the classes that are added by the local users.

    To merge multiple commercial libraries and locally defined classes that are derived from library classes, the corporate library will require some form of electronic documentation browsing and, if possible, electronic browsing of the implementations. The browser may be part of a development environment or it may be based on a general-purpose information tool such as a hypertext system. The browser should allow the user to travel the three fundamental relationships between classes: inheritance, composition, and messaging. The database underlying the browser will keep track of each of these relationships and allow the user to specify which relationship to follow. In Chapter 13 we will discuss additional properties of tools.

The difficult part of this integration is the location of similar classes in separate libraries. When multiple commercial libraries are available, there may be several different implementations of list classes, for example. These will not be in a single inheritance structure since they come from several libraries. The browser should allow for "affinity" browsing[92] as a means for locating classes that are similar in behavior, but may not be related via the inheritance mechanism. The techniques for describing characteristics to the browser so that it can locate classes that satisfy that criteria is an open research question.

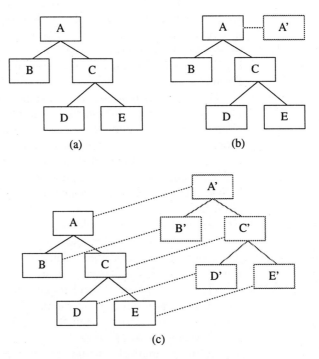

Figure 11.7: A hierarchy of classes.

CLASS EVOLUTION

The reuse of classes in slightly different contexts will eventually lead to the need to modify the classes. The modification of a single class could be managed via a single subclass; however, consider the complications of managing change in a complete hierarchy such as that shown in Figure 11.7(a). Suppose that class A is modified slightly by changing a public attribute such as a parameter. The resulting class, A', should be considered a *version* of A, Figure 11.7(b). One question that now must be considered is whether a new version is automatically created for every subclass of A. This could result in a "shadow" structure for the entire hierarchy, Figure 11.7(c). How to efficiently create these new versions from the old is an open question. Casais[14] provides a discussion of these and other issues pertaining to versioning of classes.

A related issue is how to maintain multiple implementations of a class. It is easy to conceive of several possible implementations of a class Stack. Array-based and dynamic list-based are two standards. Multiple implementations and multiple versions are similar but different problems. As with versioning, one recommended technique is the use of subclasses. The Booch components refer to bounded and unmanaged storage managers as variations for each class[12]. These are really different implementations of a single concept. One technique to handle varying the implementation of a class has been proposed by Kennedy[55]. These are issues that development environments that claim to support the object-oriented approach will have to address.

MORE GRAPHICS: REUSE

The draw program is a simple system, but even here we can see reuse. The shapes drawn by the program user are held in a linked list. The menu of selector boxes is also held on a linked list. The general linked list class we borrowed from Stroustrup is used to produce two new subclasses, one for holding shapes and one for holding selector boxes. The need for these separate subclasses will go away in C++ when templates are added to the language. They are already unnecessary in languages like Eiffel and Smalltalk.

We have pointed out the role of Rectangle in the system. It is used directly to provide borders in the interface and serves as the parent class for the selector box classes. And, let's not forget that it may be used to draw a picture!

InterViews Library

Libraries can also play an important role in the development of the draw system. Libraries of graphics routines have been around for many years, but an object-oriented library provides larger grains of functionality that make their reuse much more beneficial. The InterViews library[66] is a user interface library written in C++. It can be used to provide a new output device that will display the user interface of the draw program using the X-window system as the basis.

The InterViews library makes extensive use of inheritance; Figure 11.8 shows a portion of one of the inheritance structures. Only a small number of the classes in the

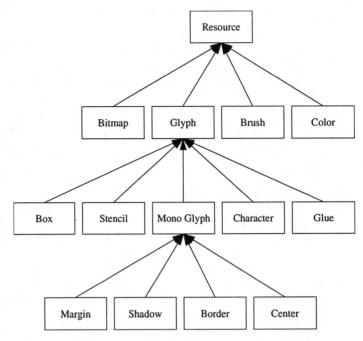

Figure 11.8: The InterViews glyph hierarchy.

library are required to provide the interface of the draw program. Each output device is assumed to provide the concept of a shape and the primitives of dot and line, setting a drawing color, and clearing the screen. InterViews allows the designer to create a subclass of the Display Device class to provide each of these required capabilities in the X-window system.

Refinement

We have said repeatedly that object-oriented design is a process of refinement. When we are designing with abstractions it takes much experience and many attempts to arrive at the appropriate abstractions. The InterViews library is an example of this refinement process. In recent months a new release of the library has presented a greatly refined design. Many changes have been made to the classes and the inheritance structures. The result is a much more comprehensive design that will support future extensions.

We have also seen the refinement process in this text. From its initial requirements in Chapter 4 until now, the draw application's classes have evolved. We began with the GKS primitives and along the way we have considered several possible designs, including using multiple inheritance. What has not changed in the system is the contract between the shape classes and the output-device classes. This has allowed us to modify one part of the system without affecting other pieces.

SUMMARY

Reuse should be a fundamental objective of the software development process in the 1990s. Many features of object technology support reuse. The encapsulation and information-hiding properties of classes support the easy integration of a concept. The polymorphic substitution property supports the flexible design of subsystems as parameterized units that can be reused in a variety of ways.

Libraries are an essential support technology for reuse. Libraries of classes are logically arranged models of a problem domain. The classifications represented in the libraries promote learning the domain as well as locating appropriate abstractions within the domain. We presented some criteria to be used in evaluating commercial libraries that are also criteria for the development of libraries.

FURTHER READING

Reuse is a very broad topic with many facets. Hewlett Packard's Kiosk product and the writings of Martin Griss[24] address a comprehensive view of reuse from analysis to implementation and maintenance. Deutsch[26] discusses frameworks in the context of reuse as does Garlan[31]. As already mentioned, Johnson and Foote[53] discuss the design of reusable classes.

12

An Example

In this chapter we develop a simple application to demonstrate the techniques and principles we have been describing. We have chosen to implement a computer-based Tic-Tac-Toe game for two players. The game is simple, but it comprises enough to illustrate what we have been describing.

We have followed the basic goals of our design philosophy, considering reuse as one of our criteria for designing the classes in this application. The resulting design is more elaborate than what is needed to simply implement the game of Tic-Tac-Toe.

It is difficult to capture all of the processes and decisions that go into the design of an application. Good design arises from experience and insight into the problem. We have tried to capture the most important decisions in this chapter.

REQUIREMENTS

We want a computer-based application to play Tic-Tac-Toe. The application shall support two players, accepting moves from each in turn, ensuring that each move is legal, and ending the game when one player wins or the game ends in a draw. The rules of Tic-Tac-Toe are:

> Two players take turns placing crosses (**X**) and ciphers (**O**)
> in the unoccupied compartments of the figure

> and each player tries to get a row—up, down, or diagonal—
> of three crosses or three ciphers before the opponent does.

If no player has three in a row before all compartments
are occupied, then the game ends in a draw. The player
placing crosses moves first.

The application is required to display the board at the beginning of the game and
redisplay it after each move. It shall also provide an indication of which player's turn
it is and terminate the game when a winner emerges or when the game is a draw.

ANALYSIS AND DESIGN

Given these requirements, we now turn to the high-level design for the Tic-Tac-Toe
application. We want to approach the design using domain analysis to identify entities.
Our goal is to identify those classes that we need for our application and develop them
so that they are as reusable as possible. We will use entity relationship diagrams and
finite-state diagrams as our notation for describing the results of our analysis.

Domain Analysis

What *is* our domain? Tic-Tac-Toe is a game, so maybe "game" is our domain. Football
is also a game, but perhaps outside of what we might want to consider for our current
application—unless over the long term we might want to implement applications to
simulate athletic games. We'll focus our interest on games that are similar to Tic-
Tac-Toe—board games such as Chess, Checkers, Monopoly™, Trivial Pursuit™, and
Sorry™. We have mentioned that identifying a domain is difficult, but it seems
appropriate that we address the games in the light gray region of Figure 12.1. This
domain includes games played on some sort of board and excludes athletic games,
card games, and party games. The border is indeed hazy. We might want to include
Hangman, for example, but we won't have to be that precise. If we omit an important
component from the domain, we can always retrofit it later. Any expansion certainly
will include the analysis we had done up to the point at which we decided to expand
our domain.

What are some of the entities in our domain of interest? These come immediately
to mind:

> game board
> cards
> spinners
> dice
> tokens
> players
> play money
> rules

Cards, spinners, dice, and money have no roles to play in Tic-Tac-Toe. A game board,
players, rules, and tokens—crosses and ciphers—are necessary. So we don't spend all of
our resources in analysis addressing a large domain, let's restrict our problem domain
a bit further to games played on a board in which players take turns and in which

Figure 12.1: The domain of games, board games, and strategy board games.

chance has no role. We are addressing games of strategy—Chess, Checkers, Chinese Checkers, and the like. These games are included in the dark gray region on Figure 12.1. A game such as Risk™ and other "war games" that many people might consider to be games of strategy, but that involve dice to decide the result of a move, is on the boundary of our strategy game domain. We will exclude them because they involve dice. Of the entities listed above, those that are relevant to the strategy board game domain are:

> game board
> tokens
> players
> rules

Some of the relationships between these entities are:

- Players *move* tokens.
- Tokens *occupy spaces—components—on* the game board.
- Players *abide by* the rules.
- Players *look at* the game board to determine a next move.
- The rules *specify* the game board and how the game is played.

An ER diagram to represent this is shown in Figure 12.2. However, from this first diagram we can identify some other entities:

> moves
> spaces on a game board

We will also add to these the notion of a "match" (for lack of a better name) by which we mean an instance of a specific game being played by specific players. We just want

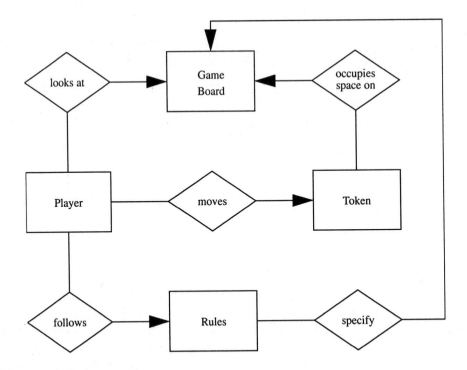

Figure 12.2: An entity relationship diagram for the strategy board game domain.

to be careful not to use the term *game* to mean both the game itself—for example, Tic-Tac-Toe or Checkers—and the occasion of two people playing it, so we'll use *match* for the latter. A revised ER diagram incorporating our newly identified entities is shown in Figure 12.3. This diagram seems to express what we know about the domain of strategy board games. We might want to show it to some game experts to see if anything is missing or wrong, but since we don't have ready access to an expert, we'll use the basis of our own experience with strategy board games and accept it for now.

An interesting property of ER diagrams is that relationships are bidirectional, even though only one direction is shown on a diagram. For example, the *makes* relationship between *Player* and *Move* can also be expressed as an *is made by* relationship between *Move* and *Player*. We have chosen to express the relationships specifiable using the active voice because they seem to more directly reflect the direction of message passing in the object-oriented paradigm. However, low-level design may indicate that the relationship expressed in the passive voice is needed instead of, or in addition to, the relationship expressed in the active voice. Some of our relationships were chosen arbitrarily—for example, Player *follows* Rules could just as easily been expressed as Rules *constrain* Player.

State diagrams for the seven entities are shown in Figure 12.4. Note that rules have only one state since we can safely assume that they don't change during a match.

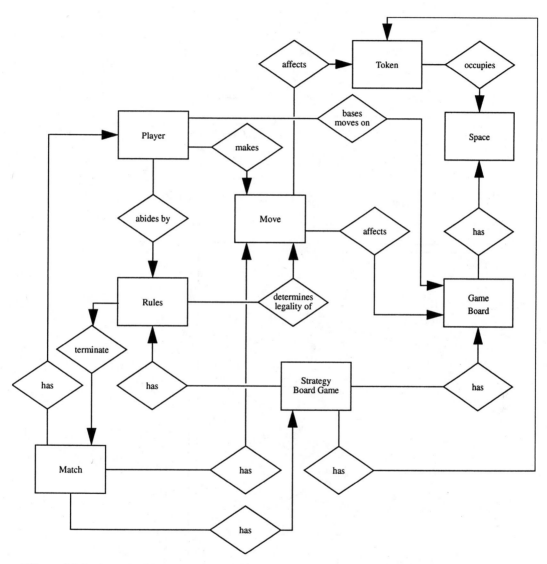

Figure 12.3: A revised entity relationship diagram for the strategy board game domain.

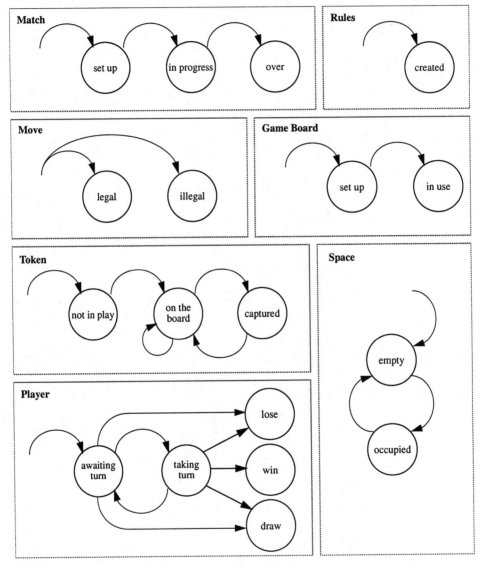

Figure 12.4: Finite-state diagrams for the strategy board game domain entities.

A move is either legal or illegal. We don't consider the possibility that a legal move becomes illegal, or vice versa, because a move is created in the context of a given match and it has to be either legal or illegal in that context. This is distinct from the notion of a "possible" move. In Tic-Tac-Toe, a player can place his token on any space during a move, but depending on the point of play in the match, some of those possible moves are illegal. At the beginning of the match, all possible moves are legal, but after the first move is completed, some possible moves have become illegal—namely, placing a token on the space used in the first move.

LOW-LEVEL DESIGN

Given the ER diagram in Figure 12.3 and the state diagrams in Figure 12.4, we want to specify classes and their attributes—variables and methods—for the domain. We are just as concerned with our domain of strategy board games as we are with our Tic-Tac-Toe application. We will even consider the broader domains of board games—and games in general—as part of our analysis. If we design to our domain, then the specifics of Tic-Tac-Toe should fit into our design very easily—as should other, similar games.

Figures 12.5 and 12.6 show one possible set of inheritance structures for the classes of objects we identified in our design. We developed these structures from a straightforward classification of Tic-Tac-Toe within the domain of games. It will serve as a "first cut" at defining a structure for our domain of strategy board games. Within these structures we have designated where the classes specific to Tic-Tac-Toe "fit." Some classes for other games are penciled in to show how they might fit. There are many abstract classes in these structures—a good sign that we have recognized so many concepts so quickly. Most of the structures parallel one another. This is not uncommon in object-oriented design and provides a benefit of eliminating polymorphism[1] when it is undesirable. For example, a Tic-Tac-Toe Game object should contain only a Tic-Tac-Toe Board object, Tic-Tac-Toe Token objects, and a Tic-Tac-Toe Rules object and not, for example, a Checkerboard object, Chessman objects, and a Chess Rules object. Thus the Tic-Tac-Toe Game class can restrict parameters to any values returned by its methods to Tic-Tac-Toe-specific classes—for example, to the Tic-Tac-Toe Rules class rather than the more general Rules class. The availability of all these classes in the hierarchy lets us restrict objects to those classes that are meaningful. The consequences of this structure are especially beneficial in typed object-oriented languages such as C++.

We could develop our Tic-Tac-Toe application with only a few classes, each having Tic-Tac-Toe-specific functionality. This type of development is discussed by McGregor for a Rock-Paper-Scissors game in [70]. Such a development would be object-oriented, but would not take into consideration the planned reuse of this application's classes for the implementation of other games. However, if we assume that we are in the business of developing game applications for computers, then the design illustrated in

---

[1]Recall that inclusion polymorphism permits an object of class to be used wherever an object of one of its ancestor classes can be used. For example, in the hierarchy of Figure 12.6, an object of class Tic-Tac-Toe Board can be used in any context that a Strategy Game Board can be used

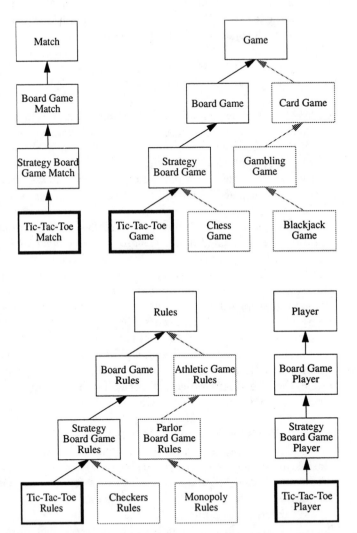

Figure 12.5: A possible set of inheritance structures for strategy board games.

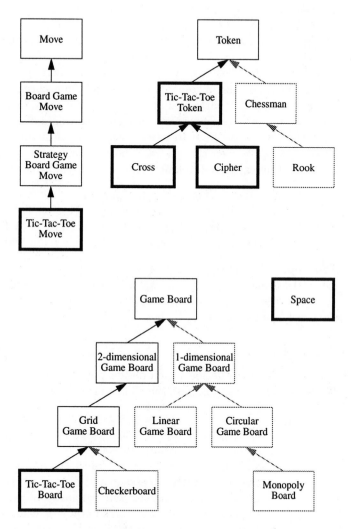

Figure 12.6: A possible set of inheritance structures for strategy board games *(continued)*.

Figures 12.5 and 12.6 is more general and more cost-effective in the long run.

The relatively large number of abstract classes indicates a source of the costs associated with a comprehensive development of classes for a domain. When we decide to implement another strategy board game such as Checkers or Chess, then we can reuse many of these abstract classes, adding only some new subclasses. Then we will begin to recoup some of our initial investment.

Since Tic-Tac-Toe is the only game of immediate interest to us, we don't want to apply all of the resources it would take to implement each of the abstract classes. Therefore, we will implement only those portions of the abstract classes that pertain to our application—that is, we will develop our class library incrementally. We will identify methods and instance variables for these classes that will directly support our application, but with an understanding that more methods and variables can be added at a later date. If we were sure that we would be implementing more games in the future, we might want to put a little more effort into implementing the abstract classes more fully even though we won't need all the functionality for Tic-Tac-Toe.

In our incremental development, we will use a three-step approach:

1. Choose a general design paradigm.
2. Identify the attributes for each Tic-Tac-Toe class.
3. Generalize application-specific attributes by fitting their attributes into the class hierarchy at the highest level in which we can make them fit.

This approach is fairly typical, though it may change from development to development. In using this approach, we want to avoid focusing too much on the current application—that is, designing specifically to Tic-Tac-Toe. Instead, we want to try to elevate relationships to the highest level in our hierarchical structures.

Step 1: Choosing a Design Paradigm

Our first step is to decide which design paradigm is best suited for our application. We have at least two choices: the client-server model and the master-slave model:

- The *client-server* model was first mentioned in Chapter 3. In this model, all objects in the system are equal and interact with each other via messages to accomplish work. The receiver of a message is a "server" and the sender is a "client" of the server. The server performs the work associated with a message and normally returns some sort of result to the client. The server will ordinarily become a client of other servers to perform its work. In this paradigm, each server works for its clients. Major decisions about the flow of control are shared by all objects in the system under this model.
- The *master-slave* model designates some object—the "master"—to be in control of the processing performed by other objects—the "slaves." The slaves operate under the client-server model for the most part, but the master is responsible for the major decisions that have to be made.

With respect to our Tic-Tac-Toe application and our strategy board games applications in general, a master-slave paradigm seems more applicable. It's easy to

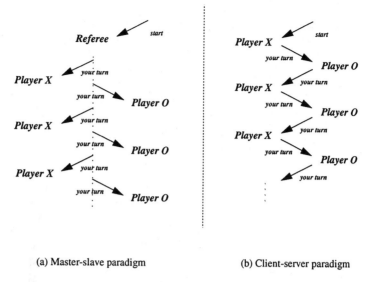

(a) Master-slave paradigm   (b) Client-server paradigm

Figure 12.7: Message passing patterns for two design paradigms.

see how a match could be controlled by a single agent—a sort of referee–who determines which player moves next and decides when the match is over. Each player is a slave to this controller, taking a turn only when told to do so. The controller is not particularly interested in knowing what move a player makes during the match, but only in knowing that a move was made. The message patterns associated with the master-slave model for the Tic-Tac-Toe application is shown in Figure 12.7(a). On the other hand, a client-server paradigm is harder to adopt for this application because distributing control for play among the players would result in a lengthy sequence of messages between players before any reply is received; each reply has no real use to the sender of the corresponding message. For Tic-Tac-Toe, a player would make a move, then send a "your turn" message to the other player. Nothing is returned from a "your turn" message until a match ends, as illustrated in Figure 12.7(b).

Step 2: Identifying Application-Specific Attributes

Having adopted a master-slave model for our design, we now direct our efforts toward the specification of classes. We will first consider how we might combine some of the entities we identified during high-level design with the idea of a referee. Consider the algorithm for the Tic-Tac-Toe application presented in Figure 12.8. This algorithm should work quite well for Tic-Tac-Toe. It is expressed in a procedural style, using expressions such as, "place a cross in space S of B" instead of the more object-oriented, "tell B to place a cross in space S." This is not serious and indeed seems to be a natural way of expressing the processing. One criticism of this algorithm, however, is that it uses very few of the abstractions and the relationships between them that we have identified. For example, it recognizes that a board has spaces and that a match has

Let B be an instance of a Tic-Tac-Toe board and P_X and P_O be players. To play a Tic-Tac-Toe match M do the following:

    set up the game; display the board;
    while there are empty spaces on B and
          there are not three crosses in a row and
          there are not three ciphers in a row **do**
      repeat
        accept a space S from P_X;
      until space S is unoccupied;
      place a cross in space S of B;
      display the board;
      if there are empty spaces on B and
        there are not three crosses in a row
      then
        repeat
          accept a space S from P_O;
        until space S is unoccupied;
        place a cipher in space S of B;
        display the board;
    if there are three crosses in a row **then**
      declare P_X the winner;
    else if there are three ciphers in a row **then**
      declare P_O the winner;
    else
      declare the match a draw;

Figure 12.8: A first cut at an algorithm for the Tic-Tac-Toe application.

a board and players, but it ignores the notion of a token or rules. A match is just a run of this algorithm. This points out the difference between our approach to problem solving and the traditional procedural approach, even as it is applied to the object-oriented paradigm. The traditional approach uses the data associated only with the application under development. Our approach, by contrast, considers the application in the context of a set of related applications—even if only one application is to be developed in the shorter term.

Consider the algorithm in Figure 12.9 to replace the one in Figure 12.8. This algorithm will work for Tic-Tac-Toe, but should also work for other strategy board games—if not for board games in general. We have purposely tried to address other games in our algorithm by raising the process to use other abstractions—that is,

Let $\mathcal{M}$ be an instance of a Tic-Tac-Toe match with players P_X and P_O, and Tic-Tac-Toe game $\mathcal{G}$ which has Tic-Tac-Toe board $\mathcal{B}$, and Tic-Tac-Toe rules $\mathcal{R}$. Then $\mathcal{M}$ is played according to the algorithm:

$\mathcal{G}$ setup;

$\mathcal{B}$ display;

while $\mathcal{R}$ allows $\mathcal{M}$ to continue **do**

    check $\mathcal{R}$ to see which player P moves next in $\mathcal{M}$;

    P move, answering m;

    $\mathcal{M}$ record m in the moves for the match and

        update $\mathcal{B}$ to reflect m.

    $\mathcal{B}$ display;

declare the outcome of the game as determined by $\mathcal{R}$ using the configuration of $\mathcal{B}$ and the last move in $\mathcal{M}$;

Figure 12.9: The referee algorithm for playing a Tic-Tac-Toe match.

avoiding any reliance on the fact that we're playing Tic-Tac-Toe and not some other game. The fact that we use the rules to determine the next player to move might even let us use this same processing for games having more than two players, such as Chinese Checkers. This algorithm essentially provides the referee we decided to use in Step 1 of our low-level design process. We'll refer to this algorithm as the "referee algorithm". We won't introduce a class for a referee both because this processing seems to fit nicely as a method in the match class and because the idea of having an explicit referee is not appealing since most people don't use a referee in a Tic-Tac-Toe match. For now, we will place a method start to implement this processing in the class TicTacToe Match. During Step 3, we will move this method—and others we identify subsequently—to the appropriate class in the hierarchy for a match.

Class specifications for the Tic-Tac-Toe application are presented below in the format:

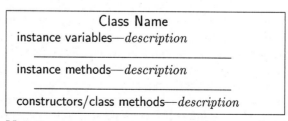

Notes:

1. *Comments about the class.*

The variables and methods listed in the classes that follow are a result of our domain analysis, our decision to use the class hierarchy structures shown in Figures 12.5 and 12.6, and our decision to use the referee algorithm. Remember that we are addressing our specific application in what follows, although we have not qualified variable and method names with "Tic-Tac-Toe." Using what we develop here, we will refine this design in Step 3 to extend it to other classes in our hierarchy structure.

TicTacToe Match

game—the game being played
moves—the sequence of moves made in this match (so far)
playerO—the player in this match placing ciphers
playerX—the player in this match placing crosses

---

display—display the game and the players
getMoves—answer the sequence of moves
getPlayerO—answer the player placing ciphers
getPlayerX—answer the player placing crosses
record(aMove)—record aMove in the list of moves
start—begin play
whatIs(aPlayer)—answer the token associated with a player
whoIs(aToken)—answer the player associated with a token

---

new(playerX, playerO)—construct a new Tic-Tac-Toe match showing no moves so far

Notes:
1. There are no methods to set the instance variables because we don't allow the game or the players to change once the match is instantiated.

TicTacToe Game

ciphers—the cipher tokens in this game
crosses—the cross tokens in this game
gameBoard—the game board
rules—the rules of this game

---

display—display the game—that is, display its components
getCiphers—answer the four cipher tokens in this game
getCrosses—answer the five cross tokens in this game
getGameBoard—answer the game board
getRules—answer the rules of this game
getTokens(aPlayer)—answer the set of tokens in this game belonging to a player
setup(playerX, playerO)—set up the game board for play in accordance with the rules, assigning crosses to playerX and ciphers to playerO

---

new—answer a new game having a board, five crosses, four ciphers, and rules

Notes:
1. There is no way to change the game board, the tokens, or the rules for a game. This class serves primarily to associate a game board, some tokens, and some rules for Tic-Tac-Toe. A box might make a good model—the get$X$ method takes X out of the box.
2. The setup method arranges the various components in accordance with the rules. We could have designed the rules to set up a game, but it seems more natural to put that functionality in this class—who would think to tell a set of rules to set up a game?[2]   However, a game might expect the rules to help in the setup.
3. When a game is created, the tokens are not assigned to players.

TicTacToe Board
spaces—a network of spaces
display—display the game board in its current state examine(aSpace)—answers the content of the space—a set of tokens getSpace(aName)—answer the space having a name make(aMove)—update the board to reflect a move and answer either **true** or **false**, depending on whether the move is legal or not eastOf(aSpace)—answers the space east of a space northeastOf(aSpace)—answers the space northeast of a space northOf(aSpace)—answers the space north of a space northwestOf(aSpace)—answers the space northwest of a space southeastOf(aSpace)—answers the space southeast of a space southOf(aSpace)—answers the space south of a space southwestOf(aSpace)—answers the space southwest of a space westOf(aSpace)—answers the space west of a space
new—answer a new board having nine spaces numbered 1 through 9, numbered left-to-right, top-to-bottom

Notes:
1. The network used to connect spaces is a library class—probably something as simple as a two-dimensional array class.
2. The navigation methods (eastOf, northeastOf, etc.) answer **nil** if there isn't any space in that direction. We could have chosen to use a special off-the-board space, but that does not seem to reduce the need for checking the result and introduces a new global constant in the process.
3. The make(aMove) method implementation has to know the rules for a move, so in some sense the rules of the game are distributed across the classes for any particular game.

---

[2]Of course, only object-oriented thinkers would consider telling a game to set up itself!

Space

contents—the token occupying this space (if any)
gameBoard—the game board to which this space belongs
name—the name of the space

---

display—display this space on the screen
getName—answer the name of the space
getContents—answer the token occupying this space (if any)
getGameBoard—answer the game board to which this space belongs
moveTo(aToken)—move a token onto this space
moveFrom(aToken)—move a token from this space

---

new(aName, aGameBoard)—answer a new space on a game board having a name
   and no contents

Notes:
1. A space is assumed to remain in the same game board throughout its lifetime and
    to keep the same name.
2. It is important that when a token changes its location, that token be informed
    of the move. Method moveFrom should notify the token. Method moveTo should
    behave similarly.

TicTacToe Rules

---

check(aMove, aMatch)—check to see that a move is legal in the context of a
   match
isDraw(aMatch)—answer **true** if a match has ended in a draw
isOver(aMatch)—answer **true** if a match is over
nextPlayer(aMatch)—answer the next player of a match—the first player to move
   if the match is just starting
winner(aMatch)—answer the winner of a match (if any)

---

new—answer a new set of rules

Notes:
1. Objects of this class maintain no state. All decisions made by rules are made
    within the context of a match. The match is provided in each method. Thus, for
    any given game, one set of rules could be shared by all matches. We could have
    a Rules object maintain the match in which it is being applied, but this ability to
    share rules has some appeal.
2. The requirements don't specify that the match is to end as soon as it can be
    recognized that neither player can win, so we assume that the match will continue
    through nine moves before isDraw will consider an answer of **true**.

TicTacToe Player

name—this player's name

---

display—display this player
takeBack(aBadMove, aMatch)—answer a move to replace a bad move that was
  made for a match
yourTurn(aMatch)—answer a move (it's this player's turn to move)

---

new(aName)—answer a new player with a name

Notes:
1. A player maintains no state other than his name. A match is provided to set
    the context for the next move to be made. Note that a player does not even
    remember his last move—it is provided to him by the match. The advantage to
    this design is that a single player can participate in more than one match without
    any confusion.

TicTacToe Token

owner—the player to whom this token is assigned
space—the space on which this token resides, if any

---

display—display this token—implemented by subclass
getPlayer—answer the player to whom this token currently belongs
getSpace—answer the space on which this token resides

---

new—answer a new token having no owner and occupying no space

Notes:
1. This abstract class has two subclasses—Cross and Cipher—that inherit everything
    from this class except the text of the method to display itself.

TicTacToe Move

player—the player making this move
space—the space on the board on which the token is placed in this move
token—the token involved in this move

---

display—display this move
getPlayer—answer the player making this move
getSpace—answer the space involved in this move
getToken—answer the token involved in this move

---

new(aToken, aSpace, aPlayer)—construct a new move with the indicated objects

Notes:
1. There is no provision to change a move once it is constructed. One advantage to
    this design is that a move recorded in a match cannot be changed inadvertently.

Step 3: Generalizing Application-Specific Attributes

Now that we have specified the classes we need for our Tic-Tac-Toe application, we will try to generalize the attributes by moving as many as we can to higher positions in the class hierarchy. This is a fairly straightforward process. We re-examine each class specification produced in Step 2 and identify which variables and which methods can be moved to an ancestor class. In most cases all classes in a hierarchy are abstract except for those at the lowest level. The abstract classes provide a specification for each of its descendents and support polymorphism among instances of descendent classes. In Step 3, we look for attributes that, if generalized, can qualify for being promoted in the hierarchy—for example, changing the idea of a token on a space to a *set* of tokens on a space will apply the relationship *on a space* to games that allow more than one token to occupy a space simultaneously. Such generalizations improve the specification of abstract classes because they increase the functionality of all subclasses in a uniform manner.

We present the results of this step using the same format to represent classes used in Step 2. We use an arrow to represent the inheritance relationship between two classes.

Match

game—the game being played
moves—the sequence of moves made in this match (so far)
players—a collection of the players in this match

---

display—display the game and the players—implemented by subclasses
getMoves—answer the sequence of moves
record(aMove)—record a [presumably legal] move in the list of moves
start—begin play—and serve as referee!

---

new(aGame, thePlayers)—construct a new match involving the players showing
   no moves so far

BoardGameMatch

tokenAssignments—the association between tokens and players

---

assign(aPlayer, aToken)—associate a player with a token
whatIs(aPlayer)—answer the token associated with a player
whoIs(aToken)—answer the player associated with a token

StrategyBoardGameMatch

TicTacToe Match

---

new(playerX, playerO)—construct a new Tic-Tac-Toe match showing no moves so
   far

Notes:
1. All matches seem to involve a game, players, and moves, so we have transferred
    these variables and their associated methods to class **Match**. Not all games involve
    tokens, but all board games seem to, so we have moved the attributes associated
    with linking tokens and players to class **Board Game Match**. These changes estab-
    lish a protocol for all matches and all board game matches, respectively. We can't
    implement all of the methods in the abstract classes, but each of these methods
    will be available in instances of any subclass. Players and a game are provided to
    a match constructor because this models the real world—players "sitting down"

to play a specific game.

2. We have generalized the two Tic-Tac-Toe players to a collection of players, replacing playerO and playerX with players and tokenAssignments.

    In generalizing to a set of players, we realize that for some board games the arrangement of the players around the board is important—for example, to determine which player moves next—but we have deferred details of this until some later date when we need to implement it.[3]   For our current application, there can be only one arrangement for two players.

3. We are assuming that in any board game match players move in turns, though this does not preclude the same player from making multiple moves in a row within the sequence.

4. At some point we might want to consider adding a *save* function to save a match (allowing a match to be interrupted or archived) and a corresponding *open* function to retrieve a saved match. A *resume* capability would be needed to continue an interrupted match. We might also add a *replay* function to Board Game Match to enable a saved match to be replayed. The class would have to be able to reconstruct the initial configuration of the game for a replay capability to be provided, necessitating the addition of instance variables. There are many possible extensions. We will be able to add them as we see a demand for them and as resources become available to implement them. For now, we will concentrate on meeting the minimum requirements for our application.

---

[3] When we implement a game having more than two players, we might find it appropriate to modify the hierarchy to distinguish between two-player and two-or-more-player games. We just don't want to design too far ahead with our only real consideration so far being our Tic-Tac-Toe application.

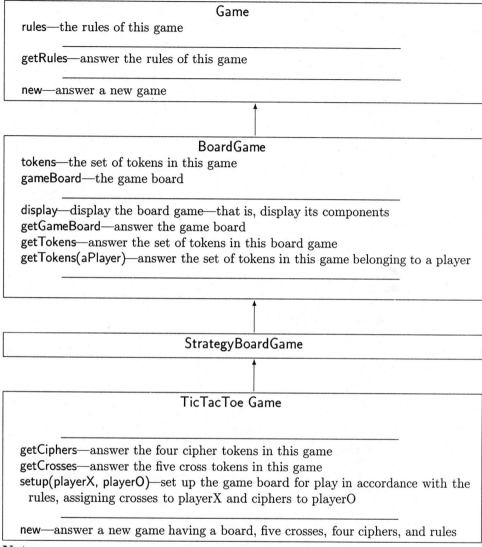

Game

rules—the rules of this game

getRules—answer the rules of this game

new—answer a new game

BoardGame

tokens—the set of tokens in this game
gameBoard—the game board

display—display the board game—that is, display its components
getGameBoard—answer the game board
getTokens—answer the set of tokens in this board game
getTokens(aPlayer)—answer the set of tokens in this game belonging to a player

StrategyBoardGame

TicTacToe Game

getCiphers—answer the four cipher tokens in this game
getCrosses—answer the five cross tokens in this game
setup(playerX, playerO)—set up the game board for play in accordance with the rules, assigning crosses to playerX and ciphers to playerO

new—answer a new game having a board, five crosses, four ciphers, and rules

Notes:
1. We have allowed class **Strategy Board Game** to remain in the hierarchy even though it has no attributes because—oddly enough—it has been the focus of our domain analysis! When we eventually address more games—perhaps games more complicated than Tic-Tac-Toe—we may find some suitable attributes for the class.
2. There is no way to change the game board or the rules for a game. There is no way to change the tokens used in a board game.
3. The **setup** method arranges the various components in accordance with the rules. This method is specific to class **TicTacToe Game**. We could see no way to generalize this method except in some artificial way.

GameBoard

---

display—display the game board in its current state—implemented by subclasses
examine(aSpace)—answers the content of the space—a set of tokens
getSpace(aName)—answer the space having a name
make(aMove)—update the board to reflect a move and answer either **true** or
  false, depending on whether the move is legal or not

↑

TwoDimensionalGameBoard

↑

GridGameBoard

spaceGrid—a two-dimensional array of spaces

---

display—display the game board in its current state
examine(aSpace)—answers the content of the space—a set of tokens
install(aSpace)—put a space in the next portion of the grid (by rows) in which
  there is no associated space
eastOf(aSpace)—answers the space east of a space
northeastOf(aSpace)—answers the space northeast of a space
northOf(aSpace)—answers the space north of a space
northwestOf(aSpace)—answers the space northwest of a space
southeastOf(aSpace)—answers the space southeast of a space
southOf(aSpace)—answers the space south of a space
southwestOf(aSpace)—answers the space southwest of a space
westOf(aSpace)—answers the space west of a space

---

new(rowCount, columnCount)—answer a new grid of specified dimensions
new(rowCount, columnCount, spaceCollection)—answer a new grid of specified dimensions and with the spaces in the (ordered) space collection tiled by row

---

↑

TicTacToe Board

---

new—answer a new 3-by-3 grid having spaces numbered 1 through 9, numbered
  left-to-right, top-to-bottom

Notes:

1. The network used to connect spaces in a grid is a two-dimensional array.
2. The getSpace method implementation could be implemented at each level in order to take advantage of any regularity in the arrangement of spaces on a board.
3. The navigation methods (eastOf, northeastOf, etc.) answer **nil** if there isn't any space in that direction. We could have chosen to use a special off-the-board space, but that does not seem to reduce the need for checking the result, and it also introduces a new global constant in the process.
4. Class TicTacToe Board retains only those attributes specific to a Tic-Tac-Toe board. All others have been elevated to ancestor classes. The constructor creates the proper size game board for Tic-Tac-Toe.

Space

contents—the collection of tokens occupying this space—possibly an empty collection
gameBoard—the game board to which this space belongs
name—the name of the space

---

display—display this space on the screen
getName—answer the name of the space
getContents—answer the collection of tokens occupying this space
getGameBoard—answer the game board to which this space belongs
moveTo(aToken)—move a token onto this space
moveFrom(aToken)—move a token from this space

---

new(aName, aGameBoard)—answer a new space on a game board having a name and no contents

Notes:

1. We have generalized the concept of a token occupying a space with the concept of a *collection* of tokens occupying a space and respecified the variable contents accordingly. Had we not done this, we would have a problem with games such as Clue in which multiple tokens can simultaneously occupy a single space during a match.

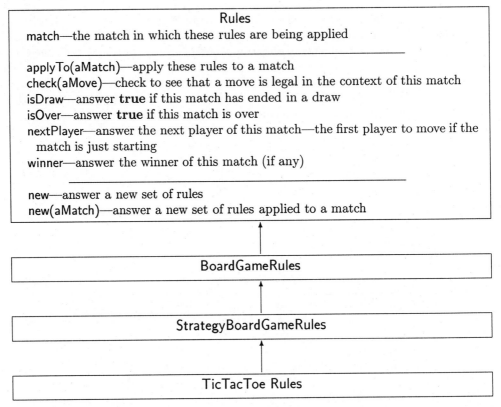

Rules

match—the match in which these rules are being applied

---

applyTo(aMatch)—apply these rules to a match
check(aMove)—check to see that a move is legal in the context of this match
isDraw—answer **true** if this match has ended in a draw
isOver—answer **true** if this match is over
nextPlayer—answer the next player of this match—the first player to move if the
  match is just starting
winner—answer the winner of this match (if any)

---

new—answer a new set of rules
new(aMatch)—answer a new set of rules applied to a match

BoardGameRules

StrategyBoardGameRules

TicTacToe Rules

Notes:

1. We have changed our minds about having rules maintain state and added a variable to hold the match for which these rules are being applied. It was annoying to require that a match be a part of every message and it seems reasonable to expect that a set of rules for a match might want to maintain state information anyway. The way we had designed it earlier, the rules would have to re-analyze the moves in the match in order to make a ruling. As a very simple example, consider the rules for Tic-Tac-Toe. In order to determine the next player, the rules would have to look at the list of moves made so far and determine that the match was not yet over and, if not, which player was the last to move. The rules could simply keep some state information—for example, remembering who made the last move. This mechanism does make the assumption that a match will consult its rules at appropriate times during play.

2. We provide a constructor without parameters and a method applyTo(aMatch) because a class **Rules** instance created by a game will not, in general, have an associated match. [A game can exist outside a match.]

Player

match—the match in which this player is participating
name—this player's name

---

display—display this player
getMatch—answer the match in which this player is participating
getName—answer this player's name
playIn(aMatch)—set the match in which this player is participating

---

new(aName)—answer a new player with a name
new(aName, aMatch)—answer a new player with a name and participating in aMatch

---

BoardGamePlayer

lastMove—the last move made by this player in the match

---

tryAgain—answer a move to replace this player's last move which was disallowed.
yourTurn—answer a move (it's this player's turn to move)

StrategyBoardGamePlayer

TicTacToe Player

Notes:

1. A player maintains state in contrast to our earlier design, remembering the match and the last move. These two objects were provided as parameters to the methods takeBack and yourTurn in our design in Step 2. We have interpreted the requirements so that both players are human. However, there is nothing to preclude one or both of the players being a computer. If we assume that a player can be a computer, then an instance will probably want to maintain a strategy across turns to move. Once we get clarification about the requirements—or some indication that we can have a computer for a player in some future set of requirements—we will add some subclasses to represent human players and machine players.

2. It is tempting to require a match as a parameter to the constructor, but with the design we have in mind, a player will be provided as a parameter to a match constructor. If we required the match parameter, we would have a Catch-22.

```
┌──────────────────────────────────────────────────────────────────────┐
│                              Token                                     │
│  player—the player who "owns" this token                               │
│  space—the space on which this token resides                           │
│  ────────────────────────────────────────────────────────             │
│  display—display this token—implemented by subclass                    │
│  getPlayer—answer the player to whom this token currently belongs       │
│  getSpace—answer the space on which this token resides                  │
│  ────────────────────────────────────────────────────────             │
│                                                                        │
└──────────────────────────────────────────────────────────────────────┘
                                    △
                                    │
┌──────────────────────────────────────────────────────────────────────┐
│                         TicTacToe Token                                │
└──────────────────────────────────────────────────────────────────────┘
```

Notes:

1. Every attribute has moved to the Token class. We have retained the TicTacToe Token class for now to keep polymorphism for the Cross and Cipher classes while still being able to restrict the amount of polymorphism.

2. We are assuming a one-to-many relationship between players and tokens as well as a one-to-one relationship between a token and a space, although we allow multiple tokens to occupy the same space.

3. A token might not be on any space and/or might not have any owner.

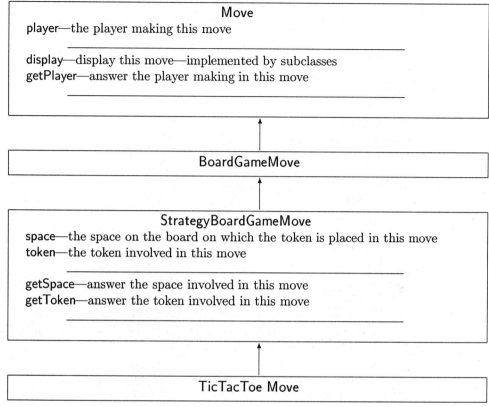

Notes:

1. There is no provision to change a move once it is constructed.

2. In all of the strategy board games we can think of, a move involves only one token.[4]   In other board games—for example, Scrabble™—more than one token and more than one space can be involved in a single move, so we didn't elevate any attributes other than those associated with a player beyond class **Strategy Board Game Move**. We are assuming—we hope safely—that only one player makes a move at a time in any board game. Note that this implies that a match is a sequence of moves made one after another—that is, no two can be made simultaneously.

3. We don't need class **TicTacToe Move** because its parent class provides all the functionality that we need, unless we want to customize one of the methods—most probably **display**.

   With all the class specifications designed, we would ordinarily move next to describing the algorithms for each of the methods. We omit this part of the design for

---

[4]We want to distinguish that the *consequences* of a move may involve multiple tokens—for example, sending an opponent back to "Start"—but a move involves only a single token. If we find a game that violates this assumption, we can always refine our definition of "strategy board game" to exclude it! Or we can redesign the class **Move**, perhaps introducing the idea of a "turn" to aggregate a group of what we have called "moves" made at the same time.

the sake of brevity, noting only that we have adopted the referee algorithm to implement the start method and that the processing required for at least most of the other class methods is straightforward—if not obvious.

IMPLEMENTATION

We have completed the design of a set of classes that hold promise for getting our Tic-Tac-Toe application up and running. We now need to realize this as a set of classes in our implementation language.

An interesting aspect of our design is that we have avoided any mention or consideration of our implementation language. We have based our design on a pure object-oriented paradigm in which all of a class's instance variables are private and all binding of messages to methods is done dynamically. This is not necessarily a good idea because the implementation language can indeed have an impact on the design. If we were a shop that programs exclusively in one language, then we might have embedded implementation language considerations into our original design in order to avoid this effort during implementation. If we use a variety of languages—or want to decide which language to use *after* we have completed design—then our approach is reasonable. Let's consider the impact of choosing C^{++} as our implementation language for this design. For illustration, let us address implementation of a Match structure.

The realization of a class in our design as a class in C^{++} is a straightforward exercise. In our design we have provided class names and parent class names. It also specifies the instance variables, though the class of each instance variable is not provided explicitly. In a "typed" object-oriented programming language such as C^{++}, we need to specify a class for each instance variable. Furthermore, once we have identified a class, we must decide whether an instance variable should be an object of that class or a *pointer* to an object of that class. As a consequence, we must perform another pass on our design in order to implement the application in C^{++}. In the case of a Match, we need to make its instance variables game and players pointers because these objects are provided as parameters to a constructor and hence are created outside of this instance. We will choose to make the instance variable moves a pointer as well because this object is accessible through the method getMoves and we want to be certain that the lifetime of the object providing moves can be longer than the lifetime of a match.[5]

---

[5] A class destructor in C^{++} usually destroys all of its component objects. The situation we have here is a bit messy. We use a pointer to keep moves accessible to clients of this class, so we have to rely on some external agent to destroy the object referenced by moves—even though no external agent created it! This illustrates the importance of documentation in classes designed for reuse. Unless users of a class are aware of such responsibilities, "garbage" can easily begin to collect in a C^{++} application. Alternatively, we can return a *copy* of the moves to a caller and destroy the object referenced by moves. This second solution is appealing and has the benefit of preventing the sequence of moves from being modified in any way and of providing a snapshot of the moves at the time the message was sent—probably just what we had in mind when we designed the class! This points out an important facet of class design: Sometimes it is appropriate for methods to answer a copy of an attribute instead of the attribute itself. Again, it is important to document that a client who receives such a copy is responsible for destroying it.

Having realized the instance variables in a class, we next address the realization of the methods. Again, since the design does not explicitly do so, we must now specify the class of each member function parameter and of the return value of the member function, if any. We must also decide whether a member function is *virtual* and/or *inline*. For the class Match, we have five methods to consider:

Match(aGame, thePlayers) This is the class constructor, renamed from "new." Class constructors are virtual.

display The design specifies that this method is implemented by subclasses, requiring it to be virtual. We assume there is no return value since the design does not specify an "answer."

getMoves This method provides access to instance variable moves so its return type is the same as the type of moves. There is no need to make this member function virtual.

record(aMove) This method appends a move to the sequence of moves given by moves. The type of the parameter should be a pointer to a class Move object. There is no return value specified. Apparently all the processing can be done by this class, so there is no need to make this member function virtual.

start This algorithm implements the referee algorithm for a strategy board game. This member function needs to be virtual.

We need to specify a destructor as well:

~Match This method is virtual and each subclass will implicitly invoke its parent class's destructor after it finishes its own processing.

We will postpone any decision to *inline* any member function until we get the application running and note its performance. Our implementation of class Match is shown in Figure 12.10. We have made all our instance variables private and all our member functions public in class Match, meeting what seem to be the assumptions of the design. Had the design for each method been more complete, we might have identified some private methods or some additional instance variables for some of these classes. As we implement, we might introduce some private and/or protected member functions to improve the design.

Implementation using C++ and other strongly typed languages can have an implication on design (other than the ones we handled above) to determine the class of each attribute and parameter and the binding to be used for member function calls. Inclusion polymorphism has slightly different behaviors between languages that use strong typing, such as C++, and languages that use no typing, such as Smalltalk. Consider the design and implementation of the class TicTacToe Match. Its ancestor classes Match and Board Game Match set up the complete protocol for TicTacToe Match except for a constructor that allows us to specify players individually rather than as a set. We designed this constructor mainly as a convenience—it constructs a game and a player set and invokes the constructor for a Match. Suppose we want to add two more methods for convenience to TicTacToe Match:

playerX to answer the player placing crosses
playerO to answer the player placing ciphers.

```
class Match {
 private
  Game *game;      // the game being played
  List *moves;     // the sequence of moves in this match
  List *players;   // the players in this match
 public
  virtual Match *Match(Game *aGame, List *thePlayers);
  virtual void ~Match();                                    }

  virtual void display();
  List *getMoves();
  void record(Move &aMove);
  virtual void start() = 0;
```

```
virtual Match *Match::Match(Game *aGame, List *thePlayers) {
 // construct a new match involving the players
 players = thePlayers; game = aGame; moves = new List;
}
virtual void *Match::~Match() {
 // destroy the moves recorded here
 moves->destruct();
}
virtual void Match::display() {
 // display the game and the players---
 // implemented by subclasses
 // this is a very simple default implementation
 game->display;
 players->display;
 moves->display;
}
List *Match::getMoves() {
 // answer the sequence of moves
 return moves->copy;
}
void Match::record(Move &aMove) {
 // record a [presumable legal] move in the list of moves
 moves->append(aMove);
}
```

Figure 12.10: A C++ implementation of class Match.

Consider a code segment that constructs a Tic-Tac-Toe match:

```
Player          *john    = new TicTacToePlayer("John");
Player          *gayle   = new TicTacToePlayer("Gayle");
TicTacToe Match *m       = new TicTacToeMatch(john, gayle);
m->start;
                    .
                    .
                    .
```

We can send a message m->game->playerX to find john, but if somewhere in the processing we used inclusion polymorphism to pass m to a member function having signature foo(Match *aMatch), then within foo we cannot send a message aMatch->game->playerX because the member function playerX is not in the interface for class Match.[6] This inability to address methods added at lower levels from a class being used to provide inclusion polymorphism is characteristic of object-oriented programming languages that support strong typing. In implementing our design in C++, we must be careful in choosing classes for instance variables, return values, and especially formal parameters to member functions to ensure that class provides all the functionality needed.

TESTING

We need to test our classes and our application.

For testing our application, we can instantiate a TicTacToe Match and send it a start message and play, verifying that as we play all the requirements have been satisfied. This is such a simple application that requirements are easy to check. We could probably get away with three test cases: one in which the player placing crosses wins, one in which the player placing ciphers wins, and one in which the match ends in a draw. We might want to include the pathological case in which the two players are the same, just to see what happens. For a more extensive set of requirements, the techniques described in Chapter 9 can be used.

If we were to develop our set of abstract classes more fully than required to support our current application, then we would want to invest some effort into testing them more fully. Refer to Chapter 9 for a description of how to approach this.

MAINTENANCE

Assume that we have successfully completed implementation of our Tic-Tac-Toe application. Somebody has decided that the user interface is just not sophisticated enough. The requirements called for the game board to be printed after each move, so we took the easy route and printed out the board using characters:

---

[6]If we *know* that aMatch is indeed a TicTacToe Match, then we can coerce the type of aMatch and send the message. The problem in general is knowing *for sure* since in C++ no checking is done at run time for such conversions "down" the class hierarchy.

```
    X |   |
   ---+---+---
    O | O | X
   ---+---+---
    X |   |
```

What our customer really wanted was something graphically more sophisticated:

Our job is to improve the look of the output.

This has no effect on the analysis we have already done. No new application-level entities have been introduced. We just have a new "look" for the Tic-Tac-Toe board and the tokens. This change is an implementation-only change, which we can easily identify as a change to three methods: the display method for class TicTacToe Board, the display method for class Cross, and the display method for class Cipher. These are similar: We need to display a graphic to represent the object.

The first step is to see if there are any classes in the library to do what we need. As we explore the library, we come across the graphics classes that were associated with the draw program application described in earlier chapters. These look promising. We can use circle objects to form the ciphers and line objects to form the crosses. The shading will be a bit tricky. We'll have to do that by drawing dots. Using dots is a little troublesome because it will take a lot of them and that means a lot of messages have to be sent. We don't want a token to take very long to display itself, or displaying the board will take an unacceptably long time. What we really would like to have is a way to draw a token once and then display the picture on the screen in a single operation instead of as a series of messages.[7] What we want is a virtual display screen on which we can draw and whose image we can transfer to another screen—either a real screen or another virtual screen. What we are after is a "bitmap" object and a method to transfer one bitmap to another.

Our next step is to identify the changes we need to make to the graphics classes to incorporate a bitmap. If we start with the class hierarchy in Figure 5.15, then we might consider a bitmap to be an object similar to a rectangle or a line—that is, a bitmap is another kind of shape. On the other hand, we might consider a bitmap to be a special kind of rectangle, one that is neither solid nor a selector box. However, since most people would not consider the "inside" of a rectangle to be a part of a rectangle, we can't really say that a bitmap *is a* rectangle, and so we won't make a bitmap a subclass of a rectangle. Besides, some of the operations for a bitmap such as testing a bit are not meaningful for a rectangle.

---

[7]Ideally, we could save this picture somewhere and not have to recreate it each time a token is instantiated. *Persistent* objects are discussed in Chapter 14.

We can add a new bitmap class to the shape class hierarchy quite easily—just add a new subclass of **Bitmap** to class **Displayable Shape**. This addition will have no effect on any other classes in this structure. As such, we can implement only the portions of the **Bitmap** class that we need for the current application. Since this is a new class in an existing hierarchy structure, we should make sure that we follow the same philosophy that was used when the other classes were developed with respect to the methods that are available in the class.

Assuming we have a class to provide bitmaps, we need to incorporate a bitmap into each of the methods we identified for change. We have two mechanisms for adding the bitmap capabilities:

1. We can use an additional instance variable.
2. We can use inheritance—including multiple inheritance in the case of C++.

Consider the class **TicTacToe Board**. We need a bitmap to represent the board. A new instance of the class should contain a bitmap of an empty board. As moves are made, tokens should appear in the image. Which of the two mechanisms should we use?

The answer lies in how we want to model a Tic-Tac-Toe board. If we want to treat it as a displayable object, then it makes perfect sense to make **TicTacToe Board** a subclass of **Bitmap**. Indeed, we would make the class **Game Board** a subclass of **Bitmap**. If we want to treat a game board as an abstraction with a capability—but not an intrinsic property—of being displayed, then the first choice is the more appropriate one. Since we are interested in implementing computer-based games in which graphics play an important role and in which the picture of a component on a screen is essentially the way we think about that component, then we choose to use inheritance. Notice that we are not inheriting from the class **Bitmap** for purposes of implementation! We use inheritance because in our view a game board *is a* graphical object. If our view of the domain of games were separate from an ability to display their components—for example, we want to be able to simulate games for the purpose of developing strategy and not for providing entertainment, then we would reflect that view in our class structure in a different way.

SUMMARY

In this chapter we have sketched the development of a simple application in the object-oriented style. We have described some of the decisions that went into the design and implementation of the classes for the application. While it has been difficult to capture all the decisions that we have had to make in the development of classes for this application, we have tried to show that a design does change during the process.

Prior to developing the Tic-Tac-Toe application, one of us had participated in the domain analysis for an object-oriented Chess application. That experience was part of the input to the domain analysis of the current application and contributed to the preliminary decomposition of classes. The Tic-Tac-Toe design was accomplished by the other author from the ground up and did not reuse any of the design or implementation details from the Chess application that was being developed in parallel.

Interestingly, many of the structures of classes from the two applications closely resemble one another. The second effort reflected the important role that refinement plays in design. Even the relatively small amount of overlap between the two projects resulted in more meaningful abstractions that can encompass not only the Chess and Tic-Tac-Toe games but many others as well.

13

Tools for System Development

Over the past few years, many tools have been developed to support the software development process. The language tools have been available the longest and are the most mature. More recently, computer-assisted design tools for design documentation and test management have been used by a growing number of developers. Automated documentation aids have also been developed. The object-oriented paradigm will benefit from those tools as well as from those designed specifically for the paradigm.

In this chapter we survey several categories of tools that are being used to support the development of object-oriented applications. We will present actual tools as well as "virtualware," which represents the tools we would like to see built but that have not yet been developed. We will discuss support for the languages that we presented in Chapter 7 as well as tools to support the analysis and design activities. First, we will consider the place of tools in the object-oriented development process and how they can contribute to improving the development process.

THE NEED FOR TOOLS

Why do we need tools more with object technology? The discrete encapsulated nature of objects seems to lend itself to manipulation by tools. There are three reasons why tools will play a more important role in object-oriented development than they have in the procedural approach.

- *There are more modules to manage in the object-oriented approach than in the procedural approach.* Many of the modules in object-oriented systems are smaller than the units referred to as modules in the procedural paradigm. A typical Ada package often has several type and structure definitions while a class is a single structure definition. Even if the class is not smaller than a procedural module, the object approach results in more abstract modules that describe increasingly larger portions of the system. The layered design model, supported by class inheritance, results in several modules where one might have been sufficient in the procedural paradigm. The result of these two phenomena is that the system developers must coordinate more modules.

- *The incremental nature of the object-oriented paradigm requires the coordination of several modules to produce a new one.* The use of inheritance to define a class combines the previous definitions of one or more classes with the definition of a "modifier" to produce the new class. The developer must be able to see these various pieces brought together for viewing, but each piece must be maintained separately to preserve modularity. Tools are needed to give access to the various increments of several products. The "definition by pieces" also leads to incremental pieces for documentation and testing, all of which must be managed.

- *The emphasis on reuse requires tools for cataloging, maintaining, and accessing the reusable components.* A methodology that results in numerous products that are combined in a variety of ways and that must be coordinated requires tools to provide access. The large number of classes means that we cannot remember all their names so techniques must be developed for finding the appropriate classes. In a corporate development environment many small modifications will be made to classes, resulting in a need for version control.

ANALYSIS AND DESIGN TOOLS

The most common support used in the analysis and design phases is a tool that enables the designer to draw diagrams in one of the design notations. Excelerator™ provides this capability using several of the popular notations including the ER diagrams we use for recording classes and their relationships. Software Through Pictures™ provides a similar set of capabilities for structured object-oriented design.

The support for domain analysis must include the recording of the entities in the problem domain and the relationships between them. The supporting tool should provide a representation that can follow the entities into the succeeding stages of development. This is easy to accomplish since the entities identified at the domain analysis level are mapped directly onto the classes at the design and implementation levels. The representation should include a conceptual description that would result from the domain analysis that would eventually be associated with a class specification and still later with a class implementation.

The data dictionary available in many CASE tools is the start of such a tool; however, no comprehensive system is in widespread use. Several systems are available that claim to provide some portion of this functionality. Software Through Pictures™ includes a data dictionary that retains sufficient detail to automatically generate a class specification in a given language. These specifications can then be the basis for an implementation of the class, and for communication between developers.

IMPLEMENTATION TOOLS

There are many languages that support the object-oriented approach, as we pointed out in Chapter 7. The success of a language is partially attributable to the quality of the available language tools. These tools must support the development process in a number of ways:

- *Tools must be available to transform the source code that expresses the concepts of the paradigm into an executable form.* This is an obvious requirement, but how it is met is not so obvious. There are several alternatives, including translators, compilers, and interpreters. These tools must be developed for a new set of ideas that in the early stages are not well formed, so the tools will be modified many times. The object-oriented paradigm has reached a level of maturity in which these tools are good implementations and the languages are relatively stable.
- *Source code development tools that go beyond simple editing are needed.* Debuggers, profilers, and other utilities can increase the productivity of the developer. The tools should be specialized to support the unique characteristics of the development technique. In the object-oriented approach, relationships are an important part of the models being developed. Therefore, tools that illustrate these relationships would be very useful. Even though a class need not know about its subclasses, it is often useful to be able to develop a list of all the subclasses of a given class. Environments such as SaberC++ keep this information for a set of classes in memory, but it does not support the long-term storage or manipulation of this information.
- *The tools should assist the developer in optimizing the implementation of a design.* One technique for this is to transform the source code of the "new" language into that of an established language. The optimizing techniques of the established language can be used to optimize and then generate an executable image from that language. AT&T took advantage of this approach by transforming C^{++} code into C code before compiling with optimizing C compilers.

In the remainder of this section we will briefly discuss the range of transformation tools available. The choice of one of these tools can significantly impact the development time and the performance of an application.

Translators

The original implementation of C^{++} by AT&T Bell Labs was in the form of a program that translated from the C^{++} syntax into standard C syntax. This approach follows the incremental style that characterizes the object-oriented paradigm because it does not require the modification of the existing C compiler. It accounts for the rapid spread of C^{++} in its early years. The port of the translator to a new platform requires an existing C compiler for that platform and a small number of modifications to the translator. Thus, C^{++} quickly became available on a wide range of systems and was easily updated by AT&T as the language matured. The use of the existing C language as a base enabled users to access existing libraries, optimizers, and other tools that would have had to be developed for a new language. One disadvantage of the translator approach is that it is often difficult to correlate the original source code and the executable code. For example, a symbolic debugger often cannot match original names with the names generated by the translator.

The translator approach is feasible in many situations, but it typically is of most use when the new language is very similar to the existing language. As a superset of C, C++ required a minimal amount of translation to be valid C code. On the other hand, a language with very different syntax and structure from C would have been very difficult to translate into C syntax and the process would be inefficient. Although native code C++ compilers are available from several vendors now, AT&T and several other vendors have remained with the translator approach.

Compilers

The "usual" language transformation tool is the compiler. It reads source code written in a language and produces object code suitable to be directly executed on the target machine. The compiler often will scan the source code—or some intermediate form—multiple times before generating the object code. During these passes, a number of transformations are performed on the program, including optimizing the structure of the code to increase the performance of generated code. These transformations are typically more complex than those performed by a translator. A translator typically relies on a compiler for its target language to perform these transformations.

The compilers for a new language are slow to mature. Optimization depends upon identifying typical usage patterns that can be replaced by more efficient patterns. These emerge after some experience with programming in the language. One useful optimization that can be performed by compilers of object-oriented languages is the substitution of the body of a function for a call to that function. C++ provides the "inline" declaration that can be attached to the definition of a member function, giving the programmer some control over optimization at the source code level. The compiler will analyze the member function and, if possible, it will generate the object code for the body of the member function instead of a call to function. The overhead of the call is eliminated in the executable, but the integrity of the design is maintained in the source code. This optimization can be carried out in any language, but the messaging approach will particularly benefit from the efficiencies produced by this technique. Of particular note are those methods that provide access to instance variables—that is, those functions that simply return the value of or assign a value to an instance variable.

A second optimization is the replacement of dynamic binding with static binding. Dynamic binding is used to support polymorphic handling of function calls. This can be specified in the class definition. C++ provides the "virtual" attribute for member functions in support of dynamic binding. In some contexts a compiler can determine exactly which method to call and eliminate the need for dynamic binding, thereby removing the overhead associated with dynamic binding. In Eiffel, the need of dynamic binding is determined by the compiler based on use of a particular instance of a class. In C++, however, the programmer must decide about the use of dynamic binding; this may not be altered without recompilation.

Interpreters

A third transformation tool is an interpreter, which provides for the transformation of source code statements into executable code for a target machine and for the immediate execution of that code. This interpretation and execution is performed on a statement-by-statement basis, which precludes optimizations. This inherent inefficiency can be partially eliminated through the use of "p-code," a form of partial compilation, and the use of cacheing. Code for a loop can be compiled, cached, and used repeatedly until the loop terminates rather than reinterpreting each line of the loop on each iteration.

The encapsulated approach of objects makes the use of an interpreter particularly appropriate for development and debugging. The user can define a class, create an instance of the class, and send messages to that instance to test the implementation without waiting for compilation. Even small pieces of code can be executed and checked for proper operation without writing test frames required for complete compilation. Smalltalk is used almost exclusively as an interpreted language, and a methodology for prototyping systems has grown around that environment. C++ has been primarily a compiled language, but we will discuss an interpreted version below.

SOME SPECIFIC OBJECT-ORIENTED TOOLS

In this section we consider two implementation environments: SaberC++ and Parc-Place Systems' Objectworks\Smalltalk. These are not intended as product reviews, nor are we endorsing these particular products over others. The two languages represented are very different, but their environments are quite similar and represent a good start at providing a comprehensive set of tools for object-oriented system development. The differences between the Smalltalk and C++ environments reflect the differences between the cultures and approaches of the typical users of each. The Smalltalk environment provides access to a large number of classes, including those that constitute the environment. The environment itself can be modified or pieces of it can be reused in other applications. The C++ environment comes with only a few classes and the environment is only modifiable by adding a user-defined button to the menu system. The user has no direct access to the environment's implementation and cannot incorporate parts of it into an application.

Having already discussed the languages in Chapter 7, in this section we turn our attention to the environments and the support they provide the user.

SaberC++

The SaberC++ environment provides a combination of compiled and interpreted operation that supports the development of classes from prototype to the final product. These basic language facilities are accompanied by a set of tools to provide information to the tool user and an interactive debugger to support the development process.

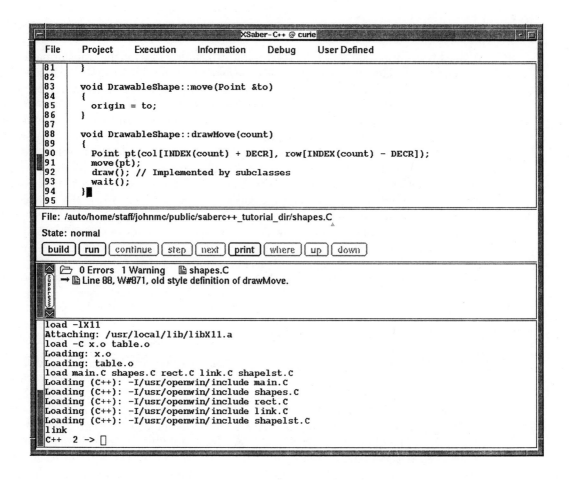

Figure 13.1: The SaberC++ X-Windows interface.

The tools provide some of the traditional support used by procedural development environments such as cross-reference information. These tools, however, provide much of this information in a graphical format that is easy to understand. The debugger also provides many of the traditional services of a source level debugger, including single-step execution and examination of variable values at breakpoints.

Figure 13.1 shows the X-Windows user interface for the SaberC++ environment. The interface is divided into four windows named (from the top) source window, menu window, status window, and command window. This interface is the central component in an environment that spawns browser windows to list project files, examine class definitions, and edit files.

The command window provides control of the environment as well as access to operating system commands. The command window accepts, interprets, and executes statements in C++, C, and the environment's command language. The command window in Figure 13.1 shows a short sequence of C++ commands, which are interpreted and executed as they are entered. These commands load files of C++ code. The code is partially compiled into a p-code representation as it is entered. During the loading process, any errors are reported in the status window.

The status window provides information from the interpretation of the source code into p-code format. Figure 13.1 shows a list of errors and warnings that is displayed when a file folder icon is selected. By selecting various folders to open, the user can move from one source file to another. Errors that occur at runtime are also listed in this window. Because of its interpreted status, the code may be executed even if there are errors in some of its statements. The erroneous statements will cause execution to halt, but the "*continue*" button in the menu window can be used to resume execution.

The menu window provides a set of quickly accessible actions that are the commonly used commands to control execution of the code. Each of these buttons enters a command that could have been entered directly in the command window. A set of menu selections is also located at the top of the source window.

The source window provides an edit facility for modifying long sequences of statements that can then be interpreted and executed. This window is also used for setting breakpoints for the debugger. The mouse cursor is placed beside the line at which the breakpoint is to be set and a simple click sets the breakpoint or later removes it. The source window is used to display source files that are loaded into the environment. When an error is discovered, the offending line from the appropriate file can be displayed by selecting the error message listed in the status window. The source window provides access to a variety of information. For example, the user can highlight a class name in the code and see the specification of that class in a pop-up window. The menu selections above this window again provide quick access to commands that can be typed directly into the command window. One advantage here is that a highlighted symbol is automatically entered as the argument to the command selected from one of the menus.

This environment has several interesting features:

- The interpreter is an unusual feature in a C++ development environment. Until the availability of SaberC++, all C++ implementations were based on compilers and a complement of tools running at the command level of an operating system. SaberC++ is the first implementation to embed C++ into a program-development environment. Developers will have to change their approach as they use an environment such as the one provided by the SaberC++ approach to implementation. The ability to test small—even incomplete—pieces of a system will change the way systems are developed using C++. This interpreter does not have access to the wide range of ready-made classes that are typically available in Smalltalk environments, but it is still a useful tool for developing systems.
- A useful feature is the ability to replace portions of the source code

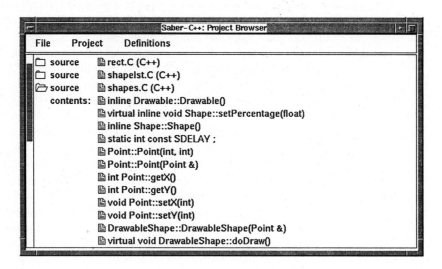

Figure 13.2: The project browser of SaberC^{++}.

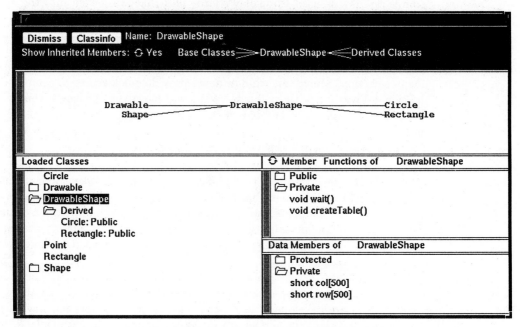

Figure 13.3: The class browser of SaberC^{++}.

running in the interpreter with object code. As each class is debugged and tested, the developer can choose to replace the source code with the object code. This greatly improves the speed of execution. As the system is developed, the code executes faster and faster as a greater portion becomes object code.

- A third powerful feature is the toolset available in the environment. Figure 13.2 illustrates one of the tools available in the environment. The environment provides a project browser that lists all the files in a project, and each file can be expanded to show the member functions in each file. Figure 13.3 shows the class browser, which provides information on a single class. This information includes the data and member functions of the class. The inheritance hierarchy is also shown so that the user can determine the position of the class in relation to other classes. The cross-reference tool provides information about all the classes that refer to a particular class, and which classes the current class references. Combined with the interpreter, these tools provide the developer with much control over the development process.

Many of the users of C++ are former C users. The SaberC++ environment will provide them with a very different approach to system development. The interactive nature of this environment will encourage an incremental, information-intensive approach that will maximize reuse of components.

Objectworks\Smalltalk

The Objectworks\Smalltalk system available from ParcPlace Systems is a good example of an object-oriented development environment. Many of the tools provided by SaberC++ were originally developed for use with Smalltalk.

Smalltalk-80 is a "non-typed" language in the sense that any variable can hold an instance of any class and can change its class over its lifetime. The availability of the tools provided by Objectworks\Smalltalk is important in this context because there is no comprehensive compilation system, nor are there any "types" to provide warnings of mistaken uses of instances of classes. The programmer must coordinate all the information that would be checked by a typing system. Browsers, multiple windows that can present information side by side for comparison, and an integrated code interpreter provide the developer with access to information about every aspect of the system development process to support this coordination.

The Objectworks\Smalltalk environment revolves around a "Launcher" window that supports the creation of multiple, independent instances of the basic tools:

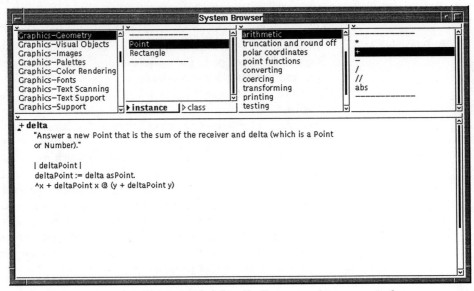

Figure 13.4: An Objectworks\Smalltalk system browser window.

> System browser
> System transcript
> Workspace
> File list
> File editor
> Change list
> Inspector
> Debugger
> Project

The principal programming tool is the system browser, which provides the ability to examine class definitions, and then edit, compile, and print them. A sample browser window is shown in Figure 13.4. Each window has five panes. From left to right, top to bottom, these panes are:

- *Class categories.* Each class is placed into a category to assist in the organization of the large number of classes. The figure shows the category "Graphics–Geometry" as being selected. A menu associated with the pane includes a selection to locate a class directly.
- *Classes.* The classes in the currently selected category are listed in this pane. Classes **Point** and **Rectangle** belong to category Graphics–Geometry.
- *Message categories.* In the same way that classes can be categorized, the methods for a class can be categorized. The environment defines a set of predefined category names to make classifications consistent across all classes. For example, the "accessing" category is used to group those

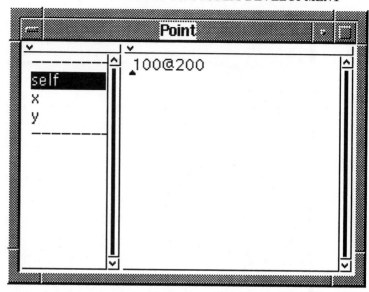

Figure 13.5: An Objectworks\Smalltalk inspector window for a point object.

methods that provide information about an instance of a class. A user can define additional categories.

- *Messages.* The methods in the currently selected category are listed in this pane.
- *Code.* The text of the definition for the selected method is made available in this text editing pane, which supports a full range of operations, including compilation. The figure shows the definition of the method "+ delta" for a Point class. This pane is also used in connection with class definition and for displaying information about a class, for example the class hierarchy "above" a selected class.

A system has a number of menus that provide selections for "filing"—moving—class definitions in and out of the environment, printing, adding categories, getting information about all users of a class, and so on. More than one system browser window can be opened at a time. The browsers provide direct access to the source code of the classes.

An inspector is a window that allows examination of the contents of an object. It displays a list of the instance variables and provides access to their values. An example of an inspector for a point object is shown in Figure 13.5. Inspectors are very useful both for debugging and for developing instances of classes for which code has not yet been completely developed. The information printed in an inspector can be customized by changing the definition of the putString method for a class.

When a program error occurs, the conditions that led to the failure can be examined using a debugger. A debugger window displays the current stack of message sends, a code view that supports the immediate editing of the code for a class, and

Figure 13.6: An Objectworks\Smalltalk debugger window.

two inspectors—one for instance variables and one for temporary variables. The window shown in Figure 13.6 resulted from an attempt to add a string 'oops!' to a point (100@200). Within a debugger program, execution can single-step, stop at breakpoints, and resume from the most recent message send. The debugger capability takes full advantage of the interpreted nature of Smalltalk to make program development and testing fully interactive.

The remainder of the basic tools provide capabilities for accessing the underlying operating system and its files and provide windows in which class instances—and hence application objects—can be created.

Objectworks\Smalltalk provides a comprehensive set of tools for object-oriented software development. This type of environment is particularly well suited to rapid prototyping because of its highly interactive nature. The main drawback is the execution speed of the interpreter—although the cacheing and garbage collection techniques make the performance of this system quite acceptable for most applications—and the difficulty in getting an application to run *outside* of the environment.

THE "TOOL OF THE FUTURE"

Our preference obviously is for an environment that supports the entire object-oriented software development life cycle. However, until that is a reality, we can consider what we require in such a program development system. The environment must support the implementation of classes from concept to source code. The environment is the manager of all the information about the system. Requirements, documentation, and test plans are part of that information. In this section we will consider several types of tools that could be of help and, in some cases, we will illustrate with current tools. The "tool of the future" can be characterized by the functionality that it should supply.

- *Support object-oriented constructs.* The environment should "understand" and support the constructs used in the object-oriented approach. The separation of class specification and implementation, the linkages between class definitions and multiple implementations, test suites, and documentation must all be explicitly supported in the environment. The environment must be sufficiently general to begin this support with the fuzzy concepts in domain analysis and continue to support through the maintenance and evolution phases of class development. The environment should support the incremental nature of inheritance by providing links between information about a class and its subclasses.
- *Language facilities.* Our ideal tool would provide both interpreted and compiled language facilities. The interpreted component would support the development and testing of individual classes in a quick-response prototyping approach. The compiler should provide an optimized executable that is the final product.
- *Diagramming and description facilities.* The tool should provide support for the development of the ER diagrams, state diagrams, and class graphs that are useful in describing an object-oriented design. The ER diagrams should be capable of being clustered—that is, an entity in one diagram could be "exploded" to provide a lower level with several entities that represent details of the higher level entity. This facility would also support the description of concepts even before they are identified as such in the system.
- *Storage facilities.* All of the information produced in the environment should be persistent. The relationships between classes, test results, and documentation should all be available in the environment.
- *Interactive access.* The browser concept provides a reasonable approach to creating, viewing, and modifying individual classes and applications. The environment should also provide browsers that can "walk" through the network of relationships that exist between elements in this information base. This graphical tool should allow the design process to proceed visually with the developer connecting definitions. The environment should support access to multiple commercial libraries that were not developed in, or in anticipation of, the environment.

Various versions of such systems and specific pieces of this functionality have been developed and tested. Our list is ambitious but involves existing techniques, although no one has yet fully integrated all of these features into a single environment. This type of support will allow application implementation to become more a constructive process and less an original creation process. It will also recognize the importance of communication in the development of very large systems.

SUMMARY

This chapter has reviewed a number of tools that are available for object-oriented system building. In many cases these tools are modified versions of procedural products and do not provide a natural approach to the paradigm. Language environments still do not talk to design environments, and most design environments are sophisticated drawing programs.

We have presented a list of capabilities that an object-oriented support environment should possess. These capabilities are not radically new ideas but together they form a formidable piece of software to develop in its own right. Progress is being made to realize this type of environment and it will provide significant increases in system development productivity.

FURTHER READING

One of a series of research monographs from the University of Geneva[92] provides some additional requirements for an object-oriented development environment, along with descriptions of prototypes developed. A language-specific programming environment is reported by O'Brien et al[76]. Kleyn and Gingrich[59] and Kappel and Schrefl[54] present tools that provide useful information to a developer using an environment.

14

Persistent Objects

This chapter considers techniques for the storage of objects created by an application. The literature has come to refer to this as *persistence* of objects. The term conveys the idea that we must explicitly be concerned about managing the lifetimes of objects. The objects must be available when the application needs to use them whether they are in memory or on secondary storage. The goal in developing persistence mechanisms is to make them as natural and as transparent to use as possible. There are several choices for the architecture of these mechanisms.

One possibility is a direct interaction with the traditional file system, associated with an operating system. This technique is somewhat awkward due to the mismatch between the object data model and the data model assumed by most file systems. This requires some type of interface between the object-oriented application and the file system. This "impedance mismatch" can also be found in most of the existing database products. Relational databases, for example, support a data model that is quite different from that of the object model. Storing objects from an object-oriented application in a relational database would require a significant overhead in data transformation.

A second type of architecture provides a persistent storage facility that directly supports the object data model. This architecture is supported by a number of categories of facilities. The use of an object-oriented database management system (ODMS) as a storage manager for an application provides a much more natural correspondence to the object model. However, ODMSs are in their early stages of development and require much effort to integrate into an application framework. A second category of facility that embodies the object data model is an *object manager*. The object manager provides a store for objects, but it does not provide the full services of a database, such as a query language.

In this chapter we will consider each of these approaches to persistence, but we will emphasize the developments in the area of object-oriented databases. We will not consider the basic architectures and implementation details of these systems, but we will survey their component parts and their use as the persistent store for a software application. ONTOS, from Ontologic, Inc. will be used as an example to illustrate the various points we wish to examine. Before exploring possible techniques for storage we want to consider some of the factors that influence our choice of technique.

LONGEVITY OF OBJECTS

Different applications will have different needs for persistent objects. Some may require that objects be held only for the lifetime of the current process. A need for a virtual memory of objects to expand the amount of available primary memory may be satisfied by current operating systems. Longer storage requirements brings the need for additional services from the manager of the storage. The following three levels provide an insight into these varying needs:

- *Persistence across program blocks.* Many objects simply have a lifetime limited to a single "block" of a program. At the end of each program block, some objects created within it are destroyed. Intermediate results of calculations are short-lived objects that are destroyed quickly. Other objects are retained for use outside the block. They might serve as the return value from the block or by having been dynamically created on the process stack.

  The runtime environment is usually charged with the retention of these objects as one block ends and another begins. The rules for changes in format vary with the language. An integer may be transformed to a floating point as it is passed from one block to another as the return value of a function, or it may be passed as a parameter.

- *Persistence across transactions.* Objects may need to be placed in secondary storage by one application to await processing by a subsequent application. Both applications understand the protocol and format of the objects. The format will only be changed by informing both applications of the change. This is accomplished by redefining the data types that are common to the two applications. If changes are made to the format while objects are stored, a customized filter will be needed to transform the stored objects to the new format. These objects represent intermediate results and are not intended to be generally available to applications outside this family of applications.

  For example, an order processing system may include numerous programs that each modify the data in clearly specified ways. An order entry process establishes a file of objects that represent orders. Additional processes will access the objects and invoke the appropriate methods to perform additional transformations on them. These objects will need to reside in secondary storage for an indefinite period of time with no application actively in control of them. A file system must be able to represent them in some format and provide them to another application that understands the same data formats. There is no need for the file system to be able to modify the format of the data. Only one application will access the information at a time. Since the data are homogeneous, the operating system's file permissions can be used to maintain the security of the data.

- *Persistence across format modifications.* Some objects are intended to be used over a long period of time by many different applications, including some that may not even be written when the objects are created. Over time the content and protocol of these objects may be changed. Because these sets of objects are usually very large and represent a significant investment, the modifications must be accomplished without extensive assistance from outside the persistence system. The existing objects must be modified to reflect the changes that are made to the class to which they belong.

  For example, consider a library of classes in a program development environment. Entries in the library describe the classes that can be used to create objects in an application program. This class information will be retained over long periods of time. As the program evolves, so may the kinds of data needed by the environment. As classes are modified in support of the library itself, existing instances of those classes—the objects in the library used to hold information about application class specifications, for example—must be updated to conform to the new class representations. Database technology was developed to handle this type of data storage update requirement.

CONTROL OF THE PERSISTENCE MECHANISM

The more interaction required between the persistence system and the application, the more automatic that interaction should be . The paging in a virtual memory operating system would not be very effective if the application had to explicitly recognize the need to page and do something to initiate it. On the other hand, the overhead of automatically checking for garbage in memory is excessive if most of the objects created by the application live through the entire application.

Program Control

Many applications only use persistence to store the end results of their processing. This only occurs at a few well defined points in the processing. It is easy for the design of the system to anticipate these uses and to explicitly invoke actions that store the objects. Writing to a file or updating a database are the typical actions taken under program control.

Automatic Control

Automatic control of the persistence mechanism introduces an overhead that is usually only tolerated in operating systems. Objects that have not been referenced recently or that are stored in a particular section of memory may be automatically written to secondary storage. The notion of paging in a virtual memory system has been modified somewhat in that complete objects—rather than an arbitrary section of memory—are stored.

FILE SYSTEM SUPPORT

Object-oriented applications can be designed to provide persistence through the use of a traditional file system. This is an acceptable technique if the application has been designed in the object-oriented style but implemented using a procedural language. The most efficient implementations result when the data structures of the application and the data model of the storage mechanism are compatible.

Practically speaking, however, until object-oriented databases mature, many applications will be implemented in an object-oriented language but will have to rely on the ordinary file system for persistence. Gorlen[38] did this in his implementation of the NIH Class Library. In making the system somewhat transparent to the user of instances of a library class, a large amount of overhead had to be added to the process. The example presented later in this chapter will not provide the elaborate system that Gorlen did. It will illustrate the problems with the mismatch of data models.

In this section, we will give examples of creating the interface to the file system for cases in which the application will read from the file and create a file. We will assume that the interface to the file system will be in the form of a Unix-like stream.

Output

The output of information from objects into a file assumes that the object-oriented language provides a means of writing its primitives to the underlying file system. Each class implements a method that might be named "storeOn"—borrowed from the NIH Class Library—to write the state of the object onto the stream. Since this method is part of the class, it has access to all the data of the class. It will write each primitive datum onto the stream. For parts of the state that are implemented as instances of other classes, we simply require that those classes define their own storeOn method. For example, the segment of C^{++} code to store a line

```
// pt1 and pt2 are instance variables of class Point
Line::storeOn(stream aStream) {
    '(' >> aStream;
    pt1.storeOn(aStream);
    ',' >> aStream;
    pt2.storeOn(aStream);
    ')' >> aStream;
}
```

relies on the storeOn method for class Point and would represent a line on a stream as:

$$((1,2),(100,200))$$

if we assume a point (x, y) is stored on a stream as (x, y). As long as the data is to be read by a non-object-oriented application that has knowledge of the internal implementation of the classes, this scheme is sufficient. The data can be read sequentially into the other application and processed there. However, most often the data will be used by another object-oriented application or even by the same application during its next execution. When this is the case, the concepts of object identification and class membership are needed.

Input

"Objects" residing on a conventional file system will be in the form of primitive data. If an application is to read these "objects" from a stream, the application must be able to identify the class of which this object is an instance, it must create an instance of that class, and it must read the information from the stream and load it into the new instance. This additional information must be on the stream to identify the class of each object. This activity should be hidden within an interface that reads the stream and produces class instances for the rest of the application. The design will facilitate moving the application to a more natural approach when this becomes practical.

In order to be able to determine the class of an object to be read, the storeOn methods must write a class identification field on the file for each object. For example, the output of storeOn for the class Line might use the string:

$$(\text{Line (Point 1,2),(Point 100,200)})$$

to indicate the class of each component, or even

$$(\text{Rectangle pt1.(Point x.1 y.2) pt2.(Point x.100 y.200)})$$

to designate the class and name of each component. The interface in the reading application can be a very simple case statement that uses the identification information in the file to create a class instance. The interface has a case for each class that the writing application is capable of creating:

```
classID << strm;
switch ( classID ) {
case "Point":
    makePoint(strm);
case "Rectangle":
    makeRectangle(strm);

        :
        :

}
```

The cases correspond to tokens written on the stream by the writer. Each token identifies the class of the data to follow. The switch statement creates an instance of the appropriate class and passes it the stream from which it is to read its required data. This simple interface provides a quick way to provide input of "objects" into the system, but it is lacking in at least two aspects:

1. Any objects used in the implementation of a larger object must be written within the data of the larger class. This makes the sharing of objects quite difficult. In the previous example, the two Point objects that define a rectangle were written to the stream. If the class Line were to have *pointers* to points in an instance instead of the point objects themselves, then it would be difficult to establish the proper link if, say, the point associated with pt1 had already been read in as a component of another line.

2. Any time the range of classes produced by the writing application is expanded, the reading application must be modified and recompiled.

DATA MODELS FOR DATABASES

Database management systems have evolved out of the need for long-term storage and manipulation of data. In addition to basic storage facilities, a database management system provides services such as data format modification, concurrency control, transaction control, and data security. Each management system assumes a particular model of the data that it is managing. This model determines the assumptions that can be made about the structure and organization of the data and the constraints that must be observed as the data is manipulated.

The network, hierarchical, and relational database models[25] have provided the basis for numerous database management systems such as IDMS™, IMS™, and ORACLE™, respectively. These models have made progressively more restrictive assumptions about the organization of the data. The relational literature illustrates the many "normal forms" into which the data must be decomposed in order to satisfy increasingly rigorous integrity constraints. The hierarchical model imposes a hierarchical arrangement of record definitions for the data elements it stores. The network model provides a more flexible organization, but at the expense of data independence.

Kim[57] lists six shortcomings of the above models:

- The relational is too simple to capture the complex structures needed for today's applications. In particular, computer-aided design(CAD) and computer-assisted software engineering(CASE) applications need nested definitions that are very cumbersome if not impossible to represent in the relational model.

- The database systems described above support only a few atomic data types—for example, numbers, strings, and dates. They do not provide the same support as an application programming language for more general data types and they especially do not support the storage of binary large objects (BLOBs) that are used for the storage of audio and video information.

- These models do not support the concepts from the semantic data models such as aggregation and generalization. These relationships must be represented and managed explicitly by the application program and must be passed from one application to another via conventions rather than automatically in the data representation.

- The performance of database systems using conventional data models is not acceptable for large systems that require integral persistence as they dynamically manipulate the data.

- There is an impedance mismatch between the models provided by databases and those supported by application programming languages. This requires a translation interface between the data representations in the program and those in the database. This further impacts the perceived performance of the database.

- The concept of a transaction in conventional databases is not sufficient for the lengthy transactions needed in applications such as CAD and CASE environments.

Two types of database models have been proposed to overcome these difficulties. The extended relational model[20], as the name implies, extends the relational model to support many of the semantic concepts missing from the relational model. In particular, the concepts of entity, associations (or relationships), and subtypes are supported. Date[25] provides an extensive discussion of this model. We will not consider it further because it still does not explicitly support many of the concepts that are integral to the development of object-oriented applications. Rather, we will concentrate on the second proposed model, the object-oriented data model.

OBJECT-ORIENTED DATABASES

In this section we will consider the object-oriented data model and how it is incorporated into database technology. Many of our applications do not need the full services of a database management system, so we will explore the concept of an "object manager." A set of requirements for an object data management system are used to illustrate how the object model contributes to a new database model. The ONTOS™ object-oriented database is used to illustrate a number of the concepts presented in this section.

Object-Oriented Data Model

Our object-oriented data model has already been expressed in previous chapters. It centers around objects, encapsulated data values, and the legal operations on that data that are grouped together in sets of objects, termed *classes*, that share common behavior. Objects can be related to each other via references. These references are defined abstractly at the class level and realized at the object level in a number of forms. Three of the major relationships between objects are inheritance, composition, and messaging. While this is *our* object data model, it is not universally accepted.

The object-oriented data model is not as formalized as the relational data model. There is no object algebra or object calculus upon which to base formal reasoning about data manipulation. There also is not total agreement about what constitutes "the" object data model. These disagreements have led to the development of databases that enforce a variety of assumptions.

Requirements for the Management of Objects

Cattell[15] provides a number of requirements for what he calls an "object data management system" (ODMS[1]). These requirements point out the features that satisfy many of the shortcomings, presented in the preceding section, of previous data models. We will modify that list to combine some points and paraphrase others to illustrate the requirements for any system for persistence. Several will be elaborated upon in succeeding sections.

- *Unique object identifiers.* Many objects are created dynamically with no user-defined name while others may have their name changed during processing. The use of a unique object identifier (UID) to identify each object stored in the database removes the need, found in relational systems, for a unique key that is extracted from the data. These identifiers are not meaningful in the application context and thus should be replaced by a more natural form—memory references—when being accessed by the application. UIDs are logical pointers and thus are not reused, while the memory references are physical pointers and are reused. This makes the UID a more reliable basis for garbage collection and the enforcement of integrity constraints.
- *Support for the object data model.* Semantic concepts that constitute the object data model are inheritance, composition, and messaging. Composite objects—that is, objects that contain other objects—are integral to the object model. This relationship and others between objects must be expressible in the object management system. The management system must maintain the integrity constraints between objects, such as how the deletion of one object affects the existence of other objects. For example, the deletion of an object could result in "garbage" in the database. The system should recognize the dependencies among class definitions and should support the incremental definition of these classes via the inheritance relationship. Each of these techniques must be supported by the object data management system if it is to transparently implement the model provided by object-oriented programming languages. This removes the impedance mismatch between the programming and database languages.

---

[1]It is unfortunate that this acronym is also used for an object-oriented database management system.

- *Representation for ordered aggregates.* The object data model supports the development of structures that are much more complex than those in the relational data model. The relational model requires that each cell contain only single instances of primitive data items. The object data model supports the aggregation of data instances in a number of forms— for example, lists and hash tables. The ONTOS ODMS even provides a separate facility that optimizes the manipulation of these groups of objects.

- *Compatible database and programming language representations.* The representations of data in an ODMS must be compatible with the data's representation in the programming language being used. The schema of a database includes the definition of the fundamental entities of the representation and the relationships between them. The schema of an ODMS is made up of class definitions that include the inheritance, composition, and messaging relationships between the various classes. Changes to class definitions require changes in the schema. The ODMS should also support the reformatting of objects that are already in the database when the schema changes, but most current ODMSs do not support reformatting under many of the changes that can be made to a schema.

   The interface to applications should also be a natural extension of the language in which the application is written. In the object-oriented approach, the "natural" approach is to include methods in the interface of the class that will place an object into persistent storage or retrieve it from the database. This is often provided by requiring every class that is to have persistent instances to be a subclass of a class provided by the database. ONTOS provides a C^{++} class, Object, that provides a number of virtual methods that must be defined before the user-defined class can create persistent instances. These methods support the reading and writing of instances to a persistent store.

- *Efficient system performance.* ODMSs need to provide performance that is superior to that obtained by writing objects directly into the file system, and they should support the distribution of the database across multiple machines. A number of techniques, including the special storage techniques for aggregates, can optimize the performance of an ODMS. The network of relationships between classes that may not be modified dynamically allows the ODMS to use techniques that are similar to the older network data model to provide for the rapid composition during retrieval of a complex instance that contains instances of other classes.

Database Schemas

The schema for a database is a representation of the entities to be stored in the database and the relationships between the entities. The schema of an object-oriented database is more complex than that of a relational database because of the rich set of interdependencies that the database supports. In the relational model, interdependencies are reduced through the normalization process. The schema designer must modify the data representations into a set of tables that often have no direct correlation to application data representation. The relational schema represents a set of normalized entities as rows in a table. The relationships are not between tables but between individual instances in a table. The modification of the schema in a relational database is a set of isolated changes to individual tables.

The schema for an object-oriented database consists of class definitions. Included in these definitions are the representations of the inheritance, composition, and messaging relationships. These relationships link the entities together. Schema modifications are not isolated as in the relational model. Modifications of one entity can affect another entity. Any change to the definition of a class is a schema modification. Adding a new attribute, deleting or modifying an attribute, or modifying the inheritance relationships are all schema changes. Actions such as adding a new attribute to a class will not only change that class definition, but the definitions of all of its subclasses.

ONTOS provides a utility, *classify*, that builds a schema from a set of C++ class definitions. This utility parses the classes to determine the encapsulated data values and the relationships. These new pieces are added to the kernel schema provided by ONTOS because any new persistent class must at least be a subclass of **Object**. ONTOS 2.0, the version we have utilized, does not support the reformatting and reloading of data in existing instances following a schema modification.

A Model of an ODBMS

Traditionally, database management systems have been modeled with three levels: external, conceptual, and internal. These are illustrated in Figure 14.1 as they relate to an object-oriented environment.

The *external* level is not an actual part of the database, but considers the context in which the objects that will be stored in the database are viewed. The persistent objects will interact with other, nonpersistent objects that manipulate the state of those objects. The external level includes the definition of classes in the application programming language.

The *conceptual* level is the schema defined as the database's view of the data. This is defined in the database programming language. An important feature of an ODMS, such as ONTOS, is that the application programming language and the database programming language are the same language. The schema reflects all of the relationships between class definitions, and thus the ODMS can manage all of these relationships between the objects. This relieves the application program of some effort.

The *internal* level is the actual storage of the objects on the disk. This layer will either be an interface to the existing file system or have direct access to handle raw disk IO. This level needs to consider the effect of page size on object retrieval.

An ODMS has the three abstract components illustrated in Figure 14.2. In this section we will briefly describe the function of each.

- *Object manager.* The manager level processes messages and dispatches object requests to the server level. The manager performs the definition and modification of schema, and ensures that newly modified classes and preexisting instances are structurally consistent.

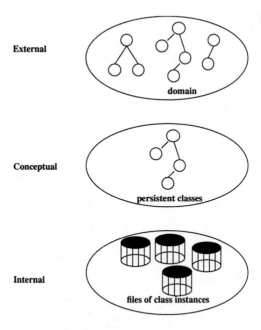

Figure 14.1: Three levels of a DBMS.

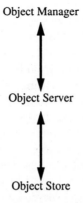

Figure 14.2: A high-level view of an object-oriented database management system.

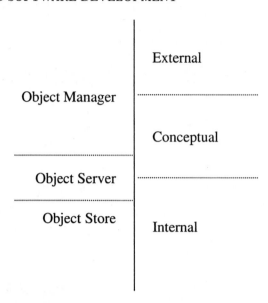

Figure 14.3: Relationships between the functional areas of an ODMS and the conceptual levels of a DBMS

- *Object server.* The server controls the interaction between the the outside world and the database. In a distributed database there usually will be a server running on each machine handling requests from any application. The server provides transaction management, storage management, and security.
- *Object store.* This low-level component provides the interface to the host file system. This level includes the interface to the actual structures that will store the data.

Figure 14.3 relates these functional areas of an ODMS to the three conceptual levels of a DBMS. The Object Manager level provides most of the features needed to support the conceptual level of the DBMS. That means it supports the maintenance of the schema. ONTOS provides *DBDesigner*, a database design tool that provides a graphically oriented environment in which the schema can be viewed in a variety of ways. New classes can be added to the schema and the C++ definitions of those classes can be automatically generated. The Object Server area is present to manage transactions that are routed to it by the Object Manager. In a distributed database, these servers will be available on each system that contains a portion of the database. *DBATool*, in ONTOS, provides the functionality to administer the registry of information about the logical and physical areas in the database. *DBATool* goes beyond the conceptual level to provide support for the creation of files to store objects on the various systems that comprise the distributed database.

Most ODMSs also have both application programming languages and query languages that provide some of the functions of these internal languages. ONTOS uses C++ as its programming language and provides an optional SQL query language.

ONTOS is a database management system that follows a programming language approach. The major techniques for adding items to the database, the techniques for schema definition, and other functions are performed from an application via the use of functions written in the programming language.

Each ODMS should provide three languages that provide the semantics of the system. These languages support the definition, manipulation, and control of entities in the database.

- *DDL*. The Data Definition Language supports the specification of the schema. Since in the ODMS the schema is the set of class definitions including inheritance relationships, the DDL can be that portion of the interface language that is required to define classes. In ONTOS the DDL is the C^{++} class-specification syntax.

- *DML*. The Data Manipulation Language supports the "manipulation" of the instances that populate the database. This includes the declaration of instances, their modification, and their destruction. Much of the syntax of C^{++} deals directly with the creation and destruction of instances and with the manipulation through activating the methods of the object. The basic concept of messaging supports much of this manipulation, including assigning and updating data values.

- *DCL*. The Data Control Language supports the statement of integrity constraints and other controlling abstractions such as security authorizations and transactions. These statements may be a part of the database assumptions or they may be stated as part of the implementation of the classes. ONTOS uses the library functions *OC_transactionStart*, *OC_transactionAbort*, and *OC_transactionCommit* to provide the semantics of transactions.

In order to make the classes persistent in an application, several additions must be made to the class definitions. We will assume the ONTOS mechanism that persistent objects will be subclasses of Object. The Object class provides several virtual functions to the interface of each shape, and these must be implemented for the instances of the class to be persistent. The following alterations must be made to a class using ONTOS. They are representative of the changes that would be required with many of the ODMSs.

- *Activation constructor*. The developer must define a constructor that will be invoked when an instance is retrieved from the database. The activation of an instance must include the resolution of all pointers, the creation of all internal instances of classes, and the invocation of all parent constructors. The implementation of this constructor is usually very simple.

- *New instance constructor*. The new instance constructor is used for creating any new instance of the persistent class. It must call the constructor of its base class and it must initialize the pointer from this instance to a representation of its class—that is, it must provide linkage so the database can ask an instance to which class it belongs.

- *Destroy member function.* This virtual function is part of the exception-handling system. It must provide the capability to clean up when the instance is to be deleted during the handling of an exception.
- *putObject.* The virtual putObject method must provide the capability of writing the object to the database. This is performed by writing the individual instances in the object's representation to the database. This method need not be redefined for the majority of new class definitions.
- *deleteObject.* The virtual deleteObject method must provide the capability of deleting the object from the database. The existing method from the base class is satisfactory for most new class definitions.

The exception-handling capability is optional and thus the overhead of adding persistence to an existing class can be limited to the implementation of the new instance constructor, which is always required for any class we intend to instantiate, and the standard implementation of the activation constructor. For ODMSs, this is a typical overhead. There are "object managers," as opposed to databases, for which the overhead is greatly reduced. While providing low overhead, persistence has a cost: The full features of a DBMS, such as queries, concurrent transactions, and security, are not provided.

Integrity Constraints

One of the important services that a DBMS can provide is the enforcement of integrity constraints. Referential integrity refers to being certain that references to other entities are valid. Relational databases will check that the so-called "foreign key" refers to an actual entry in an existing table. The composite nature of most complex objects requires referential integrity checks that an object's reference to part of its internal representation is valid. The UID supports this process. Each memory reference can be replaced by the UID of a persistent object when the object is placed in the database. This makes checking referential integrity straightforward since UIDs are not reused, and it expedites the process of retrieving complex objects from the database. The UID can also support the process of deletion ensuring that all parts of a complex object are deleted as appropriate.

Querying an Object-Oriented Database

From the user's perspective, querying an object-oriented database can be very similar to querying a relational database. Many of the ODMSs provide an SQL query language. The techniques for supporting these queries differ from the implementation for a relational database. While this is beyond the scope of this text, one comment about efficiency is in order. The discrete tables of the relational database must be combined—"joined"—during interactive queries. In an object-oriented database, most of the allowable relationships between entities can be represented explicitly and can be traversed during a query many times faster than the typical relational query language can *construct* the required information. Additional techniques in object data management have already been mentioned, including the use of a special storage manager to optimize the retrieval of groups of data such as lists.

While interactive querying of collections of data are of interest, our more immediate focus of interest is in the use of queries to provide data input to an application. This can be handled in ONTOS with SQL function calls in the application code, including all of the usual conditions and constraints. ONTOS also provides a technique for indexing all the instances of a particular class. Without the overhead of an SQL query, an application can iterate over a list of instances of a class via the index. In a sense, this is a container class that exists only in the database but is available to an application. This both simplifies and optimizes the process of accessing a group of data. Individual instances of classes can be accessed using the names given them in an application.

MORE GRAPHICS: ADDING PERSISTENCE

Of the classes we have defined for the draw system, only a small number of them will create instances that need to be persistent from one execution of a system to the next. Three inheritance structures have played a major role in our design of the draw program: input devices, output devices, and the shapes structure. The instances of IO devices need not be persistent because there is little data about these devices that needs to be retained. The major need for persistence is to retain the picture that is being drawn. That means that the shape instances should be persistent.

File System Interface

For a single application with a simple need for persistence, a database is not required. A simple interface to the underlying non-object-oriented file system can be easily and simply built (see above). The file of shapes will be simplified by the use of some form of variant record that has a case for every type of shape. A method can write out each shape on the current file by traversing the list of shape objects and having each object write out an instance of the variant record type. This does require that the shape instance be able to write out a token that indicates its class, but this is preferable over maintaining a list of each type of shape. The function to reconstruct the list of shapes when the application is restarted reads the file of variant records and uses a case construct to select the appropriate class to instantiate. Unfortunately, this requires that the input routine have knowledge of all of the shapes available in the system and quickly limits the flexibility of the application.

Object-Oriented Database Interface

Consider how this problem might be handled if an object-oriented database is available. Figure 14.4 shows our earlier view of a shape hierarchy that uses multiple inheritance to introduce the methods needed to make the shape instances persistent. The Storable Object class might be the Object provided by ONTOS, or a similar class from another database.

The shape classes can be made persistent with relative ease. The inheritance structure provides a seemingly redundant structure. The class Displayable Storable

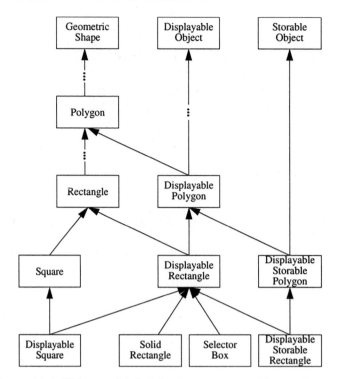

Figure 14.4: Using multiple inheritance to provide persistence.

Rectangle inherits the virtual functions described above, and they are implemented for that class. These are then inherited by the specific persistent subclasses. It is even more likely that these implementations of the functions will not need to be redefined in the shape classes since the function has been specialized for shapes.

Two possible modifications of the draw program need to be performed to make the shape objects persistent. One involves storing the shape objects and one involves the user interface.

1. The list of shapes that is currently an ordinary list implementation could make use of the group storage manager of ONTOS to provide an optimized aggregation retrieval. However, most of our drawings are sufficiently small so as not to require that power. The special aggregate storage manager would be useful because the shapes will never be retrieved individually. Either we will want to load the entire drawing or we will not want any of the instances. Shapes are added to the list as they are created. For large collections, this optimization would be worth the modification.

2. The second addition requires adding two system-level menu entries. The *load* selection utilizes the database retrieval process to retrieve the set of shape instances that have been previously stored. The *save* selection invokes a method that traverses the shape list and sends the **putObject**

message to each of the instances.

A Comparison of Persistence Techniques

We have considered two different techniques for providing persistence to an application: the file system interface technique and the object data management technique. The first alternative may require some additional effort on our part, but it is virtually as portable as the remainder of our application. It also has an advantage that if a drawing is saved as a file, it can be manipulated as an entity outside the application—for example, we can copy a drawing just by copying a file. If a database is used to store a drawing, then manipulating a drawing requires some support from either a query language and/or an application. The second alternative merely provides a sophisticated realization of the first. The need to determine the class of an object when it is stored and when it is retrieved is still there; it is just handled by software we do not have to write. For this convenience, we may sacrifice some degree of portability and convenience. Our method now requires that a version of a vendor's software product be installed on the system to which we wish to port our draw program. If interfaces to ODMS were standardized, then applications would also be portable across databases.

SUMMARY

This has been a very brief look at the issues of persistence and the concept of an object-oriented database. The development of these databases is a natural outgrowth of the use of a new data model. Building the interface between an application that supports one data model and a file system that supports a different one is a costly process. For applications that will handle large quantities of a variety of different data types, the overhead and loss of portability that derive from the use of an object data management system may be compensated for in the efficiency of implementation in a system that is intended for a special purpose: the storage of objects. These database management systems provide an additional capability, easy extensibility. The file system approach requires too much codification of systemwide knowledge in an application. Object-oriented database systems have much maturing to do, but they do represent a viable new option in persistence that naturally supports the object data model.

FURTHER READING

The literature on object-oriented databases has only recently shifted from a purely research perspective to a more application-oriented perspective. The October 1991 issue of the *Communications of the ACM*[16] was devoted to descriptions of a number of commercial implementations of object-oriented databases. The use of a common problem in each of the articles provides a basis for comparing the models that underly the implementation. Won Kim, a leading researcher on object-oriented databases, has written a readable survey of object-oriented database issues[57].

15

Summary, Conclusions, Prognostications

We will end as we began with some statements of philosophy and with a broad view of the development process. We will use our life cycles to synthesize many of the issues that have been encountered across the chapters. Finally, we will attempt to forecast where these developments will lead the discipline of software engineering.

In Chapter 1 we provided a philosophy of software development. That philosophy goes well beyond many of the traditional definitions of "object-oriented." The traditional definition of classes, objects, and inheritance is sufficient to discriminate this methodology from others, but it is not sufficient to fully describe a complete methodology. Our initial statement of philosophy included three levels:

- *Problem-centered.* The solutions to problems that are developed in the structured approach include arbitrary decompositions into tasks. The resulting tasks are seldom meaningful pieces on their own. They are not meaningful to other developers, and maintenance is complicated as a result. Developing descriptions of concepts that are present in the problem domain of the problem results in components that cannot be arbitrary and that can be understood by other developers working in the same domain. These components capture expertise in the problem domain and make that expertise available for use in a range of applications.
- *Reuse-oriented.* Our philosophy includes the consideration of reuse at each phase in the development process. The focus is the development of reusable software components as described in the previous item. Reuse is an explicit criterion in design and implementation decisions. This focus is surrounded by secondary objectives that seek to develop reusable support information. Parts of this emphasis are management issues that

must be addressed to provide the appropriate environment for reuse. Developing for reuse requires more resources for the initial development than in the usual disposable development process.

- *Engineered.* Software engineering principles have been developed that should be followed regardless of the analysis and design philosophies being used in the development of the software. These principles result in software that has been engineered in the sense that it has been developed based on agreed-upon professional standards and practices. These standards include such principles as the use of typing systems that seek to assure the appropriate interactions of various types of data, the rational naming of components and attributes, and the development of separately compilable units with independent specifications and implementations.

We will consider these three parts of the methodology in more detail below. First, we will consider technical issues associated with the application and class life cycles introduced in Chapter 3, including some we have not discussed so far. We will also look at some management issues.

TECHNICAL ISSUES

The application and class life cycles we presented are not intended to be formal models, but they are intuitive models that should assist in developing an understanding of the object-oriented style of software construction. The two separate life cycles emphasize that the life of a class should be considered independently of any other class that may interact with its instances. This independence supports the view that the class should be reusable in other contexts, but it also imposes additional requirements in areas such as testing. Realistically, few classes are truly independent of other classes. Classes collaborate to provide the functionality needed by one class or by the application. Our techniques must address and manage this collaboration.

Each of the life cycles implicitly assumes that, while the main flow through the life cycle is sequential, there is often a need to repeat steps to provide additional details. Additionally, many instances of the class life cycle may be operating in parallel since many classes may be developed simultaneously. As we have seen, classes may be identified at any of the analysis, design, and implementation levels in the development process. Thus the class life cycle may be initiated at many different times in the application development process.

Blending Development Styles

In a pure object-oriented approach, our final application will be represented as a class from which we create one instance. In a hybrid approach, the application may combine some elements of other styles with the object-oriented style. For example, Figure 15.1 shows a process architecture and objects being combined to provide an application. This figure illustrates that the development of the process architecture is independent of the development of the classes. As the classes are developed, the actual functionality

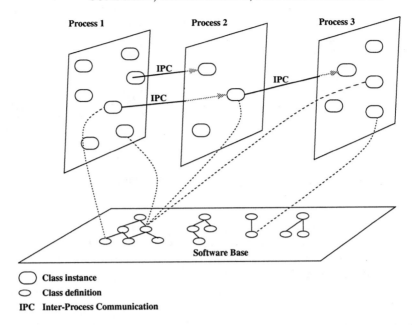

Figure 15.1: Blending the process and object-oriented styles of development.

of the system is created. Once the classes have been developed, their instances may be distributed over a set of processes in a manner that provides acceptable system performance, provides for concurrent execution, and can be used to reduce the memory requirements for execution. Our guide in developing the functionality that solves the problem is the object model and the guide to constructing an efficient solution is the process model.

If we are developing in a pure object-oriented environment, the application life cycle will include the class life cycle for the application class as well as life cycles for each class that is necessary to the definition of the application class. These may proceed more or less in parallel as long as the initial phase of determining the specification of all of the classes is done prior to the low-level design and implementation phases for the classes.

Incremental Development

As we have seen at numerous places in our discussions, the concept of incremental development provides opportunities for economics in the development process. This seems to run counter to our previous statement about parallel development, but incremental development takes place within an inheritance structure while parallel development occurs across structures. An incremental approach to developing a class assumes that some previous work has been completed and can be used as the basis for this new effort. The incremental approach can be applied to many parts of the object-oriented development process. The most obvious is in the definition of classes

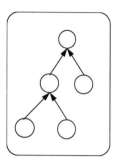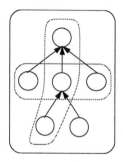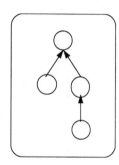

Figure 15.2: Independence in a set of classes.

via the inheritance relation. The definition of a subclass is incrementally developed from the definitions of existing classes. The inheritance relation defines a mapping of attributes from the parent classes to the new class that can be used to determine many of the characteristics of the resulting class.

In sections of this text on documentation and testing, we have seen the value of the incremental approach. The documentation of a class can be developed incrementally from the documentation of its parent classes. The process of forming this information concatenates the documentation of the individual methods that are inherited from the parent classes. When the documentation of the public interface is required, inheritance mapping is used to determine which of the methods in the parent classes are public methods in the child class; the documentation for these methods is presented. The technique also identifies the new methods that require new documentation.

The development of a test suite of a class can also benefit from the perspective of incremental development. In Chapter 10 we described a hierarchical, incremental testing technique that developed the test suite for a class by using the test suites of the parent classes to provide many of the needed test cases. This incremental process reduces the amount of effort needed to test a class by reusing test cases rather than creating new ones, and it reduces the amount of time needed for testing by determining those portions of the class that do not require retesting.

Parallel Development

Many pieces of a system may be developed in parallel provided this parallelism is coordinated with the incremental development process. The incremental process assumes previous work and thus there is a dependency between the component being developed and the existing components. Parallel development assumes an independence among the items being developed. If we consider a set of inheritance structures, such as those shown in Figure 15.2, the incremental development process proceeds in a vertical manner and the dependencies run in a vertical thread through the structure. Two classes that are subclasses of the same class can be developed independently of each other. This independence produces a set of classes in a horizontal layer that can be developed in parallel, and it extends across the many structures in the set of inheritance graphs.

Maintenance

We have not discussed maintenance because the activities required in maintenance are the same as those that have been described in the other phases! Maintenance activities on a released product include bug fixes, modifications to existing features, and the addition of new features. Many of the mechanisms of the paradigm can provide support for new approaches for each of these activities.

- *Bug fixes.* There are at least three schools of thought on the use of inheritance to fix software faults. One view is that once a class is in use, it is never modified. Any modifications are accomplished by creating a subclass in which the bugs are fixed. Inheritance is used to provide the unchanged code to the new class and the code containing the bug is overridden.

  A second view supports multiple implementations of a class body—one with the bugs and one with the fixes. In a way, this is equivalent to a software release for a class. This approach allows applications that have reused the class with the bug, but that operate properly despite it, to remain unchanged until a problem arises. New applications or existing applications that need the fixes can make use of the new implementation of the class. A disadvantage of this approach is the complexity of managing multiple versions. Care must also be taken not to implement too many variations, each catering to a specific application.

  Another view points out that the creation of a subclass leaves a class available for use that contains an error. In this third approach, the existing class is "broken open" and the bug is located and repaired. The disadvantage of this approach is that changes can be made to a class that is being used by other developers. The advantage is that no class exists with known faults. This is the preferable technique. The existence of a "buggy" class in our collection is not desirable.

- *Maintenance of features.* The inheritance mechanism can play an important role in the modification of existing features and the development of new features if the original design has an appropriate decomposition. One technique for this type of design is the client-server model. The server provides a service to all its clients. For example, in a menu system, the style of the menu, its actual display, and the handling of mouse events within its display are the behaviors provided by the server. The clients of this server contain actions that are to be taken when a certain selection is made from the menu. The client must provide certain information for the server to support the services needed by the client.

  Consider the design of the menu system. The system can be designed using two abstract classes: Menu and Menu Item. The menu class represents the server. It provides the display facilities—perhaps a window on a display device—and the ability to detect the selection of a particular menu item. The menu class serves as a container of menu items that will be displayed in the menu. The number of items in a menu is flexible and depends solely on the number of items placed in

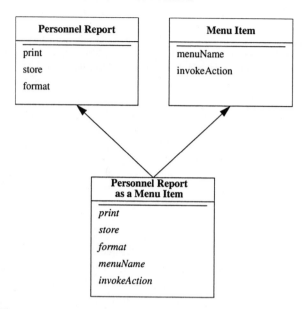

Figure 15.3: Integrating existing classes into a menu.

the container. The requirement on the menu item classes—that is, the clients—is that they provide a string that the menu can use to display the client as a menu choice and a function that is to be invoked when that menu item is selected.

An existing class can quickly become the source of a menu item through the use of multiple inheritance. The inheritance structure shown in Figure 15.3 develops a class in which the interface can be viewed in layers. One layer is the interface of the "existing class"—in this case Personnel Report—and the second is the set of behaviors that characterize a Menu Item. This second layer consists primarily of two methods: One returns a string that is the entry to be displayed as part of the menu and the second is the method to be invoked when this menu item is selected. These two methods must be implemented by the developer of the new class, but the first requires only a definition of a string and the second need only return the address of one of the methods that already exists in the first layer of the class's interface.

The maintenance of this menu system can now include a number of modifications. Each of these can be accomplished without modifications to other classes.

Addition of new menu items. New menu items can be quickly developed by using multiple inheritance to add in the needed interface, thus providing the polymorphic substitution that allows a Menu Item to be handed to a Menu.

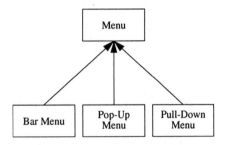

Figure 15.4: A set of menu classes.

Addition of new kinds of menus. Inheritance can be used to develop specialized subclasses of the abstract **Menu** class. Figure 15.4 shows a small hierarchy of specialized menu classes. Each class operates in a slightly different manner. All have the same interface as **Menu** and are interchangeable with it and with each other.

Modification of a menu's contents. This is a programmatic change. More, or fewer, selections may be added to the menu instance as it is constructed. This will typically be via an **Add** message to send a new **Menu Item** into the collection.

Modification of a menu's appearance. Characteristics of the menu that are controlled as attributes, such as the colors used, may be modified programmatically. The attributes of the menus can be modified permanently by modifying the **Menu** class. The changes are then inherited into each of the menu subclasses. These modifications are encapsulated and do not require modifications to related classes such as **Menu Item**.

Modification of a menu's method of operation. If the change is to be major, an instance of a different menu class can be used in place of the current one. Polymorphic substitution allows the new instance to be passed anywhere the old instance was passed, provided the abstract **Menu** class was specified as the formal parameter. A minor modification may be handled as a modification of the code of the class.

MANAGEMENT ISSUES

We have alluded to the need for changes in management practices to maximize the benefits possible in our methodology. The following three areas are representative of the kinds of changes that will better support the goals we have set.

Project

	#1	#2	#3	#4
				window class
Library Manager		menu class		
			file locking class	

Figure 15.5: A matrix management approach.

"Investment" View

High-level management in a company should view the software development process as an opportunity for investment. Resources can be allocated in ways that produce positive returns for the company. One example of this view is the allocation of resources to support "complete class development." In the typical development process, developers on a project design and construct only the pieces of functionality required by the project. In a reuse-oriented methodology, each component is developed independently of the concerns about a particular application. The functionality to be developed depends on what is required to model the concept rather than on the current solution to a specific problem. Should a project be responsible for supporting development of functionality that is not required for the project? That would make a company's first object-oriented product *very* expensive!

One way to address the expense is to establish a process for funding the development of the extra functionality. Figure 15.5 illustrates a matrix management organization in which the project manager is responsible for funding the portion of the development that will be used by the project, and the library manager is an investment manager who makes decisions about which classes to develop more completely. Using this approach, the investment costs can be easily tracked as future projects "pay" for the right to use library classes. The library manager can provide many of the services provided traditionally by a configuration manager. A software base that monitors component usage would supply information about investment returns through class reuse.

Evaluation Measures

The company should examine the measures used to evaluate developers to determine whether those measures promote the appropriate goals. Surveys[91] have shown that the analysis and design phases in the object-oriented paradigm require more resources than the actual coding. This requirement is even greater in our methodology. Measures that are based on lines of code do not accurately reflect the appropriate emphasis. If this type of measure is used, developers will have little motivation to properly analyze and identify the abstractions that will promote reuse. Measures should be adopted that recognize the amount of effort spent analyzing and reusing rather than the amount of code produced for the project.

Supporting Technology

As an extension of the investment view, the company must invest in technology that supports the development process. Computer-assisted software engineering (CASE) is moving into more companies, but very slowly. The management of large numbers of classes that belong to a number of complex structures requires a variety of development tools. Classes will not be reused if they cannot be found. Browsers are required, but the typical alphabetical listing of classes—or even a hierarchical listing only by name— is not a satisfactory approach. In our discussions of libraries and tools we have made several suggestions that point to technology that will support the development process. These tools should sit on top of the software base of classes and should understand the kinds of relationships that exist in that base.

DEVELOPMENT METHODOLOGY

We return to our outline of a development methodology to summarize the variety of techniques that have been discussed in the text.

Content-Centered Designs

- *Domain modeling.* The concept of domain modeling has appeared in discussions about analysis, design, documentation, testing, and libraries. It is a central concept for our methodology. Our basic premise is that the content of the domain that is the focus of an application should guide the system-development process. Classes that model the concepts of the domain should be given the names of those concepts so that they improve the readability of analysis and design documents. Instances of these classes should appear in the implementation of the application to improve the developer's ability to trace requirements into the final application.
- *Libraries of expertise.* The libraries that are currently available with most object-oriented languages and those that are available with procedural languages provide fundamental features and data structures, but they only represent the tip of the iceberg. Large companies develop many pieces of software within the same problem domain. Their software engineers develop an expertise within that domain. This expertise can be readily captured in sets of classes and inheritance structures. These class libraries serve as the repository of the company's expertise within the

domain. The libraries may even become sources of standard knowledge within a field if the company decides to sell its expertise. Alternatively, a company may want to use a library developed externally as a way to cut its own costs and make use of existing domain expertise, perhaps even in a domain tangential to its real business.

Reuse-Oriented Components

Most of the techniques we have discussed have improved the reuse potential of the components being produced. The techniques listed here are representative of those improvements.

- *Abstract root classes.* Inheritance structures are more robust if the top-level classes are abstract. That is, they are conceptual models with little or no implementation details, and they provide entry points into the classification schemes used to give order to a collection of classes. These entry points can be used by librarian tools as well as by browsers to support development activities. These classes also provide an opportunity for polymorphic substitution of a range of subclasses.
- *Well tested.* Components that are intended for reuse should be more completely tested than components often are. Testing techniques often test a component within the context of its use. Reusable components need to be tested across the range of their inputs and across their state space. This testing, combined with the hiding of implementation components, provides a high level of confidence in the integrity of the components.
- *Well documented.* Components intended for reuse need different types of documentation than do single-application components. We want developers to pick an item off the shelf and use it without understanding how it works. This requires some documentation about performance. Graphs of the component's response under load will provide information about the performance of specific methods. Also important is documentation about the component's relationships with other components— which components it relies on, which components it supports.

Engineered Software

In this section we will return to the fundamental implementation devices that make up the traditional definition of object-oriented programming. We will summarize about each device now that the reader has a broader view of each concept.

- *Classes.* The class is the unifying concept in object technology. It is used in the analysis, design, and implementation phases. The class provides a unit of abstraction that at the same time is a syntactic unit in the language. It provides the technical means for the encapsulation of concept and the hiding of implementation details. It is the basic unit of reuse and the basic component in libraries of reusable software components.

- *Objects.* Objects are the runtime structures that support the development of applications. Instances of classes themselves are always represented in the execution of an application as objects and, in some languages, classes are also present in the runtime as objects. Objects are the manipulatable entities in an object-oriented application that maintain their state between periods of active use.
- *Inheritance.* Inheritance is a relationship between definitions. We have focused on *class* inheritance, which creates a dependency between existing definitions and a new definition. This relationship is the feature that most characterizes the object-oriented paradigm. The object-oriented style defines components in layers. The inheritance relation defines those layers and provides a path for building larger components by composing the definitions along the path.
- *Polymorphism.* While we want to use a strongly typed language for implementing classes, we also want to recognize the special relationship of a class and its subclasses. Inclusion polymorphism and dynamic binding support the substitution of instances of subclasses where an instance of the parent class was specified. This mechanism provides a design technique that supports the development of interchangeable components and decomposes a system into classes that provide features and classes that manage those features.

FUTURE DIRECTIONS

Much research and development effort is being exerted in the area of object-oriented software development. Although the paradigm is being widely used, many areas of the technology remain to be fully developed.

Generalization of the Inheritance Mechanism

Inheritance is an example of the very general concept of incremental definition that goes well beyond the characterization of class inheritance that we have given in this text. It is possible to generalize so that any objects, not just classes, can be related; this relationship is termed *delegation*. This mechanism has been realized in the *actor* family of languages. An object may choose to handle a message it receives or to pass it on to an acquaintance who will handle it. The actor model is significantly different from the model used by most object-oriented programming languages. A good introduction to these concepts can be found in [65].

The use of class inheritance is by no means a standard process. Each object-oriented language has its own inheritance "mapping." The mapping is the set of rules that determines how attributes of the parent classes are inherited by the subclass. Languages that provide a wider range of mappings will probably appear. In fact, the languages that support instance inheritance usually provide a class inheritance mechanism that is very general.

Concurrent Object-Oriented Languages

Object-oriented techniques have gained popularity at the same time that there is much interest in multiprocessor computers and distributed computing. Thus it is natural that the two ideas are being combined in a number of language implementations. The encapsulation and information hiding of the object technology facilitates the decomposition of the application into schedulable "grains." This natural parallelism leads to an approach in which objects are identified, after which the need for synchronization is considered.

Several languages have been developed that employ a variety of models for the synchronization and for the underlying hardware. Concurrent C++[32], POOL[3], ConcurrentSmalltalk[103], and the ABCL family of languages[104] are examples. The development of libraries of classes that add multiprocessing capabilities to existing languages has provided C++ developers with classes that can provide parallel execution[4]. AT&T has provided a set of task classes with its translator that support a coroutine style of programming. Languages such as ABCL/1 support both synchronization and asynchronous messaging, providing a diversity of computational models. Some, such as Concurrent C++, support shared memory while ABCL/1 supports only distributed memory models.

Many problems still remain to be solved with parallel object-oriented languages. Current techniques for incorporating synchronization into classes do not lend themselves to inheritance. Each class must have a custom-designed scheme for handling synchronization. These problems will be solved and better implementations will become available. Agha[2] provides an overview of this area and Yonezawa[105] provides a detailed account.

Integration, Standardization, and Sell-Out

As object technology matures, it will progress through the same stages that any innovation experiences. Pioneers in the field will describe radically new approaches to system architecture and *ad hoc* design practices to develop these architectures. As the audience for these techniques grows, they will integrate these radical techniques with the established technologies that they have been using. Some of the expected benefits will not be recognized, since the radical techniques are being adapted to work with the established procedures. An interesting example of this phenomenon can be found in the technique termed "object-oriented structured design"[94].

Experimental language implementations will give way to standards that constrain the language and slow the process of change. This is a necessary part of widespread acceptance. Standardization—as long as it does not happen prematurely—promotes the use of a technology. The standardization of languages such as C++ indicate a maturity in object technology. We hope that this will not slow the pace of improvement in that and other languages. Other areas of informal standardization include the treatment of inheritance. The clear majority of design texts and articles agree that, in typed languages, the inheritance relationship between classes should be used to model the subtyping or specialization relationships between concepts. These design techniques will evolve into accepted methodologies as more and larger system-development efforts are completed.

Our use of "sell-out" as part of the section title may seem a bit strong, but it is there to remind us of the need to push for the modification of existing techniques. The methodology described in this text cannot be achieved overnight and without effort. It calls for practitioners to view the software development process from a perspective— that of the problem—that is different from that they have traditionally used—the solution. Reuse orientation requires that there exist libraries of reusable pieces that will not be available at first. The methodology also calls for the use of an engineering discipline that many have not developed. It is easy to try a new methodology without proper training, techniques, or support and then quickly return to the established, comfortable processes. Managers as well as practitioners must approach this process of fundamental change with attitudes that will support innovation rather than be suspicious of it.

Diversity and Division

There continues to be great diversity within the arena of object technology. There are many analysis techniques, design methodologies, and implementation languages. As subareas develop there will be divisions into separate methodologies. This is an ongoing process that has already been experienced. In the early stages of the popularity of object-oriented techniques many claimed that Ada was an object-oriented language and proceeded to produce systems that failed to achieve many of the improvements possible with the object-oriented style. When the importance of inheritance—which Ada does not currently possess—became obvious, the division between languages that support incremental development of components and those that do not became obvious as well. We have nothing against Ada, but it is necessary to identify and use the essential elements of a technology.

CONCLUSION

This text has attempted to survey the various aspects of object technology over the entire life cycle. This is an ambitious task and we will not have satisfied everyone with the level of that coverage. We have attempted to provide pointers to much of the useful literature where the reader can find detailed accounts of techniques. It is important that the person or company that is considering using object technology get a complete perspective of the impact across the life cycle. Object-oriented analysis, object-oriented design, and object-oriented programming have each been used independently of the others and can result in some measure of improvement in the software development process. The comprehensive, life cycle-wide approach described in this text will compound the economies and successes of the individual methodologies to provide a substantial improvement in the way software systems are developed.

Bibliography

[1] Harold Abelson, Gerald Jay Sussman, and Julie Sussman. *Structure and Interpretation of Computer Programs*. MIT Press, Cambridge MA, 1985.

[2] Gul Agha. An overview of actor languages. *SIGPLAN Notices*, 21(10):58–67, 1986.

[3] Pierre America and Frank van der Linden. A parallel object-oriented language with inheritance and subtyping. In *OOPSLA '90 Proceedings*, pages 161–168, 1990.

[4] Ian Angus. Personal communication.

[5] Phillip J. Beaudet and Michael A. Jenkins. Simulating the object-oriented paradigm to Nial. *SIGPLAN Notices*, 23(6), 1988.

[6] Kent Beck and Ward Cunningham. A laboratory for teaching object-oriented thinking. In *OOPSLA '89 Proceedings*, pages 1–6, 1989.

[7] E. Blake and S Cook. On including part hierarchies in object-oriented languages, with an implementation in Smalltalk. In *European Conference on Object-Oriented Programming 1987*, pages 41–50, 1987.

[8] D.G. Bobrow, L.G. DeMichiel, R.P. Gabriel, S.E. Keene, G. Kiczales, and D.A. Moon. Common LISP object system specification. *SIGPLAN Notices*, 23(Special Issue), 1988.

[9] B. W. Boehm. Software engineering economics. *IEEE Transactions on Software Engineering*, 10(1):4 – 21, 1984.

[10] B. W. Boehm. A spiral model of software development and enhancement. *IEEE Computer*, 25(5):61 – 72, 1988.

[11] Grady Booch. Object-oriented development. *IEEE Transactions on Software Engineering*, 12(2):211–221, 1986.

[12] Grady Booch. The design of the booch components. In.*OOPSLA/ECOOP '90 Conference Proceedings*, Reading, MA, 1990. Addison-Wesley.

[13] Luca Cardelli and Peter Wegner. On understanding types, data abstraction, and polymorphism. *Computing Surveys*, 17(4):471–522, 1985.

[14] Eduardo Casais. Managing evolution in object oriented environments: An algorithmic approach. Technical report, University of Geneva, 1991.

[15] R.G.G. Cattell. *Object Data Management*. Addison-Wesley, Reading, MA, 1991.

[16] R.G.G. Cattell. Special section: Next-generation database systems. *Communications of the ACM*, 34(10), 1991.

[17] Thomas J. Cheatham and Lee Mellenger. Testing object-oriented software systems. In *Proceedings of the 1990 Computer Science Conference*, pages 161–165, 1990.

[18] P.P. Chen. The entity-relationship model: Toward a unified view of data. *ACM TODS*, 1(1), 1976.

[19] Peter Coad and Edward Yourdon. *Object-Oriented Analysis*. Yourdon Press, 1991.

[20] E. F. Codd. A relational model of data for large shared data banks. *Communications of the ACM*, 13(6):377 — 387, 1970.

[21] Bruce Cohen, Douglas Hahn, and Neil Soiffer. Pragmatic issues in the implementation of flexible libraries for C++ In *USENIX C++ Workshop Proceedings*, pages 193–202, 1991.

[22] D. Coleman, F. Hayes, and S. Bear. Introducing objectcharts or how to use statecharts in object-oriented design. *IEEE Transactions on Software Engineering*, 18(1):9 — 18, 1992.

[23] Brad J. Cox. *Object-Oriented Programming: An Evolutionary Approach*. Addison-Wesley, Reading, MA, 1986.

[24] Michael L. Creech, Dennis F. Freeze, and Martin L. Griss. Using hypertext in selecting reusable software. Position Statement for OOPSLA '91 Workshop on Reuse, October 1991.

[25] C.J. Date. *An Introduction to Database Systems*. Addison-Wesley, Reading, MA, 1982.

[26] L. Peter Deutsch. Design reuse and frameworks in the Smalltalk-80 system. In *Software Reusability Volume II*. ACM Press, 1989.

[27] Margaret A. Ellis and Bjarne Stroustrup. *The Annotated C++ Reference Manual*. Addison-Wesley, Reading, MA, 1990.

[28] P. Feldman and D. Miller. Entity model clustering: Structuring a data model by abstraction. *The Computer Journal*, 29(4):348–357, 1986.

[29] Mary Fontana and Martin Neath. Experiences in the design of a C++ class library. In *USENIX C++ Workshop Proceedings*, pages 179–192, 1991.

[30] Phyllis G. Frankl and Roong-ko Doong. Testing object-oriented programs with ASTOOT. In *Quality Week 1991*, San Francisco, CA, 1991. Software Research, Inc.

[31] David Garlan. The role of formal reusable frameworks. In *Proceedings of the ACM SIGSOFT International Workshop on Formal Methods in Software Development*, pages 42–44, 1990.

[32] Narain Gehani and William D. Roome. *The Concurrent C Programming Language*. Silicon Press, Summit, NJ, 1989.

[33] Carlo Ghezzi, Mehdi Jazayeri, and Dino Mandrioli. *Fundamentals of Software Engineering*. Prentice-Hall, Englewood Cliffs, NJ, 1991.

[34] Jean Jacques Girardot and Sega Sako. An object oriented extension to APL. 1987.

[35] Adele Goldberg. *Smalltalk-80: The Interactive Programming Environment*. Addison-Wesley, 1984.

[36] Adele Goldberg and David Robson. *Smalltalk-80, The Language and Its Implementation*. Addison-Wesley, 1983.

[37] Adele Goldberg and David Robson. *Smalltalk-80, The Language*. Addison-Wesley, 1989.

[38] Keith E Gorlen. An object-oriented class library for C++ program. *Software-*

Practice and Experience, 17, n12:899–922, 1987.

[39] S. Gossain and D.B. Anderson. Designing a class hierarchy for domain representation and reusability. In *Proceedings of TOOLS '89*, 1989.

[40] Brent Hailpern. Special section: Multiparadigm languages and environments. *IEEE Software*, 3(1), 1986.

[41] D. Harel. Statecharts: a visual formalism for complex systems. *Science of Computer Programming*, 8:231 — 274, 1987.

[42] Mary Jean Harrold and John D. McGregor. Hierarchical incremental testing. Technical Report TR91-111, Department of Computer Science, Clemson University, 1991.

[43] Mary Jean Harrold, John D. McGregor, and Kevin Fitzpatrick. Incremental testing of object-oriented class structures. In *Proceedings of the 14th International Conference on Software Engineering*, To Appear 1992.

[44] F. Hayes and D. Coleman. Coherent models for object-oriented analysis. In *Proceedings of OOPSLA '91*. ACM, 1991.

[45] Richard Helm, Ian M. Holland, and Gangopadhyay. Contracts: Specifying behavioral compositions in object-oriented systems. In *Proceedings of OOPSLA '90*, 1990.

[46] B. Henderson-Sellers and J.M. Edwards. The object-oriented software life cycle. *Communications of the ACM*, 33(9), 1990.

[47] Sallie M. Henry and Matthew Humphrey. A controlled experiment to evaluate maintainability of object-oriented software. *Personal Communication*, 1990.

[48] Urs Holzle. The self papers. Technical report, The SELF Group, CIS 209, Stanford University, Stanford, CA 94305.

[49] F.R.A. Hopgood, D. A. Duce, J. R. Gallop, and D. C. Sutcliffe. *Introduction to the Graphics Kernel System*. Academic Press, New York, 1983.

[50] Saber Software Inc. *Using Saber-C++*. Saber Software Inc., Cambridge, MA 02138, 1990.

[51] Jonathan P. Jacky and Ira J. Kalet. An object-oriented programming discipline for standard pascal. *Communications of the ACM*, 30(9):772–776, 1987.

[52] Michael A. Jenkins, Janice I. Glasgow, and Carl D. McCrosky. Programming styles in Nial. *IEEE Software*, 3(1), 1986.

[53] Ralph E. Johnson and Brian Foote. Designing reusable classes. *Journal of Object-Oriented Programming*, 1(2):1, 2, 22– 35, 1988.

[54] G. Kappel and M. Schrefl. Using an object-oriented diagram technique for the design of information systems. In *Proceedings of the International Working Conference on Dynamic Modelling of Information Systems*, 1990.

[55] Brian M. Kennedy. The features of the object-oriented abstract type hierarchy (OATH). In *USENIX C++ Conference Proceedings*. USENIX Association, 1991.

[56] Michael Kilian. Trellis: Turning designs into programs. *Communications of the ACM*, 33(9):65–67, 1990.

[57] Won Kim. *Introduction to Object-Oriented Databases*. MIT Press, 1990.

[58] Won Kim, Elisa Bertino, and Jorge F. Garza. Composite objects revisited. In *Personal Communication*, 1989.

[59] Michael F. Kleyn and Paul C. Gingrich. Graphtrace – understanding object-oriented systems using concurrently animated views. In *Proceedings of OOPSLA*

'*88*, 1988.

[60] Tim Korson and John McGregor. Object-oriented software design: A tutorial. *Communications of the ACM*, 33(9):40 — 60, 1990.

[61] Tim Korson and John McGregor. Technical criteria for the evaluation and specification of object-oriented libraries. Technical Report TR91-112, Department of Computer Science, Clemson University, 1991.

[62] Wilf R. LaLonde and John R. Pugh. *Inside Smalltalk*, volume II. Prentice-Hall, Englewood Cliffs, NJ, 1991.

[63] Jo A. Lawless and Molly M. Miller. *Understanding CLOS*. Digital Press, Bedford, MA, 1991.

[64] Karl J. Lieberherr and Ian M. Holland. Assuring good style for object-oriented programs. *IEEE Software*, pages 38–48, September 1989.

[65] Henry Lieberman. Using prototypical objects to implement shared behavior in object-oriented systems. In *OOPSLA '86*, pages 214 — 223. ACM, 1986.

[66] Mark A. Linton, John M. Vlissides, and Paul R. Calder. Composing user interfaces with interviews. *IEEE Computer*, pages 8–22, February 1989.

[67] Stanley B. Lippman. *C++ Primer*. Addison Wesley, Reading, MA, 1989.

[68] C. L. Liu. *Elements of Discrete Mathematics*. McGraw-Hill, New York, 1985.

[69] Dennis Mancl and William Havanas. The impact of C^{++} on software maintenance. In *Proceedings of C^{++} at Work*, 1990.

[70] John D. McGregor. Object-oriented programming with scoops. *Computer Language*, pages 49 — 56, July 1987.

[71] Bertrand Meyer. Genericity versus inheritance. In *OOPSLA 1986 Proceedings*, pages 391 — 405, New York, 1986. ACM.

[72] Bertrand Meyer. Reusability: The case for object-oriented design. *IEEE Software*, pages 50–63, March 1987.

[73] Bertrand Meyer. *Object-Oriented Software Construction*. Prentice-Hall, Englewood Cliffs, NJ, 1988.

[74] William M. Miller. Error handling in C^{++}. *Computer Language*, pages 43–52, May 1988.

[75] William M. Miller. Exception handling without language extensions. In *Proceedings of USENIX's C^{++} Conference*, pages 327–342, 1988.

[76] Patrick D. O'Brien, Daniel C. Halbert, and Michael F. Kilian. The trellis programming environment. In *Proceedings of OOPSLA '87*, pages 91 — 102, 1987.

[77] M. Page-Jones and S. Weiss. Synthesis: An object- oriented analysis and design method, 1990.

[78] Joan Peckham and Fred Maryanski. Semantic data models. *ACM Computing Surveys*, 20(3):153–189, 1988.

[79] Dewayne E. Perry and Gail E. Kaiser. Adequate testing and object-oriented programming. *Journal of Object-oriented Programming*, 1(1):13 — 19, 1990.

[80] Xavier Pintado and Dennis Tsichritzis. Fuzzy relationships and affinity links. In D. Tsichritzis, editor, *Object Composition*, pages 273–286. University of Geneva, January 1991.

[81] Ruben Prieto-Diaz. Domain analysis: An introduction. *ACM SIGSOFT's Software Engineering Notes*, 15(2):47–54, 1990.

[82] Ruben Prieto-Diaz. Implementing faceted classification for software reuse. *Com-*

munications of the ACM, 34(5), May 1991.

[83] Mary Beth Rosson and Eric Gold. Problem- solution mapping in object-oriented design. In *OOPSLA '89 Proceedings*, 1989.

[84] James Rumbaugh, Michael Blaha, William Premerlani, Frederick Eddy, and William Lorensen. *Object-Oriented Modeling and Design*. Prentice-Hall, Englewood Cliffs, NJ, 1991.

[85] Sally Shlaer and Stephen J. Mellor. *Object-Oriented Analysis: Modeling the World with Data*. Prentice-Hall, Englewood Cliffs, NJ, 1989.

[86] M.J. Stefik, D.G. Bobrow, and K.M. Kahn. Integrating access-oriented programming into a multiparadigm environment. *IEEE Software*, pages 10 –18, March 1986.

[87] Rob Strom. A comparison of the object-oriented and process paradigms. *SIGPLAN Notices*, 21(10):88–97, 1986.

[88] Bjarne Stroustrup. *The C^{++} Programming Language*. Addison-Wesley, Reading, MA, first edition, 1986.

[89] Bjarne Stroustrup. Possible directions for C^{++}. In *Proceedings USENIX C^{++} Workshop 1987*, pages 399–416, 1987.

[90] Bjarne Stroustrup. *The C^{++} Programming Language*. Addison-Wesley, Reading, MA, second edition, 1991.

[91] Dave Thomas and Ivar Jacobsen. Managing object-oriented software engineering: An oopsla tutorial. Technical report, Association for Computing Machinery, 1989.

[92] Dennis Tsichritzis et al. Active object environments. Technical report, Centre Universitaire d'Informatique; Université de Genève, Genève Switzerland, 1988.

[93] Jurgen Uhl and Hans Albrecht Schmid. *A Systematic Catalogue of Reusable Data Types*. Springer-Verlag, 1990.

[94] A.I. Wasserman. Object-oriented structured design method for code generation. *ACM Software Engineering Notes*, 14(1):32 — 55, 1989.

[95] Peter Wegner. Dimensions of object-based language design. In *OOPSLA '87 Proceedings*, New York, 1987. ACM.

[96] Peter Wegner and S.B. Zdonik. Inheritance as an incremental modification mechanism or what like is and isn't like. In *European Conference on Object-Oriented Programming*. Springer-Verlag, 1988.

[97] Elaine J. Weyuker. Axiomatizing software test data adequacy. *IEEE Transactions on Software Engineering*, SE-12(12):1128 — 1138, 1986.

[98] Elaine J. Weyuker. The evaluation of program-based software test data adequacy criteria. *Communications of the ACM*, 31(4):668 — 675, June 1988.

[99] Robert Wilensky. *Common LISPcraft*. W. W. Norton, New York, 1986.

[100] Rebecca Wirfs-Brock and Brian Wilkerson. Object-oriented design: A responsibility-driven approach. In *OOPSLA '89 Proceedings*, 1989.

[101] Rebecca J. Wirfs-Brock, Brian Wilkerson, and Laura Wiener. *Designing Object-Oriented Software*. Prentice-Hall, Englewood Cliffs, NJ, 1990.

[102] Christopher J. Van Wyk. A class library for solving simultaneous equations. In *USENIX C^{++} Workshop Proceedings*, pages 229–234, 1991.

[103] Y. Yokote and M. Tokoro. The design and implementation of ConcurrentSmalltalk. *SIGPLAN Notices(Proceedings of OOPSLA-86)*, 21(11):331 — 340,

1986.

[104] A. Yonezawa, J. Briot, and E. Shibayama. Object-oriented concurrent programming in abcl/1. In *Proceedings of OOPSLA '86*. ACM, 1986.

[105] Akinori Yonezawa and Mario Takoro, editors. *Object-Oriented Concurrent Programming*. MIT Press, Cambridge MA, 1987.

[106] Pamela Zave. A compositional approach to multiparadigm programming. *IEEE Software*, pages 15–25, September 1989.

Index